Deer, Pigs and a little bit of Bull!

Graeme Mackie

Dedication

To my Nana Bauern and her wonderful proud contented
smile as she encouraged us.
"If you start something you must finish it."

Acknowledgements

To all the members of the Hibiscus Coast writers and
their contagious enthusiasm. Thank you all.

Published by **HAIRY WAKA**
Order from www.letsbuybooks.weebly.com

Copyright Graeme Mackie – 2011

Editing, layout & cover design – Bev Robitai
www.thebookcoach.weebly.com

Made in NZ

National Library of New Zealand
ISBN 978-0-473-19657-8

Introduction

When I first placed pen to paper, there was only one incentive in mind and that was to make people laugh. Therefore the yarns I've included here come from many walks of life.

The vast majority are based on factual events, some of them very personal to the people described, but in no way can these original characters be recognised. I have enjoyed the challenge of sharing their stories with you, hopefully for your amusement and pleasure, perhaps astonishment and disbelief! Did it actually happen, you may ask?

There are quite a number of references to the smoking of cigarettes and in this day and age I cannot condone this in any way at all. But that is what the characters described were associated with. Personally I have not smoked a cigarette since New Year's Day a number of decades ago and it really appals me now the number of people who still continue to light up, stating 'No one's going to tell me that I'm not allowed to smoke!' For goodness sake wake up and look around you at how many people a year die from cancer and related diseases associated with the lungs, throat and the respiratory system. If this helps even one person to kick the habit, I will feel that my words have not been in vain.

Back when I was a young, fit, strong, outdoors type, I believed that I was bullet proof. Now into my seventies, I can remember some sage words from my Dad that I at the time thought was his waffling!

'When you're young son, you're tough for the sake of being tough but when you're old, you're tough because you have to be tough.' Now, fifty years on, I can see what he was trying to get into my thick head. Maybe he wasn't such a silly old bugger after all!

About the consumption of alcohol, I have imbibed more than my fair share over the years, so it is in here and I can't change the past. But even though I may enjoy a shandy every now and then, it's only on looking back that I can see now that I could have had just as much enjoyment if I'd stuck to the shandies! Maybe even had more fun in the long run!

I personally know that the world would be a much richer place, with a lot more humour and fun, if it was filled with heaps of laughter. Yeah! The more merriment echoing around the world the better, as far as I'm concerned. When's the last time you really enjoyed having a good laugh? I hope that my efforts will get your attention, put you in the right mood, and perhaps even lead you astray!

A brief resume on the character of Rolly. He was born and raised in South Auckland where his greatest enjoyment was fishing on the Manukau harbour with his Dad. His other major interest was the deep-throated roar of diesels, and he would cycle for miles to watch earth-moving machinery in action, dreaming of the day when he'd be behind the controls himself. Here's his story as it unfolds …

Contents

vi

CHAPTER ONE

GOOD DAYS AND BAD DAYS

Some people strike it lucky and other people don't. Me, I'm one of those that don't have it as good as it could be, or for that matter as good as I'd like it to be.

Until about twelve months or so back I'd had a not so bad job driving a Caterpillar tractor, a bulldozer if you like, for a joker down in the Waikato, and this bullie had seen better days. It was fightin' a losin' battle and was well and truly past its use by date! The tracks were shot, just about worn flat, with so little grip that every time the going got a bit on the tough or slippery side, they'd spin. Talk about frustrating. It wouldn't even pull the skin off a rice pudding. Well, to cut a long story short, I collared the boss and did a moan about it, and going by the look on his face, I thought that I'd wasted my breath.

Anyway, a week or so later when I called in at the office jacking up for a load of diesel to be delivered out to the job, the boss bailed me up an' told me a mechanic was coming out first thing in the morning an' I was to lend a hand to drop off the worn set of tracks and fit a reconditioned set. Well, wonders will never cease. The boss was not known for his generosity, but fair enough I thought, it'd make my job one hell of a lot easier and quicker. Besides it'd be a welcome change to have someone on the job to yak to other than myself. They reckon it's the first sign of madness when ya start answering yourself back!

Next day I was out on the job about ten after seven, untying the bullie's dilapidated, oil stained cover that leaked like a sieve, letting in a damned sight more water than it kept out. It looked as though someone had taken to it with a four-ten shotgun. Full of holes, it was stuffed and no doubt about that! But the boss blew his top if he found out that ya hadn't put it back on at the end of each day's grind. Was always carrying on about how it kept the leather covered seat and armrests from gettin' soaked and goin' rotten. There's no pleasin' some blokes ya know.

It was just as well that I took the trouble to put the bullie's seat in the back of my old jalopy each night, otherwise it'd be like sittin' on a flamin' underground spring all day.

Well, like I said, I took that piece of church-goin' canvas off the old girl, grabbed the dry seat out of the back of my old heap, lugged it over and onto the bullie's tracks, clambered up liftin' the seat and dropped it in place. Then deciding a quick smoke wouldn't go amiss, I perched myself on the armrest and reached into my pocket for the matches. But wouldn't ya know it. Not a single live one. "Damn!"

In disgust I chucked the useless box away, and the tobacco tin that was perched nicely on my knee slid off, hit the tracks, bounced and neatly emptied itself with the papers right into the middle of a muddy puddle. For a short time I just stared, and then out it came. "Bugger!"

Then the air turned blue, really blue! Even the birds in the scrub must've put their wings over their ears and it was just as well that I was a fair distance from the nearest farmhouse. An' no doubt about it, I'll lay you odds that that joker up there with his little black book had put another cross beside my handle! It's all right for Him, He doesn't smoke anyway, but I betcha He had a puff or two when He was down here!

2

After cooling off a bit, I clambered down from the bullie and stomped across to my old bomb to start ratting around through the accumulated rubbish under the dashboard for some live matches.

Ah, now here's a box, but no, it's full of dead ones. Aha, another box! But only the one solitary live match. I struck the match, but it was no go. I struck again and the ruddy head flew off, so once again the air turned blue.

"Go on, you up there, put another flippin' cross beside me name!"

I find a full box of live ones, and this time the match strikes first pop. I'm elated, and on lighting up take a deep drag. Boy, that's just great. What a relief! Sanity returns to me at last and even the birds seem to appreciate it, they've started singing again. In my search, I spotted a spare packet of baccy. Good. But what about the papers? Another frantic search is underway, but still no joy. Wouldn't ya know it, not a single flamin' paper. Man oh man what a day of days it had started off to be.

Then I remembered about the mechanic. I hope ta hell that he smokes. Yeah, I think he does. I'm sure I spotted him havin' a drag in the workshop the other day. Well, I damn well hope he does, cos if he doesn't he could be in for a pretty miserable time.

Hell! I looked at the time. Seven-thirty, so I'd better shake a leg and give the old girl a kick in the guts.

Slamming the car door, I strode back and climbed up onto the tracks, turned the diesel on and made sure she was out of gear, primed the petrol in the starter motor carby, and checked the water level in the radiator. Yep, enough water to float the Q E II. Righto old mate, wind the pull-cord around the flywheel, open the throttle, give it full choke, and okay, she's all set now, so pull like hell!

"Whoopee! You bloody little beaut!" Away first pop, an' you're running like a dream, well, I wonder what's gotten into you this morning?"

Now gently start to engage the starter motor with the main engine.

"Blast it all, why did you have to stall again just when things were goin' along so smoothly?"

Oh well, I might've known it was too good to last. Just the sort of luck I seem to have inherited today.

Well Rolly old chap, let's give it another go, but first you'd better disengage the starter motor or you won't have a snowball's chance in hell of getting anything up and running.

Wind the pull cord around again. Boy, what I wouldn't give for an electric starter. Just imagine if I got two bob for every time I've yanked on this damned thing over the years! Hmmm, that cord's lookin' a bit on the frayed side. But she'll be right mate so don't let it worry ya! All set? Now pull and give the old sod heaps! Blast! Nothin'. Not even a solitary cough. I just knew it, you bloody thing you, and if it's true what they say about that joker up there knowing everything that ya say and think, boy is he in for an earful. Why in creation can't these machines be fitted with electric starters? It'd sure make my life a hell of a lot simpler. Now that the cord is wound on again, she's all set for another go. Right, Rolly old son, put a bit of a sting into it this time.

I really did put some elbow into it. Then I reeled back, holding my nose. "Hell's bells, that sure hurts! You bloody starter cord, you would have to break, copping me one fair across the snorer!"

Jeez, it's really makin' my eyes water. One thing for sure, you up there, you'll run out of paper and crosses before I run out of swear words. Man oh man, that's sure bloody painful but at least the starter motor is still ticking over, so I guess that's some consolation.

"Don't you let up on me now, will you? Okey dokey, old cob, you'd better get the revs up!" That's it, engage her to the main engine, gently, gently now, gently, righty'o old cob, it's a winner so go for it. Yep you little humdinger, keep rollin', keep rollin' - now flick over the compression lever, slam the throttle wide open. Yahoo, you bloody little beaut. The sweet roar of success. I ease the throttle back a bit, that's it, she's runnin' sweet as a nut, and it's just as well because I've got nothin' that I could use for a replacement starter cord anyway. Now, what about a well-earned smoke, Rolly old pal? I reach into my pocket, but blast and damn, no papers. Ah well, looks like I might just have ta hang on for a bit longer until that damned mechanic arrives on the scene, and he sure won't be the most popular of blokes if he doesn't smoke!

Hell's teeth, time flies when you're havin' fun, it's after eight already, about time he turned up.

A couple of minutes later I spot a truck burling along the road; goin' by the speed and the dust it's puttin' up the driver must have his foot planted flat to the floor boards. Yeah, that's one of our heaps all right, and there's the boss's hotted up little Mini right behind. I wonder what the hell he wants? By crikey, that driver is really givin' the truck heaps, surely he must know the boss is right up his exhaust pipe, and if he does, he must be a flamin' idiot. The boss'll have his guts for garters, and that's for sure!

Hell's bells! He hardly slowed down at all when he turned in off the road. Whew, how he made it through that gateway without wrappin' the truck around that big strainer post I'll never know. And boy if he doesn't take

5

it a bit easier comin' over this rough ground, he'll do a set of springs in! Jeez! Now that was a beaut bump, I bet he's got a lump on the top of his scone the size of a duck's egg, must've just about put his head through the top of the cab! Ah, I can see you're gunna take it a bit slower now that you've learnt your lesson.

Well, I guess I'd better get down and say gidday to this manic mechanic, that's if and when he gets here. But on second thoughts it might be a damned sight safer for me to stay put up here out of harm's way, you never know!

As he pulled up to a stop beside me I could hear the sound of tortured and groaning metal. Switching off, he stuck his head out of the window.

"Well, it looks like I got to the right place this time. Rolly's your name, isn't it?" Getting out of the cab he extended his hand up to me. "Jim's mine."

We shook. "Howdy Jim, you're at the right place all right." Then with a bemused look, I asked, "How does it feel to try and put a truck into orbit?"

He grinned at me as he ruefully rubbed the top of his head. "I didn't see that big hump until I was right on top of it and then it was too damn late to do anything but hang on for grim death!"

Grinning back I retorted, "Well, Jim, the boss did, and goin' by the way you turned off the road, you'll be pushin' up daisies when he catches up with you. Can't you feel your ears burning? Anyway, no pain, no brain, I guess."

He stared at me for a few seconds until the penny dropped and then with raised eyebrows asked, "Whadya mean the boss saw me? You're the only bloke workin' out here, aren't you?"

I pointed behind him. "See that Mini comin' slowly across towards us? Don't you recognise it? It's the boss's, and he was right up your exhaust pipe until ya careered in through the gateway."

Turning, he looked back towards the gate. "Bloody hell, I saw that clockwork toy behind me in the dust and I thought I'd give it a run for its money, never dawned on me he'd be out here in that. Especially when most time's he's drivin' that bloody great Yank tank. I guess this'll mean I'll be presented with the DCM, eh?"

It was my turn to look puzzled. "I don't get it, what in the heck is the DCM, anyway?"

"Same as getting fired. Don't Come Monday!"

I chuckled. "Well, that's a bit different. Must remember to tell the boys in the boozer about it, especially if it turns out to be true."

Jim looked at me and giving a wry smile, replied. "Well, I guess I'd better face the music then."

The boss stopped his Mini about 40 yards behind the bullie, unfolded his bulk from behind the wheel and squeezed out. How he even managed to get into it was a mystery in itself. Then leaving the guy who had come with him standing beside the Mini, he stormed across towards us, and boy, talk about spitting sparks. He was ropable all right.

"Just who in the hell do you think you are, a bloody astronaut? My vehicles are not made to go into orbit, and I want to see you in my office tonight. You haven't heard the last of this!"

Jim said nothing. Just stood there, looking embarrassed.

Then glaring at both of us the boss snapped, "Well, what d'ya think I pay you jokers for, to stand there like a couple of wooden dummies? Get stuck in and change

7

those bloody tracks. Ya should've started half an hour ago. And you," he said, pointing to Jim, "are bloody lucky not to have got your marching orders. Next time you get behind the wheel of one of my vehicles, take it easy or you'll wind up on the end of a bunch of fives!"

He raised his clenched fist under Jim's nose, turned on his heel and muttered something about money not growing on trees as he stomped back to the guy waiting next to the Mini. They walked away towards the brow of the hill, so it looked as though they were going to give the job I was doing the once over. When they were out of sight Jim fished a packet of tobacco out of his back pocket.

"I wonder what will happen tonight?" he said, looking at me and questioningly raising his eyebrows.

I breathed a sigh of relief on seeing the roll ya owns.

"Thank God you smoke rolls Jim, could I flog a few papers off you? I'll pick some up on my way home and pay you back tomorrow, okay?"

"Sure thing, Rolly. I've got a spare book of them in my lunch bag, that'll keep you goin'. Anyway, you don't look like the nervous type to me, you're not goin' ta smoke your head off are you?"

He grinned, reached into the cab of the truck to grab his lunch bag, which had ended upside down on the floor after its rough ride, hunted out the papers and handed them to me. I was glad to see that they were the same brand that I used.

"Thanks Jim, you're a bloody lifesaver!"

As I was rollin' myself a smoke I could see Jim was turning a few thoughts over. "You know something Rolly, I hope that our boss is all piss and wind because I don't really want to be out of a job right now."

8

After I'd lit up I began explaining to Jim just how things had been working against me, the loss of the makin's, the frayed starter cord and the smack across the dummy.

He smiled. "Yeah, I know how ya feel, worse luck. I started the day off on the same foot. First off, I slept in and then there was no hot water left. Some bloody idiot had left the hot water tap trickling, so I had to do the lot in icy cold water and I'm afraid that sort of thing doesn't make me the happiest of fellas at the best of times. Jeez, the agony while shaving. If I could've gotten my hands on the ignoramus who hadn't turned off the tap properly, I'd have half killed him!"

I grinned at the big chunk of bloody tissue paper stuck to his top lip.

"Yeah, I can see the paper, you must've taken a fair chunk out all right."

"Actually it's just a little nick," Jim replied ruefully, "but the damned thing wouldn't stop bleeding. That reminds me, the next time I'm handy to a chemists I'll have to get one of those thingymebob sticks to stop the bleeding. Anyway, getting back to the story. No sooner did I sit down at the table to what is called breakfast, a couple of spoons of lumpy porridge that sticks like glue to ya ribs, and a slice of last week's toast, when the old battleaxe herself comes stridin' up to me saying, 'You'll have to find somewhere else to stay. One of my old boarders is coming back!' No beg ya pardons, no nothin'! Before I could swallow the porridge and reply, she left me to it. Fancy someone being stupid enough to return to a dump of a joint like that. The truth of it is that she's probably let the room for an extra couple of shillings more a week, probably the most tight-fisted old bat I've ever had the misfortune to meet. If only she'd been a man I'd've told her just where she could have stuck her dump of a boarding house.

Anyway enough of the moaning, the reason that I wasn't here earlier is that I turned up the wrong track and it was all one way, nowhere to turn around, so I had to back up a half mile or so. Jeez, I thought my head was going to drop off and my neck has still got a crick in it and the rest you've seen for yourself. I guess in all honesty, I can count myself lucky that I didn't get the DCM on the spot. Have to watch my step in future."

I shrugged my shoulders, "Well, Jim, perhaps the boss was in a better mood than he looked. But it's a bit on the tough side about your lodgings. So if you like I'll have a chat to my landlady - she might have a vacancy coming up. And talkin' about vacancies, we'd better do a bit and get our A into G before the boss comes back or we'll both wind up lookin' for new jobs!"

Jim grabbed a few tools out of his toolbox.

"Righto, Rolly, you back the bullie up an' I'll give you the thumbs up when the master pin is on the front idler and ready for knocking out!"

He walked to the front of the bullie and turned, watching me clambering up onto the tracks. Then, wouldn't you know it, my foot slipped on the edge of the track, causing me to bark my shin! Boy, did it bring tears to my eyes and even though Jim couldn't hear me above the throbbing engine, he could tell by the way I was vigorously rubbing my shin and how my mouth was opening and shutting, just exactly what I was feeling like.

While trying hard not to smile, Jim made out he was in my shoes acting, using both hands to stop the halo from strangling me. As the pain eased I saw the humour of it all, gave him a lopsided grin followed by a vigorous two finger sign and then dropped into the seat. Selecting reverse gear I eased the clutch out and opened the throttle, she began trundling slowly backwards. We kept going back and back. I was waiting, watching for Jim's signal to stop, but there was still no sign of the master pin, it must've been covered with mud and difficult to locate. Then the engine began to labour, so waiting and watching for Jim's signal, I opened the throttle wider, giving it few more revs, until unexpectedly the right hand track began to rise up higher and higher.

"What the hell? What's making the track lift up like that?"

I turned my head, looking over my shoulder, just as the track began to flatten what it had climbed onto. Too late, bloody hell, it can't be true. I'm seeing things. Oh no, not… it can't be, not the boss's Mini! Instinctively, I threw the bullie out of gear, but there was no way that I could get my mind around what had happened! Putting my hand over my eyes, I frantically motioned to Jim, who was staring at me wondering what was going on, to get around the other side of the bullie to look. When he came around and saw what was left of the flattened Mini under the track, he clapped both hands over his eyes and turned away. Then removing his hands slowly, he turned around to take a second look. Now that he was sure his eyes weren't deceiving him, a look of disbelief and incredulity spread over his face. He slowly shook his head from side to side.

We both looked at what had been the boss's pride and joy, now a crushed mass of metal with its wheels splayed out. Bloody hell, there was no way it could be repaired, it was a total write off.

I cut the engine, and in the deafening silence that followed, only the groans and squeals of tortured metal filled the air. I also thought I heard the bellowing of a bull, but it wasn't. What I was hearing was the sound of an enraged boss.

"You're fired! You're both fired! I'll kill both of you bastards when I get my hands on you!"

And there, about two hundred yards away, was the boss sprinting towards us waving around a big chunk of broken fence post in his mitt.

Jim was the first to come to his senses. "Let's get the hell out'a here!" he yelled. "Goin' by his threats and that bit of post he's wavin' about we'll wind up doing a twelve month stretch flat on our backs in the hospital!"

They reckon that fear lends you wings. Well, I can tell you it's true! I sailed off the bullie, but my foot rolled on a clump of dirt as I landed. Ye gods, my ankle hurt like hell, but this was not the time or place to think about that. I hobbled over to my old bomb praying that she'd start first go, and yelled to Jim, who was trying his best to start the truck, its starter whirring over and over again.

"Throw your tools and stuff into the back and come with me, forget about the truck! It's always been a bastard to start when it's hot!"

Divin' back out of the truck, he grabbed his tools and lunch bag off the tray. I've never seen a joker move so fast in all my days. His gear was in the back and him in the front next to me in seconds flat! All the time I'd been pushing the starter.

"C'mon, start you sod, start!" Then realising that in my haste I hadn't turned the ignition on I flicked the isolating switch and thankfully the motor burst into life and boy was I relieved! "You bloody beaut!"

I slammed it into gear, but it wouldn't go. By this time, our irate now ex-boss was only a short distance away and still goin' great guns for a fella who had a paunch as big as his.

"What's stoppin' her from goin' into gear?" I growled out, then watched as Jim's hand wrenched my lunch bag out of the way. Slamming it into first, I dropped the clutch like a hot potato. We took off just in the barest nick of time as the chunk of post the boss had been waving about sailed through the air and landed right where we'd been only seconds before.

"Whew, that was too close a shave!" Jim yelled above the sound of the racing motor. "It's a bloody good job that it didn't clobber us or the car, a chunk of stuff that big could do a fair bit of damage!"

"What's he doin' now?" I called while spinning the wheel from side to side trying to avoid the humps and hollows that were making the car leap about like a one legged kangaroo. Jim was lookin' back.

"He's standing there shaking his fist at us, and goin' by the way that mouth of his is opening and shutting, I'd say that he's telling someone all about it and casting grave doubts about our ancestry. One thing though, he's not goin' near the truck, so it looks like he's given up the idea of chasin' us. I think we can ease up a bit! Yeah, he's just walked over to the bullie shakin' his head and that other bloke has joined him too."

Easing off the throttle a bit I still kept my eyes peeled for any more harsh bumps.

Jim spoke again. "I don't know about you Rolly, but my ears are really burning, feels like they're on fire!"

I took a big breath. "Well, one thing for sure, we've given him plenty to carry on about! Jeez, I couldn't believe my eyes when I looked down and saw the Mini under the tracks! I've seen and done some pretty unusual things in my day but this one really takes the cake, and it's all my bloody fault. So it'll be no bloody good me thinking of lookin' for a job in this neck of the woods. The word will spread like wild fire!"

By this time I was a little more relaxed, but the ankle I had rolled was giving me gyp, hurting a fair bit.

"Jim, when we get back onto the road again do you think you could drive for a while? I must've done a bit of damage to my ankle when I leapt off the bullie, it's givin' me a fair bit of pain!"

"Sure," he replied, "I could handle one of these even if I drove it blindfolded!"

I took a quick glance at him. "Blindfolded? To hell with that, I want to get out of here in one piece!"

"Rolly! That's one thing I don't intend trying out, so you can just put your mind at rest. Anyway what in the hell happened to your ankle?"

"When I jumped off the bullie, it rolled on a damned clump of dirt. It sure hurt and is still giving me the works, but I'll tell you something, I certainly wasn't going to hang around waiting for anything or anyone, believe you me!"

Jim laughed ironically. "Well, it's no bloody wonder, the way you sailed through the air. Reckon you must've set a new world record in the broad jump and from a sitting start at that. It's a pity we can't go back and measure it," he taunted wryly.

"It may be a record, but not on your bloody life. My name might be Willy, but it's certainly not silly! Anyway, what's he up to now? Because if he gets into that truck, you'll see a new land speed record set, as well as the broad jump all in the same day!"

"She's jake, Rolly, he just turned and waved his fist at us again, but he's not goin' anywhere near the truck!"

For the next short time we had nothing much to say, we were both deep in our own thoughts mulling over what had just occurred. It certainly left a lot of unanswered questions!

Then Jim broke the silence. "You don't think he'll get the law onto us do you?"

"Nope," I replied, a little unsure of myself. "I certainly hope not and anyway if he does, all we'll have to do is stick to the truth, that it was an accident. But I really wonder just who would believe us. Another thing is that he should've had more sense and parked the damned Mini somewhere else!"

Then a thought hit me and I let go a brief nervous laugh.

"What's so funny?" quizzed Jim.

"Ya know, I was just turning over bits and pieces about today's misadventure. Can you imagine describin' it to the beak? 'Your Honour, I looked under the track of the bullie and there was the boss's Mini, his pride and joy, as flat as a pancake!'"

Even though it wasn't really funny, we both laughed and it certainly helped ease some of the tension.

As I turned the car onto the road, I caught a glimpse of our ex-boss still waving his arms around as he talked to his off-sider. I could just imagine what he was saying and I'm sure it wasn't very complimentary.

A bit further along the road, well out of sight of the bullie and our now ex-boss, I pulled over to the side of the road and swapped places with Jim. After we'd got goin' again, I asked, "Have you driven one of these jalopies before?"

"Sure, I owned one of these bone-shakers myself. Great until I rolled it and wrote the damned thing off!" he replied with a short, nervous laugh.

"Now you tell me, after I let you get behind the wheel. Are you sure you won't do it again? You're not driving under false pretences are you?" I wisecracked. "By the way, don't push this old girl too fast, the steering's a bit on the dicey side, and it pulls to the left when you brake too hard. The king pins are a bit shot, but will do another turn or two. And as for the brakes, they'll stop you in a flash, if you meet up with something like a power pole!"

"Well, Rolly, one thing for sure, I reckon you're in safe hands now as we've already written off one vehicle today!" he said with a humorous lilt to his voice.

For a couple of seconds I didn't catch on but then the penny dropped. "Now I can see what you're getting at. They reckon lightning never strikes the same place twice? Well let's keep our fingers crossed, but you'd still better take it easy or you might just tempt fate. Anyway, do you want a smoke? I'm rollin' one for myself."

"A gasper? You bet I would," he enthused.

When the cigs were lit Jim again broke the silence. "The only thing I could really do with now is a nice cool beer. An' talking of the amber ale, reminds me of how I wrote my old bomb off. As a matter of fact, the same model and make as this," he said with a ghost of a smile.

"Ya see, I went to a shindig with this sheila, a good looker too, and very well put together at that. About an hour or so after we'd arrived at the do she up and vanished into the night, leaving me on my pat malone. Someone said that she'd shot through with an old flame of hers, leaving me in the lurch feeling like a proper mug. So I proceeded to drown my sorrows, getting stuck into the booze as a consolation. But it didn't help, just made things a hell of a lot worse in the long run! I downed quite a few and don't recall a great deal about it.

Later on I was told how I'd tried to knock the block off some joker, as a result the fella whose party it was tossed me out on my neck. I can vaguely remember getting behind the wheel, where, according to a driver behind me, I was out of it and very lucky that no one was coming from the other direction. I then came to an s-bend. Went round the first part on two wheels, the second part no wheels. I was so pissed and relaxed that I didn't know what was happening and this was probably the only reason I didn't suffer any bad injuries, just a few scratches and bumps. When I came to and things started to register a bit, I realised my car was wrapped right around a tree on the side of the road. A total write off! To this day I count my lucky stars that I didn't get badly injured or find myself shaking hands with the old reaper.

"Anyway, worse luck, the cops turned up and after blood tests and what have you, I was booked and my licence was cancelled for six months. That is a lesson well learnt and it's never going to happen to me again. It was really rubbed in when the damned insurance wouldn't cough up so all I've got left is a couple of payments to the finance company and the slate will be wiped clean!

So my next move is to start stashing a few quid away in the hopes of buying myself a four-wheel drive job."

I gave some thought to Jim's tale. It certainly wasn't the brightest thing to do, this drinking and driving, but accidents can still happen even if you're stone cold sober like today.

We drove onwards not saying much initially until the thought hit me and I blurted out, "Jim, you'll have to get another job, and so will I. You can only save dough if you're earning some dosh and one thing for sure is it won't be worth havin' a shot for a job around here. Our old boss is a pretty big noise in these parts, so I reckon that I'll try my luck elsewhere and head off down south a bit. They tell me there's some good hoot to be made if you put in the hours in a construction company. Got any thoughts on what you're gonna get up to?"

"Blowed if I know, Rolly. As you say, the word'll get round everywhere, and a man'll feel a bit of a nong when his mates find out just what really happened. Yeah, it'll have to be new stamping grounds for me too, just like you, I guess." He paused in thought. "Another thing is, I've been trying to make up my mind whether or not I should risk calling back in at the workshop for my good mocka, or leave it. Do ya reckon I'd be pushing my luck too much by going back?" Jim posed, as he turned onto the main road back towards town in the direction of the workshop.

I tossed it over for a while before answering. "Look Jim, our luck can't always be this bad, surely? Might just as well give it a shot, the boss will have to fly to get there before us and besides we're nearly there."

For a while we again lapsed into thoughtful silence, and when I again gently moved my foot, I realised that the ankle was no longer hurting as much as it had been earlier.

"Hey, Jim, things are on the up and up, so I reckon our luck must be on the turn. My ankle's not hurtin' anywhere as much as it was before, don't think there's as much damage as I first thought. Reckon I'll be able to handle the old girl meself after we've dropped in at the workshop."

Jim chuckled and gave my leg a bit of a pull. "Jeez, talk about a real Hollywood job, that ankle of yours! Surely I'm not that much of a poor driver, am I?" He followed this up with more cheeky laughter.

I joined in with this light-hearted banter.

"You'll probably pass with a push," I jokingly tossed back at him. "Anyway, tell me, where did you get your license from in the first place? My guess is that it didn't cost all that much, was it a Woolworths el cheapo job?"

We turned into the depot where Jim pulled up beside the workshop. On getting out of the car we were greeted by the boss's sidekick, and not knowing what sort of a reception we were going to receive, we were on the cautious side.

But Wally, the boss's second in charge, was standing there grinning from ear to ear, so things were looking slightly better all round for us.

"Well, Rolly, you've sure got the right handle haven't you? They tell me that the boss's hot little machine looks as flat as a sardine tin with a bullie perched on top. Hell's teeth, what happened, just how did it come about? How'd you jokers do it? Until today I reckon I'd heard of everything being done in this game, but this one sure takes the cake."

I thought quickly for a second or two, and decided that it was no bloody use being fearful and replied with an 'oh so what' attitude. "I was backing up, with Jim watchin' for the master pin to come up on the front idler. Waiting, looking for Jim's signal to stop when he'd located it, I'd completely forgotten about the Mini until it was too bloody late, the result was one very flat Mini! Easy as, I still can't get over what happened, it seemed so damned simple, just ask Jim."

"Nothin' to it, easy as falling off a log!" was Jim's quick retort. "Just give us a Mini and a bullie and we'll give another demo!"

"Thanks all the same!" laughed Wally, "but don't you buggers think there's already been enough strife around this neck of the woods for one day. You should've seen the colour on the office girl's face when she was speaking to the boss on the blower, and to make matters worse, she demanded an apology for his bad language. Boy oh boy, he must've really blown his top because she slammed the phone down in his ear!"

Then with a half serious, half humorous expression on his face, he said, "Well you guys can probably guess I'm the bearer of bad news. First of all thanks for telling me how it all came about, but the bad news is you're both down the road. The office girl's already made your pays up, and I'm now off to survey the damage and to commiserate with the boss. And another thing, I don't think it would be a wise move for either of you to be seen by the boss again. See ya!"

With that, he waved his hand and climbed in behind the wheel of the boss's big Yankee heap and drove off.

When Jim had collected his good gear from the locker room we went into the office. Immediately the girl behind the counter blushed and disappeared through the door into the boss's office, she was probably as embarrassed as we were, never said a word, just left our pay and time sheets ready for signing on the counter.

With my pay in my hand, I remembered some of my own personal gear was still in the locker room so went and collected it. Back at the car I got in behind the wheel. There was no way that I wasn't going to drive.

Taking Jim back to his lodgings, I dropped him off, arranging to meet him later in the day at the pub. It was not really for a session on the booze, or to drown our sorrows about gettin' the boot, but to chew the fat about our future and what it might hold for us. And not forgetting more discussion, letting the fact really sink in that we'd squashed a Mini as flat as a pancake! One thing that I think we'd gotten a real handle on, was make sure to look behind before backing up, especially on the controls of a bloody big bulldozer!

CHAPTER TWO

A NEW BEGINNING

It was in the early afternoon when Jim and I got back together over a beer. Then later, very much later, after quite a few beers and a great deal of discussion, it was decided that Jim would accompany me southward on the following day. With our minds made up to seek new pastures, there was nothing much else worth doing, so we gave the old grog a fair sort of a hiding. It was just as well I'd left the old bomb back at my lodgings, as it was with a great deal of difficulty that I blindly made my way homewards. Definitely was in no fit state to drive!

This was much to my landlady's dismay, but she was to have the last word.

Next morning, coming slowly back to the land of the living, I moaned aloud. "Ohhhh God, my aching head!" It felt as though someone had been hammering it with a lump of four-by-two, and the bright sunlight streaming in through the window didn't help one little bit. Hell it was bright! It seemed to take hours just to get my eyes fully open, and when I did everything was a hazy red. But worst of all was the taste in my mouth. Talk about the bottom of a foul parrot cage. Yuk! Realising that something had to be done about this horrible state of affairs, I gingerly lowered my feet over the side of the bed until they contacted the floor. So far so good I thought, but then the fun really began. When I lifted my head from the pillow, my God, the agony, as everything in my head became an immense explosive mass of pain. I didn't know it then, but this was going to be nothing compared to what lay in wait. The phenomenal agony increased, and by the time I'd managed to stagger to my feet I would've, without the slightest hesitation, throttled the bugger who had given the order for an army of centipedes in hobnail boots to do a route march around on the inside of my skull. That is if I'd had the strength. Somehow, and with as little movement as possible, I gathered up the toilet gear and began to make my way gingerly towards the bathroom.

Halfway down the hall all hell broke loose. I was greeted, or should I say my nerves were shattered, as the raucous voice of my landlady assailed me at full volume.

"I've been waiting to have words with you! Pack your things and get out today, I just won't tolerate my boarders coming in drunk, creating a disturbance in the middle of the night!"

I thought my head was going to leave my body, and my stomach was performing double back-flips. I was unable to reply or make any excuses as ghastly feelings of nausea impelled me urgently into the toilet, and just like the landlady, unceremoniously evicted an unwanted tenant. Even when my stomach was empty I retched and retched violently. Beads of cold sweat appeared on my forehead, leaving me with barely enough strength to remain standing, while vowing and declaring many times over that I would never, ever drink again! Eventually a little of my strength returned, enabling me to drop my clothes and step into the shower, at least this helped to clear some of the centipedes and their many boots from my head. Unfortunately, they returned violently when I made the mistake of bending down to pick up the soap that had escaped my weakened grasp. My head was spinning like a runaway merry-go-round and again my emptied stomach heaved violently, over and over again.

"Ohhh God, please let me die! Have mercy, don't let me linger in agony! C'mon God, be a sport, to hell with all the booze. I swear I'll become a member of Alcoholics Anonymous, just lead me to the pledge and I'll sign up!"

Practically on my hands and knees with the nausea, I discovered a couple of aspirin in the toilet gear and downed them dry. Aughh, what a vile taste! The damned things just about came back up faster than they'd gone down. But very slowly the horrible throes of sickness diminished slightly, allowing me to become a little more aware of my surroundings. Then I caught a glimpse of a person in the mirror. I was confronted by a total stranger with a sallow, greenish around the gills complexion, and blurry eyes looking just like a couple of poached eggs daubed with dots and lines of tomato sauce. What an unwelcome, disturbing sight! Jeez it was horrible, like an alien from another planet. But no, it vaguely resembled someone I knew. Jeez that's you mate, and what a bloody mess. I had to look away. Then after lots of deep breaths, I managed to run some hot water into the hand basin, lathered up my dial, and with shaking hands, was able to begin removing four days growth. The end effect was a small improvement in both the head and guts, with the painkillers kicking in too. All in all, a small step in the right direction. Then gingerly I made my way back to my room, taking great care not to encounter the landlady again, or make any quick movements with my head. The bed took on a very welcome form as I collapsed in a heap, ohh, what a relief to rest one's head again!

After some time, I was surprised to feel the beginnings of a spark of optimism, at last the nausea had diminished somewhat. Rising slowly from the bed and taking my time, I began packing up my kit and then eventually when this chore was over and done with, I slowly carted out my gear to the old bomb and loaded it up. I retuned to the room for a final shufti before I made tracks, and good thing I did, because there on top of the wardrobe were a couple of old army blankets and my sleeping bag. It would've been pretty cold without these, especially as I was heading south. I'd probably have ended up with frozen ones just like the proverbial brass monkey.

On stepping out of the boarding house front door, my thoughts went quickly back over the last couple of years. No regrets, I'd made my bed and I'd slept in it. All in all, I'd had good an' bad times, but it was now time to up stakes and head for greener pastures. It felt good to be back on the road again.

Off I went down the road and there to my amazement was Jim, sitting on the kerb with his feet in the gutter, cradling his head on his arms and knees. He didn't look a very well boy at all, quite a picture of misery and suffering, but seeing someone who looked even sicker than I was made me feel a lot brighter. As I neared him, I pulled up and called out as loud as it was safe for my own state of health. "How'd a feed of greasy bacon and eggs go, Jim?"

Jim's body appeared to cringe, but after a deep shudder he replied in a most subdued voice. "Can't you let a man die in peace? I've been through enough torture for one day as it is! All I want to do is die!"

Then much to my surprise, he lifted his head and laughed. "I'm all right, just putting on a bit of a Hollywood, but I certainly wasn't acting late last night. This was one very sick guy! An' talkin' of grog, you can certainly knock it back, where do you put it all? There's nothing to you, you're built like a piece of number eight wire."

Putting on a braver face than I actually felt, I replied, "Haven't you heard of the wooden man with hollow legs? Well, that's me to a tee, but all the same believe me you, I was wanting to die until a couple of hours ago and there's a pretty rugged feeling in the pit of my guts even now! Anyway, you didn't seem to want to stop drinking last night, so talk about the pot calling the kettle black, there's not much difference between you and the way a Taranaki gate is put together!"

After the pleasantries were over, Jim climbed into my old bomb and we headed off to pick up his gear. Then with Jim's stuff loaded we headed out of town, tidying up a few things on the way. I pulled into a gas station for petrol and smokes, where the garage owner was putting the local paper onto the counter. He scanned the front-page headlines for a few moments and then exclaimed in amazement to us.

"Good God! Hey, you guys, take a gander at this would ya! Jeez, what a beaut, how in the hell did this happen I wonder?"

Jim and I looked, and there on the front page emblazoned across the paper was a photo of the bullie squatting on top of the Mini, with the headline stating, 'You big bully you!' The write up started with 'At dawn this morning there was a very one-sided duel.'

Jim and I quickly bought a couple of papers and retired rapidly back to the car.

There it was in black and white, and for a few moments we both stared. Nothing much further was to be said between us, we'd yakked about it enough the previous night. Thankfully for us, neither of our names were mentioned in the article. But we both agreed emphatically that it's not the sort of thing that one would shout from the hilltops about. Anyway with this in mind I turned on the ignition.

"Okay, Jim, let's make tracks." With that, we were on our way, only too happy to put a bit of distance between us and the scene of our infamy. We left our reputations in tatters behind us!

CHAPTER THREE

GO SOUTH YOUNG MAN, GO SOUTH

On the outskirts of town we hit a fair sized pothole. The car's exhaust system, which was on its last legs, fell to bits making one hell of a clatter, and the roar from the motor without a muffler made a sound just like a rally car. I slammed on the anchors and cut the motor. On getting out we surveyed the situation, then Jim walked back to get the muffler. He'd no sooner picked it up than he dropped it quicker than a hot potato. It was nearly red-hot, causing him to wave his hand about and mouth a few silent curses, but he was unable to say too much because two women were pushing prams along the footpath. He saw I was laughing at his actions and he whipped out a clean handkerchief, wrapped it around the exhaust and dragged it back to the car.

In a teasing tone I smilingly asked, "Why didn't you wait until it had cooled down a bit? We've got plenty of time to spare. It would've at least saved you from dirtying a nice clean handkerchief!"

Jim's retort was immediate. "And stand there like a big nong with those two sheilas laughin' their silly heads off at me?"

I couldn't resist giving his leg another pull. "Is that what they were laughing about?"

He shot back at me as he unsuccessfully tried to hide a grin. "You thought it was pretty funny too! Anyway, Rolly, the pipe that is joining the manifold has rusted right through, and we haven't got a hope in hell of fitting it back on until it's been welded up."

I agreed with him. "Okay, we'll have to leave it for now and get it seen to a bit further down the line. Hope we don't get picked up by a cop for excessive noise because it sure is kicking up a fair old racket!"

That was just a bit of wishful thinking because, as per usual, our luck was out. About three minutes further down the road, right out of thin air, there he was alongside me. A bloody cop in mufti, lights flashing, the siren blaring, with his finger pointing to the side of the road. What was that about luck did I say? If I took all but one of the tickets in a raffle, the one I didn't take would be the winner.

Pulling to one side we stepped out of the car to speak to the cop.

"Let's hope this guy's in a good mood," Jim muttered. I nodded in agreement.

Closing the door of the patrol car behind him, the cop walked toward us. "You jokers should know better than to drive around without a silencer."

I thought to myself, did this guy think that we did this sort of thing just for fun? Instead I apologised, "Sorry, officer, I do know better, but the damned thing only fell off a short distance back and it would've still been in place if a great big pothole in the road had been mended."

"Go on, is that so?" the cop replied sarcastically. "Now tell me another one. Surely it's about time you jokers learnt to come up with something a bit more original. I've heard that one at least a hundred times." And with that he began to open his ticket book and get his pen ready.

Oh no! I had to think up something pretty quick, before he wrote me out a bluey! "Look, officer, if you don't believe me, it's lashed to the back bumper. If you put your hand on it you'll find that it's still warm."

I breathed a slight sigh of relief as he walked around to the back of the car and, after taking a look, he commented, "It doesn't look very hot to me," then rested his hand on the thickest part of the muffler as it must've looked pretty cool.

"Yipes, that is hot!" He cursed, blowing on his fingers to cool them off.

Jim and I barely managed to keep straight faces.

"I see what you mean." He then turned and strode to the front of the car to check the W.O.F. I knew that the warrant was up to date as it was only about two months old, as was the rego, so he couldn't pin that one on me. He held his hand out, asking. "Could I see your licence please?"

'This joker's a thorough one,' I thought, as I fished my licence out of my wallet. He looked at it carefully, then asked, "Your first name is Rolland, right?"

I nodded an affirmative. "Yes."

"You have heavy truck and road machine licences, I see?"

What's goin' on here? I was trying to work it out, wondering what he was takin' so much care for.

"You and your mate here are heading to where?"

"Just down south a bit, we're on our way looking for work."

"You guys haven't had a confrontation with a Mini and a bullie have you?"

My heart sank to the bottom of my boots. It looked like more trouble was on its way. What a day it was turning out to be. "Ah, yes officer, we did have a slight problem."

I looked at Jim and raised my eyebrows. I couldn't understand why, but suddenly the cop's face broke into a big grin. He said, "Look, your ex-boss is my brother-in-law and last night I drove out to have a look at the mess. It certainly was a write-off, so now if you've got the time, could you give me your side of the story?"

Well, that was a load off my mind, thank goodness. When we'd finished the yarn he said. "My only regret is that I wasn't there to see the look on his face when it happened. Heaps of times I've told him that the Mini would cause him big problems one day, but I really thought he'd be the one to write it off. He was always pushing it to the limit!"

All the time we'd been telling him the story, he had a grin and a half on his face.

"Thanks for that, and by the way, I haven't told him yet but I managed to salvage the four hub caps off the Mini and I intend to present one cap to him on each of his next four birthdays, just as a little reminder." Then, still grinning from ear to ear he proceeded to write out the infringement ticket for the lack of adequate silencing!

Bugger, I thought, so much for being obliging. But no, he surprised me by taking all the copies out and screwed up the duplicates! "Here, this might just come in handy if you get stopped by another cop further down the line. Good luck, have a good trip but keep a watchful eye out for Minis!" He then shook hands with us and was on his way.

We climbed back into my old bomb, very relieved to have gotten off scot-free but somewhat bemused by the turn of events.

"Crikey, Jim, that is what I call a lucky escape, it's a pity I'm still not feeling well enough for a beer or two."

"You can say that again, Rolly! That is, all but the part about the beers, I don't think that my insides are quite up to it. What with him askin' about the Mini, I thought we were right up to our necks in it. Man he sure put the wind up me for a while!"

"I agree. He had me really worried at that stage and I think the quicker that we put a bit more distance between our ex-boss and ourselves the better while we've got the chance!"

CHAPTER FOUR

JUST A SHORT HOP DOWN THE ROAD

By the time we'd covered about twenty miles, the racket created by the straight exhaust had just about driven us nuts! Our sign language wasn't up to much anyway and in desperation, we were forced to stop and have the exhaust seen to in a small one-horse town that comprised of a garage, restaurant, a couple of small shops and a pub.

Dropping the old bomb off at the garage, we arranged to have the exhaust repaired. I asked the unhappy-looking joker who appeared to own the joint about how long he thought the job would take.

"About six feet," he replied in a somewhat niggardly manner that got right up my nose and with an annoying Pommy accent at that.

What's with this guy, what in the hell is biting him? I thought about it for a few seconds and decided that it's about time someone gave him a bit of his own back. Smiling, and looking him in the eye, I replied, "Now you'd be a real bright spark wouldn't ya? Did ya sleep with the light on, or was it razor blades and Cornies for breakfast?" I waited for his reply.

He appeared to take a step back in his thinking, and then a little unsure of himself muttered, "It'll probably be ready in an hour or so."

"Okay pal, I'll see you in an hour." We then walked away leaving him to stew in his own juice.

When we were out of earshot, Jim looked at me and said, "Jeez, these ruddy Poms always seem to be doin' a moan or bein' smart arses. You'd think they owned the country by the way some of 'em carry on. It's a damned shame that the Maoris have given up eating them, especially the objectionable types!"

I interrupted Jim. "Tell me, did you ever hear why the old Hori gave it away as a bad job?"

"Nope, Rolly, but I heard that after the defeat of the Maori in the wars, the law was 'stop killing and eating the Pakeha or be hanged'!"

"That's only what the history books might lead us to believe. Anyway, just remember it was the Poms who recorded most of the early history in the first place. The real story was that they were too damned salty, made everyone who ate them as thirsty as, remember no pubs around in those days ya know! But the biggest problem was that they had trouble keepin' them in the hangi cooking. Ya know how most Poms are full of hot air? They just kept on drifting away with the breeze!"

Jim interjected. "Whoa, boy, just hold your horses for a minute while I get myself a shovel, I reckon the bullshit around here is getting pretty thick!"

Giving Jim a grin, I responded. "Like I said, they had a hell of a job keepin' them in the hangi, it's all that CO_2, they're full of it. Well, you know how hot air rises? They got sick and tired of seein' their lunch floating away, so gave 'em up as a bad job!"

Jim chortled away. "You're sure you're not a bloody Pom y'self Rolly?"

A few steps further down the road we were greeted by the delicious smell of grilling steak wafting through the air.

"Mmmm Jim, that aroma reminds me I haven't had a bite to eat all day and I'm feeling on the peckish side with my insides really starting to growl. What do you

34

reckon, a feed? Or is it to be the hair of the dog that bit us?"

"Which first?" he queried.

Reaching into my pocket I pulled out a coin.

"Tell ya what, let's toss a coin, heads we go for a beer, tails it's a feed?"

"Agreed Rolly, but I sure hope that it comes up tails, my belly button is about ready to touch my backbone too!"

The coin was duly tossed and turned up tails.

"A feed it is!" And we wandered into the café to enjoy a real good binder of steak, eggs and chips, followed by a decent cup of good hot coffee. Following this we ventured across the road and in through the doors of the pub. After a slow start the beer wasn't too bad a brew at all, but due to our previous night's efforts, we certainly weren't going to give a repeat performance!

Back at the garage, I paid for the repairs and received some info that the jumped-up joker who'd got on our wick was just an ordinary lube bay attendant who had big ideas of his importance. Luckily he wasn't around because we would have given him a hard time.

With my old bomb purring along beautifully we covered the miles in next to no time. After we'd been on the road for about an hour we started feeling as though another small drop of the old amber ale wouldn't go amiss, and we reckoned that another hair of the dog was just what was needed, so we called in at the next pub along the way. It was typical of the old type of a place that earlier travellers would have stopped off at for a meal but all we were really interested in was a bit of a break and a chance to see if the accommodation was up to scratch.

Leaning up against the bar, we were quietly sipping away minding our own business, generally summing the place up, and were watching the antics of half a dozen fellas enjoying their beer and generally mucking around having a bit of fun. They appeared to be a happy looking mob but were fair knockin' back the grog, some of them, and gettin' as full as bulls in the process.

The bar itself was an elongated oval shape, just wide enough for the barman to comfortably serve both sides easily. These jokers were good-humouredly slinging the bull across the bar at one another, until one flicked an unlit match over at the opposite side. In a matter of seconds tempers flared and it was all on, with the insults and flicking of more matches at each other. Boy, we just stood there, all eyes, until someone flicked a lit match and it was just like Guy Fawkes Night all over, flaming matches flying in all directions! The barman moved rapidly down the far end of the bar to get out of the crossfire. Then in a bit of one-upmanship, someone else lit up a whole box of matches and tossed it across! This was quickly extinguished by someone's beer, followed by what was left in the glasses, and then by what was left in the jugs. Then to top off, a little pint-sized fella grabbed the soda siphon, and boy, did he drench the opposing lot when he let rip! What a mess. There was beer, soda water and dead matches on the bar everywhere, all over the place. At this stage of the proceedings the barman stepped in and we could see he'd had more than a guts-full of these guys. He raised his hands for them to cease their shenanigans.

"Okay, you jokers, enough is enough, knock it off right now! If you can't take it easy in here and start acting as adults, I won't serve you any more. And you'll be barred for the next month!" With that he started to clean up the mess of beer, soda and matches.

To us, it was as funny as a fight and we couldn't have predicted what was about to happen.

I turned to Jim, "Jeez, this mob sure do take the cake don't they? And if looks could kill, boy! The barman would have this lot in pine boxes!"

"Yeah, what a go. I couldn't believe my eyes," Jim replied, slowly shaking his head from side to side in bemusement.

Then we noticed one of the revellers making an approach to the barman. "Look mate," he said apologetically, "I'm sorry if we went a bit over the top, and seein' as we made this mess, we'll clean it up for you. Now, where do you keep your mop and bucket? In fact, why don't you just leave it to us and we'll soon put it to rights!"

They collected the cleaning gear from a cupboard and soon had the mess swept and mopped up and the floors and the bar reasonably clean and dryish looking. Then the lanky joker carrying the bucket, smiling from ear to ear, walked slowly over to the bar and spoke reasonably politely to the barman, who had been glaring at every move they had made during their clean up.

Happily he asked the barman, "Now how's that for a neat job, just about spotless, eh mate?"

"It'll do," was the surly barman's terse reply.

The lanky fella with the bucket, unperturbed by the barman, kept smiling and said, "I got a feelin' that you don't like us jokers do you? Is that so?"

The barman curled up his lip and sneeringly stated, "As a matter of fact, I reckon you and your mates should be locked up!" Boy he was bloody bitter as hell!

The lanky joker looked him up and down, and still smiling stated nonchalantly, "Well now, is that so? Because we're not very impressed by you, or your bloody beer! So here, you can just have it all back!"

Before the barman could think or move, he didn't see it coming and the bucket was upended over his head! Dirty water, dregs, matches and cigarettes, what a disgusting mess! By the time the barman had the bucket off his head and his eyes clear enough to see again the revellers had all shot through, leaving the bar completely deserted, apart from Jim and me and one hell of a mess.

We'd decided that this was no place for us to hang around either, so we hightailed it out of there and continued on our way.

Both of us were somewhat taken aback and most amused by the events that we'd just witnessed. Neither of us had ever seen the likes of it before, it was a talking and laughing point for quite some while on our way further south. No doubt those jokers would have probably been banned for life!

We continued southward wondering what else we might encounter on the way.

CHAPTER FIVE

YOU NEVER KNOW WHAT'S AROUND THE NEXT BEND

Some twenty minutes later on our travels we switched our lights on, as dusk was falling and night was quickly setting in.

The road we were following was loose metal winding through the pine forest. Suddenly, without warning, I rapidly slammed on the anchors halfway round a bend trying to avoid a dog sprawled across the middle of the road. It must've been this mutt's lucky day as the car tyres screeched and scattered gravel everywhere, finally pulling to a stop barely a foot from it. But not so good for poor old Jim, he was flung forward, pounding his nose into the dashboard, trying to make a dent in it.

I hurriedly leapt out of the car, and squatting down in the glare of the headlights, I could see the old pooch had been gashed badly in two spots and there was a fair bit of dried blood matted in its fur. One of the wounds was quite long and had opened up the shoulder to the bone. The other one under its neck wasn't quite so bad, but the dog itself had barely enough strength to lift its head and feebly wag its tail.

"Hey Jim, can you come here for a mo'? This kuri is in a pretty bad way."

"What about me?" was his muffled reply. "That bloody mutt has caused me to lose at least a pint of blood!" He came around the front of the car holding a bloody handkerchief to his nose. Crouching down beside me, he gave the dog a once over.

"You're right Rolly, it doesn't look too good at all. Must've been hit by a car or something. This place is miles from nowhere and there's not even a sign of a light shining anywhere around here, is there?"

"Yeah Jim, but what can we do? We can't leave the poor old thing lying out here to kick the bucket like this. And another thing is if we leave him, another vehicle might finish him off anyway. What say we get him in the car and take him into the next town to try and locate a vet? What do you think?"

"You're right Rolly, it's probably best if we get him to a vet."

On finding an old coat of mine in the boot we gently eased the dog onto it, carried him to the front passenger door side and laid him in the floor well. Then Jim climbed in, placing a foot on each side of the dog while I closed the car door and we were on our way.

In less than twenty minutes we spotted the lights of a town and on calling in at a petrol station were given directions to a vet. Luckily for us, the vet lived right on the premises.

His first words at seeing the extent of the injuries were. "Well, well, what's this old fella been up to?"

Shaking my head I replied. "Blowed if I know, we found him lying in the middle of the main road about halfway through the pine forest and damn near ran right over the top of him!"

The vet nodded. "Ah, that stands to reason, there's a lot of pig hunting done around there and it certainly looks a bit like he's been ripped a couple times by a boar's tusks to me. As for his breed, probably a whippet mastiff cross, ideal as a pig dog. So now, what do you want me to do with him? Fix him up or put him out for the count? But remember, there's a possibility that you must take into account, and that is he still might have someone who would claim him if they spotted him. Also you know nothing about his nature, never know what he'll really turn out to be like." He stared at me, wanting an answer.

Thinking over what had been said, I asked, "First of all, do you think he's going to be all right?" It was my turn to stare.

"He's pretty weak, probably from the loss of blood, see there's not much colour in his mouth. But I'm pretty sure once he's stitched up and has got some good tucker into him he ought to come right in a few days. He hasn't had much to eat for a while going by the look of his ribs either. I've had dogs in here with their bellies ripped open, and after everything is tucked back inside and sewn up, they've come right and in fact, quite a few are still out there catching pigs to this very day!"

I was relieved with his explanation that the dog had a chance of making it. Don't know why, but I'd somehow taken a liking to him. Why? Yeah why not!

"Okay, let's go for it, he's hung in for this long already, might as well give him the chance to get back on his pins again."

While I waited at the vet's for the dog to be stitched up, Jim went around to a motel and booked us in.

I was wondering just how we could smuggle the kuri into the motel unit until the vet solved the problem for me.

"Look, I think you'd better leave the dog here for a few days so I can keep an eye on him. Fair enough?"

I thanked him and went outside waiting for Jim to come back for me.

The following morning when Jim and I dropped in to see how the kuri was doing, there was little change. So leaving the vet's we started looking for a cheaper place for us to stay.

After visiting a land agent and looking at several houses for rent, we settled on a small cottage that the owners didn't want the world for. It was ideal as far as we were concerned, and even had an old chook house that could easily be modified to house the kuri in, that's if he pulled through. It was ideal all round and we were more than happy to get it, besides we'd both had more than enough of boarding houses and irate landladies!

Over the next few days Jim and I spent time being tourists, making ourselves familiar with the district, and not forgetting to sample the brews and atmospheres of the local pubs. All in all we were quite taken with what we'd seen.

As for the kuri, we were both happy to see him getting more and more lively each time we dropped in. This improvement was just great to see and after much deliberation and thought I decided to give him a name and settled on Gray, due to his light colouring. Also he appeared to answer to it as well.

Several days later the improvement enabled us to finally pick Gray up from the vet's, he was beside himself with joy and I swear he had a grin from ear to ear, his tail wagged furiously. Immediately made himself at home, just like he owned the place, but by the same token he seemed very obedient. All in all, Gray was a dog who appeared to enjoy our company as much as we liked his.

We'd certainly had a good look around and although it'd been enjoyable, we decided most reluctantly it was about time we did something to earn our keep. The local rag had several jobs and the only one that fell into what was available was general labouring, so we applied and started the next day. It didn't pay all that well but we had to keep the inevitable wolf from the door somehow.

Another thing was Gray, he certainly greeted us enthusiastically after work. Boy had he ingrained us into his doggy heart. Everywhere we went in the car, who should be sitting up in the back seat like Jacky? Yeah, Gray.

CHAPTER SIX

A LUCKY FIND

Life rolled along very pleasantly and quietly for a while, that was until Jim and I were out on a Saturday morning having a nosey up a track then meandering along the banks of a world renowned trout stream that flowed through some scrub and secondary growth bush. I'd heard some of the jokers in the pub talkin' about the big trout that had been caught there, and wanted to see them for myself. I was half-pie attracted to tryin' my hand at trout fishing and we did spot several nice sized rainbow trout taking off at a great rate of knots when they spotted us.

As Jim and I were wandering along, lookin' around and generally chewin' the fat, there was a fair sort of a splash in the stream behind us. Turning quickly we could see that Gray was swimming flat out, makin' a beeline for the far bank. My first thought was, boy is he gunna stink, because the last time he got wet through he was ripe as and smelt to high heaven.

By then he'd scrambled up the far bank and disappeared into a dense patch of fern and bush. We were both calling and whistling, but he took absolutely no notice of us, just vanished from sight and hearing into the undergrowth. But then, after a couple of anxious minutes or so, Gray started barking loudly and steadily. Once again, we tried calling him back, but no, he just kept on barking, loudly and continuously. Nothing we did or called out convinced him to return to us.

"Well, Jim, it looks like I'll have to go over to the other bank and find out why that silly mutt won't come back. I don't know what's got into him, usually he's back like a flash."

The water only looked about ankle deep so I leapt into the stream and to my abrupt surprise found the depth was well above my waist. What a shock to the system! Talk about brass monkeys, jeez it was bloody freezing!

"Bloody hell, man, that's cold!" I squawked like a soprano.

Jim thought this was one hell of a joke and he really cracked up, just about pissing himself at my expense.

From the middle of the stream I snapped back at him. "Just you remember the old saying, Jim. He who laughs last, laughs longer, and one thing for sure, my time will come and revenge will be sweet. Just you wait and see, you bloody great laughing jackass!"

I continued wading towards the far bank then scrambled out, getting a fair covering of mud in the process. Turning, I could see that Jim was certainly enjoying things at my expense. So I gave him the universal sign 'that's two BBQs you're invited to', and continued struggling through the scrub and fern in the direction of Gray's continuous barking. The undergrowth was thick as and at times I had to back track a bit, even crawling under fallen trees to make any headway. All the time Gray's barking was getting louder as I got closer. What in the hell was up with that kuri?

At last, I stumbled into a smallish clearing and my eyes nearly popped! Gray had a pig backed up against a steep bank! I got one hell of a fright! This was the first time I'd ever seen a wild pig up close, and it was as scary as hell. Seemed to me as if it was twice the size of Gray. Bloody hell, I was scared stiff, but at least Gray was in between me and the pig. It looked pretty upset and fierce to me. Not for one minute did Gray take his eyes off the pig, but I was pretty apprehensive all the same! He gave me a little more time to weigh up all the options and one thing for sure, my legs felt like jelly.

Then a thought came to me, and they reckon that two heads are better than one, there was nothing that I could do without a knife or something to clobber the pig with, and with my mind going twenty to the dozen, I remembered the old axe under the back seat of my bomb, and also somewhere in the boot there should be a knife in a sheath.

Taking one last look at the pig and Gray, I decided it looked like he was more than holding his own so I rapidly started the mad scramble back towards the edge of the stream. It took a while and I was just about out of wind. Jim gawked at me as I gasped.

"Gray has got a pig trapped up against a steep bank!" I gulped out in between breaths. "There's an old axe under the back seat, and in the boot a sheath knife. Maybe even grab the crank handle from under the bonnet, it might come in handy too!"

For a moment he just said, "What?" Then my words must've sunk in as he replied, "Righto Rolly, I'm on my way!"

Jim streaked off back down the track towards the car and boy he could certainly move when he wanted to!

Turning, I set off back into the bush tryin' to think of some way that I might be able to help Gray and not get hurt in the process. The pig had looked bloody big and frightening to me!

Arriving on the scene for the second time, I looked around but this time with my own self-preservation in mind, and noted several small trees that just might be able to support me if needed. That fella 'Justin' was there too, just in case things got out of hand. With my heart still thumping frantically I waited for Jim to get there. It seemed like ages before he appeared out of the undergrowth, the axe in one hand and the knife in the other.

"I didn't bring the crank handle," he panted, "it looked a bit too flimsy. Jeez, look at the size of that pig! It sure looks bloody ferocious to me, Rolly. How're you goin' to knock it off?"

I didn't have a clue what to do, but surely I could work out something. "That's the sixty-four million dollar question isn't it? Tell you what Jim, if I grab one of its rear legs and flip it over, do you reckon you can stick the knife into its throat? Then hopefully it will be all over 'cept the laughing."

Jim looked at me dubiously then passed the buck straight back to me. "Tell you what Rolly, you flip the pig over onto its back and I'll grab one back leg and a front leg, then you can hold the other back leg and stick the knife in it. I've never killed anything in all my life. At least you've killed a few sheep in your day haven't you? It makes more sense that way, don't you reckon? And I must admit I'm feeling shit scared!"

Jim looked me in the eye. He was deadly serious all right and I wasn't much better!

"Okay, I guess it does at that." So taking the knife from Jim I checked it out. It was a lot sharper than I'd thought it'd be, but I still touched up the blade with the steel from the sheath. Then I was all set to give it a go, but was extremely nervous about the whole deal.

Sidling slowly and carefully along the base of the steep bank, I waited for my chance. Once close enough to the pig, I reached over and managed to grab a back leg.

Then immediately to my utter amazement, it was all Gray needed as he rushed in and grabbed the pig by its ear, and did that pig squeal! It sounded almost human, and it sure kicked like hell.

At the same time, Jim leapt into the fray, getting hold of the pig's other rear leg and between the two of us we managed to tip it on its back with the pig screaming frantically as it tried to make its escape. I was as scared as hell and very wary, but with Gray hanging on like there was no tomorrow, my adrenalin kicked in and now all I wanted was to get things over and done with! After a couple of half hearted shots at it, the knife finally drove into the pig's throat and several minutes after that with a fair bit of blood everywhere, it was all over. Gray hung on until the pig's final kick, then moved away looking at me, as though to say, well, what was all the fuss about? Jim and I stared at each other, both of us relieved that the struggle was all over, but the excitement was overwhelming! My breathing was frantic as was my thumping heart. I'd never experienced anything that was so exciting but scary at the same time!

Jim was the first to break the silence, finally able to overcome his excited breathlessness. "Hell's bells, Rolly, I never knew a pig could make so much noise, and look at my skinned knuckles." He showed me his blood-smeared fingers. "It certainly put up a fight didn't it?"

"Yeah, just like you, Jim, I had a hard time holding on and I'm more than happy that it's all over with now. I can't get over how Gray, as mangled up as he was just a few weeks back, managed to stop the pig from takin' to his scrapers, an' the way that he shot in as soon as I grabbed a leg, latching onto an ear and not lettin' the pig move one inch!"

"Come here Gray, what a great dog you are." I patted his wet fur. "Ya sure know how to catch a pig even if we don't know how to kill it! You're a bloody great mutt, all right."

Gray licked my hand, with his tail doin' nineteen to the dozen. Looking so highly pleased, lapping up all the fuss and praise, he was really making the most of it. Then he sauntered over to Jim for even more fuss.

"Look at him Rolly, does he know how to make the most of every opportunity? He's a real bloody con-dog, isn't he?"

We wiped our hands on some bushy leaves. It was time for a smoke. All in all, it had been a real exciting time and given me more than a big thrill, but it also had been a real eye opener at that!

With shaking hands I began rolling a smoke. It was only then that I noticed that Jim was wet through from head to foot and no way was I going to miss out on a golden opportunity like this. It was a fantastic opportunity to do a bit of leg pulling and get some of my own back on him!

"What happened to you, Jim? Tried walkin' on water did you? Just remember, there're not too many who've been successful at that trick." I started to laugh. "Told you he who laughs last has the best and longest laugh, didn't I?"

Fishing the tin of baccy from my shirt pocket, I was very lucky that the water hadn't been any deeper or I'd be spittin' tacks or eating humble pie at the very least. Jim tried avoiding my shots and reached for his own tin in his back pocket, but when he opened it, all he found was a soggy mass of papers and tobacco. He poured the lot out, and did he do his nana, lettin' out a string of oaths that would've put an old sea dog back on his heels. I thought to myself, that reminds me, I'd better get a set of ear protectors for that joker up there. I'm sure that He'd slammed the gates shut, or was it a stray burst of thunder? It was my turn to laugh and revenge was so sweet. Yes siree, and I held nothing back!

"You big galloot," Jim managed to splutter. "It so happens that I had the sense to find a shallowish spot in the stream but I was in such a hurry to get back to you and Gray that I slipped on the slimy, moss-covered rocks. It wasn't more than knee deep but I went right under, so you can stick that in your pipe and smoke it!"

He was trying to keep a straight face, but even he could see the funny side of it all so I passed him the makin's and said, "Oh Jim, revenge like this sure tastes so sweet."

"Go bite your bum!" he answered as he reached out for the proffered baccy tin.

After we'd both lit up and were enjoying our smokes, we discussed our next move on what we could do with the pig. Neither of us had a clue or knew of anyone to give us the info' that we needed. Then it was Jim's idea that we take the pig back to the pub. Surely someone there would know what to do with it? All we needed was a few clues from someone who could give us a few pointers.

The less said about carrying the pig back to the car the better. It was no joke, falling over branches, and we even had the bad luck to get tangled up with a bit of bush lawyer. Then to top it off, Jim wound up giving a demo of how not to cross a stream carrying a pig and over he went again. I didn't have the heart to say a thing as I lifted the pig off him so he was able to get a breath of air, stopping him from nearly drowning!

50

The pig wasn't exactly light, and seemed to weigh about as much as a bag of cement. The further we carried it, the heavier it seemed to be getting! Finally we made it back to the car, managed to get the pig partially into the boot, and lashed it in so that we didn't lose it on our way to the pub. We both agreed that if someone at the pub was willing to give us a hand, or at least show us what to do, we'd shout them a couple of jugs or even give them half the pig.

As soon as we'd walked into the public bar, Curly, one of the barmen that we'd got friendly with, called out, "Two jugs?" then he had a second look. "What in the hell have you two been up to?"

I quickly replied, "Well, it's a long story and we'll tell ya if you hurry up and pour those jugs for us."

Curly filled the jugs and handed us two glasses. "Okay, so now what's the guts on it? Spill it out, you pair of drowned rats!"

After downing a couple of quick ones, I replied, "You don't happen to know someone who's able to show us how to go about gutting and getting a wild pig ready for the oven, do ya Curly?"

"What's that got to do with you jokers covering the bar floor with water? And, yeah, I know a guy who'd be able to put you right about a pig. So?"

After we had told him our yarn, and managed to convince him that it wasn't just a line of bull that we were slinging, he grinned happily, saying. "It's probably a good thing that I don't believe all the stories that flow across this bar! But talk about a pair of tin bums, two bloody novices fluking a pig like that, so I'll make this one an exception to the rule and I'll give ya the benefit of the doubt. Okay?"

Giving an amused chuckle, he looked across the bar and called out. "Sonny, come over here for a moment will ya? A couple of jokers here that I reckon you should meet."

A wiry looking Maori guy wandered over. Curly introduced him. "Sonny, I'd like ya to meet two of the best bull slingers that this old kiwi land has produced yet."

Curly then began to retell our story, with a few more frills tossed in for good measure, and there's no doubt about it, he knew how to dress up a yarn. He had us all in fits. Sonny fired a few more questions at us and we soon filled him in on a few more details and after joining us for a few beers, he agreed to show us how to scald the pig in boiling water and in so doing scrape off the hair. After we'd finished off the last of our beers we moved out to the car where Gray was keepin' an eye on things for us.

Sonny looked the pig over. "It's in bloody good nick, and at a quick guess, weighs about eighty-five lbs. Just as well you didn't gut it, or we'd have had to singe it, because the sulphur in the hot water from the bore might've ruined the pork. Right, let's go then."

We piled into the old bomb and on the way Sonny collected his own knife from home. Arriving out at the outflow drains from the geothermal bores, Sonny tied a rope through a hole that he cut in the hock of the pig's back leg.

"Now listen, just watch where you step and whatever you do, don't fall in, because it's bloody hot and well above boiling. Also if you leave the pig in for more than ten seconds it'll start to cook!"

Sonny, with our help, lowered the pig gently into the boiling water. We counted up to ten, then dragged it back onto the bank and watched as Sonny scraped the pig with his knife. We were somewhat taken aback by how quickly the pig was already looking so clean!

"Sonny, I'm amazed, it looks as good as the chunk of pork that we got from the butcher last week, doesn't it Jim?"

"You can say that again. Can't wait to get my teeth into it."

Sonny grinned. "Slow it down a bit; you guys have to do the other side yet and after that we've still got to dress it out and break it down. Right, now it's your turn to have a shot at getting rid of the bristles!"

We followed Sonny's instructions to the letter and when we'd finished, we'd thought it looked pretty good, but not so in his eyes.

"Boy! You guys are pretty rough all right, just look at those patches of hair and bristles that you've missed!" Sonny then took the knife from us. "You want to keep a better edge on the knife and just use your wrists like this."

There was no doubt about it, already this was a vast improvement on our efforts.

"Now we'll take it over into that patch of scrub," he directed, and in no time at all we were watching Sonny back in action. The guts were out and the head came off. He salvaged the liver and heart and held them up for us to look at. "See what I mean, clean as a whistle, no sign of any disease, and good tucker for your kuri too. Besides he deserves a share, after all if it hadn't been for him you wouldn't be having a feed anyway. So if you slice up the heart like this, he'll lap it up."

Jim and I took it all in. Sonny, in quick order, had the pig broken down into four quarters. Back at the car we loaded the pork into the boot. Gray was hanging around with a begging look on his face. So, under the instructions of Sonny, I handed the sliced up bits of meat to him. Well, I'd seen Gray eating before, but this must've been like food from the Gods or something. Did he make short work of it all; it was gone in seconds flat!

We then climbed into the old bomb and were on our way back to town. We took a couple of detours, first to Sonny's so he could take a half of the pork for himself. He then had a quick wash and was back with us in no time at all.

"I thought you were going to take half of the pork, not just a little bit of it?" I queried.

Grinning from ear to ear Sonny answered. "Don't you worry about that, you'll see what's up later on in the pub!"

We dropped Gray off at home and hung the pork in the washhouse where Gray must've thought it was Christmas as we gave him another feed. Then it was back to the boozer and a few more cool enjoyable beers.

When we arrived at the pub, Sonny took his quarter of pork and headed on into the bar, held it up yelling out, "Righto you fellas, twenty tickets at five bob each for the wild pork, with the head for second prize! Also with half the dough going into the Crippled Children's box. What d'ya reckon?"

Within minutes all the tickets had been sold and as soon as the raffle was drawn, Sonny went over to the corner of the bar that held the collection box and stuck half the money into it. He was laughing as he jingled the rest in his pocket.

"This is something that the missus won't find out about!" Then he shouted us another couple of beers.

We were knocking back the beer, and also learning a bit more about the arts of becoming a pig hunter, when

54

the joker who'd won the pork walked over and spoke to Sonny.

"Give us a loan of your knife son, the boys want me to break down that bit of pork and to re-raffle it off. It's one of the choicest pieces we've seen for a while. And besides, I'm runnin' a bit short of dough!"

"Rolly's got a good sharp knife. Do you mind if Rata borrows it from you please?"

I went out to get my knife from the car and loaned it to Rata who in a short time had the pork in two and thanked me for the use of it.

Inside the bar I grinned at Jim then commented, "Well, one thing for sure, we know what to do now if we're ever a bit short of dough!"

With a big grin on his dial Sonny asked, "Do you reckon that you'll ever be able to latch onto another pig?"

"Just listen to him will you? We've still got our champ, Gray, and I'm going into the sports shop during the week to get myself a good knife," was Jim's quick reply.

"Okay then," replied Sonny, still happily grinning. "But what say you come across a decent sized boar who's eyeing you up and the dog as well? And as well, he's chompin' away with his tusks? He's a pretty tough guy to tackle. If you get between him and where he's gunna take off to, it's bang, one hell of a mess especially if he rips you or the dog and then is long gone. All I can say is I've seen some horrible gashes, so don't think it will always be as easy as your first pig!"

At that, he let the message sink in, and took another deep drink of his beer.

For a while we were thoughtful, as it certainly had put a different slant on things. A few beers later we both agreed with Sonny, and Jim asked, "Well, what do you pig hunters find is the best way to handle the pig, and what sort of gear do you suggest using?"

Sonny savoured another mouthful of beer before answering.

"The way I see it is, the jokers that have got really exceptional dogs, good finder-holders say, well all they need is a sharp knife. But for myself, I carry an old cut-down three o three. If the dogs can handle the pig okay, I reach in, grab a leg and flip it over on its back, knife's in and end of story. But, if he's too big, all it takes is just the one shot and there's fresh pork on the menu. So you're as safe as with the dogs, and there's another useful thing about carrying a rifle. Sometimes you can come across the odd deer - nothing nicer than fresh back-steaks. Or a pot of venison stew sure takes a lot of beating. If I remember rightly, there was an ad for a couple of rifles in last week's local rag. Might be just what you guys need, but take a good careful look at them, 'cause some of the barrels are so worn that the bullets just about go end over end and talk about inaccurate!"

I thanked Sonny for all the info. "We may just get hold of a copy of the paper and have a bo-peep. And now with all this talk about food and eating, my stomach is doin' a bit of a rumble so what about us getting a feed?"

Jim's face lit up. "Now that you mention it, this beer seems to be going to my head, and the thought of roast wild pork is makin' my guts feel like my throat's been cut. So, what do you say Sonny, how about coming up home for a feed and a few more beers?"

Sonny held up his spread hands. "Thanks all the same you chaps but my missus would hang one on me if I didn't eat what she put in front of me when I get home."

"Fair enough, Sonny! Thanks for all your help and the clues on hunting because without your help we'd have been totally stumped!"

"She's right, without you guys giving me the pork, I'd have to've gone home to hit the wife up for a few bob. Anyway I might just think about dropping into the TAB and put a couple of bets on the nags, never know do you, and with the luck I've struck with you two, I could hit the Jackpot and make a killing at that!"

Downing the last of our beers we wished him luck on the ponies, then called into the bottle store where we bought a dozen cold ones, and headed for home. We were really looking forward to our first taste of wild pork that we'd been lucky enough to have scored!

About three hours later we'd finished our feed, talk about a meal fit for kings. We really had made pigs of ourselves, and man, what a meal it was! This was the start of us becoming two good keen men and right into pig hunting!

The following day being a Sunday we relaxed and once again we stuffed ourselves with roast wild pork. Boy, what a life, this was sure living at its best!

CHAPTER SEVEN

MAKING THE RIGHT CHOICE

During the following week Jim and I followed up any odd snippets of information on the whereabouts and availability of rifles that might fit the bill for us. All I can say in all honesty is that I knew which end the bullet came out of, and which part that you held onto. Jim and I were both in the same boat so it was a case of the blind leading the blind.

We called into a house to look at a rifle that this joker wanted to sell, and talk about ancient, even to a couple of beginners like us, it looked bloody old, a real relic! Must've been made prior to the Boer War and wouldn't have seemed out of place as an ornament on the wall above the fireplace. Not only that, he wanted the moon for it and we wouldn't have taken it off him even as a gift!

The next rifle offered to us had the serial number ground off, so it was a definite no no. Just imagine the strife this could get one into, trying to explain that away? Ya know, they reckon that there's one born every minute. Jim and I were certainly not going down that track.

Eventually we did what we should've done in the first place, and it turned out to be the most logical step of all - trying the local sports store. We cast our eyes over the racks of new and second hand rifles, a wide range of them, plus there was a salesman who really knew his onions and had a good all round knowledge of hunting. And it didn't take him long to suss out the extent of our inexperience. He pointed out one rifle in particular that he thought would be ideal for us as it was a cut-down ex-army three o three. He was very up front, and it only took a little talking before I was the owner of the rifle, along with some thirty rounds of ammo. Another thing that helped the deal was a plastic packet attached to the trigger guard, containing a note from the local gunsmith.

'Barrel has minimal wear, reasonably light to carry and doesn't kick like a mule!'

The salesman then proceeded to give us the directions to an old disused quarry-come-rifle-range on the outskirts of town. So all that was left now was for me to learn how to use the rifle, and bone up on all the aspects of firearm safety. Jim then showed interest in a range of knives, because we were both keen to obtain a good one. The salesman came to the rescue again, pointing out which types were the most widely used for pig hunting, but also, universally suitable for dressing out deer. One thing that went through my mind at the time was, 'you've got to get the deer first, mate!' All the gear in the world would be of no help at all if we didn't find out how to bowl one over in the first place. Thanking the salesman for his assistance we carried our purchases out to the car.

On our way home, we decided to drop into the local takeaways for a feed of fish and chips, so there'd be no slaving over pots and pans tonight. Best of all, no washing up either!

Gray greeted us with his usual enthusiasm, his tail working overtime, but looked a bit down in the mouth when he smelt the fish and chips, knowing from previous occasions that there was very little chance of leftovers, but he certainly didn't waste any time in getting stuck into a big fresh beef bone that I tossed to him.

Directly after work the following night, Jim and I made our way to the disused quarry. As we got out of the car, and with a wide grin on his face, Jim strapped on his knife. "Hail the great white hunter."

I smiled. "Fair enough, Jim, but one thing you can count on is that there's a lot more water to flow under the bridge before we can claim to be hunters!"

With that thought in mind I inserted the loaded magazine into the rifle, and strolled out with an empty beer carton that I placed at the base of a large pile of crusher dust. It was ideal to absorb the impact of the bullets, no chance of a ricochet, and going by the bits and pieces of cardboard full of holes, we weren't the only fellas to go there for target practice. Walking back towards where I was going to fire my first shot from, my mind ran through the firearm safety manual that Sonny had given to us, and with the rifle cradled in my arm, barrel facing downwards for safety, I have to admit to feeling a certain amount of nervousness as I'd never fired a rifle of this calibre before.

'Before firing, identify your target, make sure that there is nothing in line with or behind the target that could lead to an injury, or deflect a bullet. Don't shoot at an animal that is on the skyline or on the top of a ridge. Always treat a rifle as though it is loaded and above all, never point a rifle at anyone even if you think it's unloaded. Don't carry a rifle in the cocked position and never rely on the safety catch!'

Jim and I had both read through the safety manual a number of times, but it was better to be safe than sorry. How many times in life had it been said, that it was 'just an accident'? Who could live with the fact that they had taken someone's life? But even so, I was making absolutely sure that everything I did was one hundred percent safe, so I pointed out a spot where I felt Jim would be out of danger.

"Okay, Jim, stand there right behind me!"

I faced toward the target, eased a round into the breech and raised the rifle to my shoulder, sighted on the beer carton, squeezed the trigger. Bloody hell! Talk about a shock! It made one hell of a lot more noise than I'd anticipated. Not only that, the rifle had a kick all right and it was only then I remembered some advice from Sonny about holding the butt of the rifle firmly into the shoulder. That's something that I won't ever forget again! It just goes to show how accidents can happen. Releasing the bolt, I ejected the spent shell, then leaving the breech open, and with the barrel pointing at the ground, I turned and walked back towards Jim.

"Jeez, I completely forgot about holding the butt firmly into my shoulder! What a bloody idiot, it copped me right on the cheekbone and believe you me, it's something I'll never forget again!"

Jim looked concerned at my cheek. "Yeah, that's quite a mouse you've got under your eye, so one thing for sure is that you'll hold the rifle a bloody sight firmer next time you pull the trigger!"

"Thanks for the sympathy, mate!" I grinned regretfully in reply as I went back for the next shot. This time I was ready for the kick, and there was hardly any movement at all. My confidence was building. The next two shots drilled holes very close to the marks on the carton. With my final shot I aimed at just one side of the mark on the container. Squeezed the trigger, bang, and I was elated!

"Look at that, Jim, right on the spot! Yahoo, that's one hell of a lot better!"

I checked out the magazine, yes it was empty. Turning back to Jim I offered him the rifle. He took it and reloaded the magazine and clipped it home. On stepping forward he raised the rifle, sighted onto the target, and talk about a deadeye dick, he was spot on with each shot. Having emptied the magazine, and then checking that there were no further live rounds, he handed it back to me, grinning contentedly.

"Ya know, Rolly, I reckon this rifle is a little beaut, especially as I thought I'd be lucky to hit a barn door even if I was inside with the door shut!"

I was more than happy to compliment him. "That was a good accurate bit of shooting, so don't sell yourself short, I'm most impressed!"

My thoughts were now a bit further down the track as we drove out of the quarry and were both feeling more than satisfied with our initial shots. How would Gray react to the sound of gunshots? According to some hunters there were dogs around that were dead scared and would head off homeward bound at a great rate of knots. Anyway, my fingers were crossed!

When the weekend came around we were both on a high, and just couldn't wait to get out hunting, it was certainly an exciting time for us both. I guess our enthusiasm knew no boundaries, this being our first dinkum hunt! Time seemed to hang tantalisingly, just out of reach.

CHAPTER EIGHT

WHERE ARE ALL THOSE BLOODY PIGS?

With the weekend on us we were off to an area of bush that had been recommended to us, where they reckoned the odd bit of pork was being nailed.

The first fingers of light were breaking the dawn and the stars were rapidly fading as we walked away from the car at the start of our first real hunt. Neither of us was saying a great deal, we were both feeling excited and looking forward to whatever the day brought forth.

The meandering overgrown track we followed led us through gullies full of thick manuka and heaps of secondary growth that we'd been told had been heavily logged in the late twenties. Boy it was certainly damned thick now. Gray seemed as happy as a sandboy, moving away into the scrub for long periods at a time. We found this a bit worrying at first, but gradually got used to it. Whenever we stopped for a smoke he turned up, usually just when we were about to resume walking, and as always looking for a bit of a fuss. It took us a fair while to recognise when we heard the sound of him returning towards us, as time and time again we stood stock still, senses on high alert, wondering if it was a pig or a deer.

By midday we'd covered a fair amount of ground and all we'd got was a bit of a thrill at what we thought was a deer crashing away through the bush. As we moved along on our way, the sun continued rising, heating up the bush and making us sweat heaps, but worse luck there were no streams in this area, and we were unable to quench our growing thirsts. Our keenness kept us moving along, and it certainly wasn't easy going as at times the rifle seemed to weigh a ton. Eventually we began retracing our footsteps into an area that certainly looked a lot more promising, we even discovered what looked like pig tracks. We looked at each other, our excitement rising again making us as keen as mustard, and what we could see were most definitely pig tracks leading into a muddy wallow. On scrutinising the sign we realised that the marks were pretty old and some of them had cobwebs in them, but those old tracks gave novices like us quite a thrill initially.

We also learnt another hard lesson, that in this area we definitely needed to bring something along to quench our raging thirsts. Talk about suffering from dehydration, we were as dry as wooden gods.

Eventually we made it back to the car, weary, thirsty, and covered in scratches. But there was one positive thing we learnt and that was our new sharp knives were ideal for scraping off the thousands of hook grass seeds that were hanging onto the hairs on our legs, even if it was at the expense of a fair bit of lost hair from the knees down. But neither of us had any smart remarks about the fact that we'd been shaving our legs!

So, as dry as hell and empty handed, we headed off to the pub where on arriving in the car park I filled a container with water for Gray. Going by the amount he consumed he was suffering as much as we were! Leaving him happily sprawled across on the backseat of the car in the shadow of trees, we thankfully entered the bar to quench our dire thirsts. Boy, I don't think a beer had ever tasted so good, and the first few drinks, well they didn't even touch the sides on the way down, nor did the next few for that matter. What more could a man ask for, apart from just catching a nice fat porker thanks, mate!

The rest of the day was spent yarning and generally chewing the fat with a few guys who were keen on hunting. It was quite an eye and ear opener for us to hear all the different ideas floating around, like what time of the day, and where to go hunting. We also learned, very much to our dismay, that the particular area we'd just been hunting in had literally been thrashed to death by every man and his dogs! So I guess it was no wonder we'd come home empty handed, but they reckoned give it six months or so, and more pigs will have moved back into the area. They also pointed out a few other likely possies on the map on the wall of the bar. I only hoped that they were a lot more productive than where we'd been hunting today.

One guy, Franno, who never seemed to have a lot to say, quietly pulled me to one side. He said that his main thing was deer stalking, and said, as long as I could keep my mouth shut about where, he'd draw me a sketch of where he'd seen heaps of signs of fresh pig rooting only two days ago. Reckoned that some patches of the pig fern and bracken had been turned over so many times the ground was bare and it looked as if it had been ploughed up and harrowed. Also, he'd caught the sound of pigs squealing in a dense patch of supplejack and bush lawyer, halfway up the side of a steep slope. He drew a rough sketch on the back of an empty tobacco packet of the area and how to get there. I was most thankful, so in return asked if there was any way we could repay him for his advice and help. Initially he shook his head and then said, "Look, if you do have any luck and do score a pig, I wouldn't mind a piece of pork. A mate of mine who's a butcher could make bacon out of it!"

It was great to get positive info like this. "Thanks Franno, if we do score, consider it done, but I'd at the least expect you to share a jug of beer with us, and another thing I must mention is that we're absolutely new comers at pig hunting, the next pig we catch will only be our second one ever!"

Franno gave a wry smile. "Everyone has to start somewhere y'know. Well Rolly, time is rolling on so I'd better make tracks for home or else the missus will be putting a flea into my ear, or maybe I'll that find she has put my roast dinner in the fridge. Also I've got another early start tomorrow. With any luck, I'll catch up with you and Jim in the near future, so good luck!" And he was on his way.

I happily related to Jim what Franno had suggested. "What do you think? Have one more beer and head for home?"

Jim was all for it. "Yeah good thinking Rolly, I'm feeling quite peckish myself, so a binder will hit the right spot and one thing more for sure, I'll be out to the count in no time at all! First thing tomorrow let's start out to this spot that Franno described. But right now let's pick up something from the bottle store, so that we can take it to wet our whistles with tomorrow. I was as dry as hell today when we got back to the car!"

Needless to say, it was a unanimous decision that we had the necessary all set for the following day!

We were up well before daybreak again, and after an enjoyable cup of coffee we loaded Gray and the beers into the car and were on our way. It was just on dawn when we arrived at the spot that Franno had suggested we leave the car. According to the sketch on the tobacco packet, it should take us close on an hour's hard yakka to be in the area that Franno said the pigs had been squealing. To us novices it wasn't going to be a walk in

66

the park but it certainly looked like the area that had been described to me.

Stopping for a break, we were just getting our breath back when I remarked to Jim, "Yesterday Gray was coming back to us all the time, but this time I haven't heard or seen a sign of him. Hope he hasn't taken off in a different direction. We haven't a hope of catching anything without him and that's for sure!"

We stood there rolling smokes, and without warning, Gray's frantic barking put an end to that. We were galvanised into action, and took off at a run, crashing our way through the bush, in and over, any way we could, boy it certainly got the adrenalin flowing! It wasn't easy going, but the sound of Gray's strong steady barking had really got us excited. We scrambled up over a small land slippage on the steep slope and were into another dense patch of supplejack laced with the inevitable clumps of bush lawyer. This slowed our progress down to a crawl, until we finally reached the edge of a deep, narrow, very steep-sided gully. We stopped, listening intently, but there was only complete silence, as Gray ceased barking for what seemed eternity.

Waiting, we strained our ears to the limit, hoping to pick up his bark. We didn't have a clue what was up. More waiting, and then much to our relief, Gray resumed his frantic barking. And we were off again, taking to our scrapers like a couple of madmen, over, around and through branches of fallen trees, until our way was halted by another steep rock-strewn slope. It left us only one way to go, so down it was, sliding, slipping, stumbling, with me cursing as the rifle seemed to get caught up and tangled in everything until finally we made it to the bottom in one piece. How, I don't know. It was pretty steep, and we found that we were slightly to one side of the pig that Gray was bailing in a fairly deep washout. A big sow, but in such an awkward possy to get at, that if cither one of us tried to get behind it, we'd wind up with the pig takin' big chunks out of our hides. There was only one way to handle this situation and that was to use the rifle. I made a mental note to thank Sonny as I scrambled slightly up to the right above the pig, where I could get a reasonably clear shot but at an awkward angle. Motioning for Jim to move behind me I raised the rifle, slid a shell into the breech, then remembering this time to hold the rifle firmly into my shoulder, squeezed the trigger. Even before the echo of the shot had died away, Gray was latched onto the pig's throat, there was no holding him back. It even looked to me as though he had a hold before the pig had actually dropped!

"You bloody beaut!" Jim exulted. "Good shot Rolly, but did you see how fast that Gray moved in, just like greased lightning, man he was quick!"

Taking a deep breath I congratulated myself, and was I elated that the shot was accurate enough to have done the trick. Even so my heart was hammering excitedly.

"Thank God Jim, I'd hate to think what would've happened if I'd missed it, and there's no doubt about it, I was bloody nervous. Just look at that Gray, he's still in there hanging on for grim death. Another good thing we've found out today is that he's definitely not in the least bit gun shy, is he?"

When the pig had given its final movement, Gray waited a few more seconds before releasing his grip and ambled towards me as though to say, 'well what do you think of that aye?' I patted him heartily and lavished him with praise. "Hey, boy, you are a bloody beaut, aren't you?"

And didn't he make the most of the fuss with his tail going like an eggbeater. Then he was all over Jim too. And talk about smiling, if Gray could've talked he would've. When finally he'd milked it for all the fuss that he could, he retired to a cool spot and stretched out, watching our every move.

"You, Gray, you're just a bloody prima donna aren't you?" said Jim. Gray's tail wagged vigorously in complete agreement.

Jim and I squatted down in front of the pig while rolling our smokes. We were both astonished at how Gray could stop a pig of this size and bail it. Just looking at it we reckoned that it was at least seven times the weight of Gray, but probably could have even been heavier!

Then you wouldn't read about it, we were astonished at the quick arrival of big black flies. They were coming in droves, heaps of the damned things zooming around. Where they'd all come from we didn't have a clue, but right up until the time that the pig had dropped, we hadn't seen hide nor hair of them. It didn't take us long to get fed up with their unwanted attentions, so we dragged the sow a short distance out to a spot that was mainly a mixture of small stones and gravel. Even with the two of us pulling, it was no lightweight, so there was not a snowball's chance in hell of lugging it back to the car in one piece.

Luckily for us Sonny had explained in detail how to go about singeing a pig, so the spot where we had dragged it to was ideal, no overhanging bush and very little burnable stuff on the ground that could cause the fire to spread. On the slip where we'd clambered down from there were a number of dead clumps of manuka and kanuka. It didn't take us any time at all to break off and gather up a fair stack of it. All the time we kept in mind the safety factor when we lit the fire and then gradually added more to it. Once we had a good base and it was burning efficiently we dragged and rolled the pig onto the fire. The flames singed and burnt some of the hair but the rest had to be scraped off with knives. It took us a fair old while, and it certainly wasn't as simple as Sonny had made it sound! A damned sight more yakka than meets the eye and the sweat was pouring out from us both. Finally with the singeing done as best we could, it was just a matter of gutting it out, cutting the head off and breaking the body down into two halves. It was going to be a real test of our mettle to lug it back out to the car, but first of all we gave Gray his due reward, and did he made short work of the sliced heart!

After we'd had a short breather, and dampened down the fire by throwing all the guts onto the embers and scuffing out whatever else was still smouldering, we gave it another ten minutes or so, then rechecked the embers, making sure that they were well and truly extinguished. With this part over and done with, we wiped the sweat from our faces, and especially from around our eyes, as it certainly stung when it had dripped into them!

I thankfully commented to Jim, "Man, am I happy to see the end of this singeing lark, it's bloody hot work. Give me the job of scalding out at the hot water bores any day, and there's no doubt in my mind it's a dammed sight easier way of doing it! Now all that I could do with is a beaut nice long, cool beer. Wouldn't it go down well right now? But seein' we've got none, I'll have to settle for second best and have another smoke!"

Jim grinned back cocking his head to one side, "Stop taunting a man will ya; my imagination is kicking up bobsy die as it is. Jeez I can just see a big cool handle sitting on the bar with beads of condensation running down the sides. Anyway there's one consolation at least and that's the half a dozen waiting for us back at the car and it's really going to hit the right spot, believe you me! Another thing, Rolly, we've still got the job of humping this pig out of here and for sure, that's going to be no joke. But one last thing before we do, that's if you're happy about it, I'd like to take a shot with the rifle, just to see if I could hit something after all the running and what have you we've been doing."

I nodded my head. "Go for it Jim, a damned good idea. You're welcome!"

Taking the rifle in hand he prepared to fire a shot. "Now do you see that rotten log about fifty yards across the other side of the gully?" He pointed the rifle towards it. "There's a knot hole about half way along, well that's what I'm aiming at. Okay, I'm all set!"

I waited, watching the target area, and heard the report echoing throughout the gully. A chunk of wood flew off about three inches above the knot. I looked towards Jim, where to my surprise he was unhappily rubbing his right cheek and moaning ruefully.

"Bugger it Rolly, you know what, I forgot all about holding the stock firmly against my shoulder too! Hell, it sure kicked all right, whacked me right on the cheek just like it did to you the first time at the quarry. Guess I should've known better and learnt from your effort. One thing for sure, I won't ever forget again so you can take that grin off your moosh!"

Even though it had happened to me, I couldn't resist pulling Jim's leg a bit, just for the hell of it. "I bet you won't, once bitten twice shy aye? And unless I miss my guess, you'll wind up with a pretty good shiner by tonight and maybe tomorrow the boys at work will start giving you heaps, especially when some nice fella hints that some dame hung one on you for not keeping your hands to yourself! You know something? It looks pretty suspicious to me!" I gave an exaggerated wink and grin to add emphasis to my words.

"Trust you to be the leader of the stirrers aye Rolly. Who needs enemies when I can have a friend like you?" He grinned back at me.

By now there were still heaps more of those bloody big black blowflies hanging around. "Anyway Jim, now that we've had a breather, I've had more than enough of these damned flies, let's make tracks. We've still got to hump these hunks of pork out to the car and it's a fair old tramp from here."

We both struggled to get the pieces of pork on our backs and they certainly weren't the smallest. I picked up the rifle with one hand and we started battling our way back up to the top of the ridge above us. It was no joke, a real gut buster with both of us collapsing exhausted at the top. At first I didn't even want a smoke and that's sure saying something. While we were gasping, trying to get our wind back, Jim managed to get out between breaths, "That bird's got a real shrill whistle, wonder what it is? I've never heard anything quite as noisy, the sound must travel for miles!"

"Jim it's a shining cuckoo, and he sure can make a ton of noise for a bird that is only about the same size as a blackbird. Just as a matter of interest, the Maori name is Pipiwharauroa and I'm not trying to be a know it all, but it just happens that it was something that I learnt from my dad years ago. Another thing is, if you can get under a tree he's in, talk about loud, it's just about deafening!"

"That's interesting Rolly, let's hope that I'll be able to see one for myself some time."

With us both lying back we lapped up the cool breeze that was rising up through the bush. I was immersed deep in thought when Jim broke the silence.

"Ya know something, Rolly? This sure is a great life. I'm bloody glad that we flattened the Mini otherwise we might've never tried our hand at pig hunting! An' it was sure a real stroke of luck that we found old Gray, because without him we wouldn't be here relaxing and enjoying nature. What a life!"

Gray, hearing his name, perked his ears up and never one to miss an opportunity, got off his haunches and came over to slurp his tongue all over my hand and then proceeded to do the same to Jim. He certainly was making the most of it all right!

"Yeah, you've echoed my own thoughts exactly about Gray. But Jim, we can't put off forever the task that lies ahead of us, gettin' this pork back to the car."

"Well, Rolly, you're not wrong there, but I'll tell you one thing. Gray's a great pig dog, but I sure hope he won't latch onto another pig on the way out, because I'm gunna be stuffed enough as it is by the time we get back to the car!"

Struggling, we got the pork onto our backs and again continued along the ridge until it dropped down into a valley. For the most part it was a mixture of flattish bits, but even then there were a couple of very steep pinches. Talk about real gut busters! When we crossed another saddle, it was again a real struggle through some more rough country that was covered in dense native scrub, laced together by long stringy pig fern that towered over our heads seeming to want us to stay in

73

there for good. It latched onto the barrel of the rifle, and tried tripping us both up, time and time again.

I could hear Jim muttering to himself, "And I thought that this was gunna be fun. Yes, folks, this is what I do to keep meself amused." This was followed by deep gasps for breath.

Always the optimist, I answered, "I don't think we've got all that far to go now, Jim."

All I heard this time was, "Just who in the hell do you think you're trying to kid?"

Neither of us was able to muster enough energy to say anything more and after what seemed like an eternity, we broke out onto the rough track that led us directly back to the car. We still had another half mile or so left, but at least it was slightly easier going. Even so we had a number of stops for breathers before at long last we made it. What a relief to unload the pork at the back of the car.

With the next thing on my mind being a beer, my mouth was dry as and filled with pollen from the pig fern. I was dying for a drink. Opening the passenger side door I reached in for the beer, wriggled my hand around, nothing! What in the hell? Where was the bloody beer?

"Hey, Jim, did you see me put the beer under the seat? I'm sure I did."

Just at that moment, Jim grabbed some newspaper from off the back seat and as he headed into the bush, called back. "Have another look, I'm sure you did just before we left. I'm dying for a beer but mother nature is calling too!"

I had another look around just to make sure that it wasn't somewhere else and began swearing.

"No bloody beer, not a drop!"

I was incensed and for five minutes I raved on about thieving ratbags who would flog a man's beer.

74

This, in my books, was a crime far worse than treason even, especially as a man could die of thirst out here. Where in the hell was Jim? He ought'a be back by now I thought.

"Hey, Jim, where are you?" I yelled, but no answer was the stern reply. Again I called. "Jim, where in the hell are you? Are you all right?"

No answer again. I listened intently, then vaguely heard something. That's a funny sound, I thought, and then there it was again, sounding like a suppressed laugh. Then the penny dropped I roared out in anger. "Jim you dirty rotten bastard!"

Then came a burst of full-hearted laughter! Like a runaway express train I headed in towards the sound. I was just about demented with thirst! I charged into a small clearing and there he was, seated with a half empty bottle in his mitt. Staring at him, initially I was lost for words then he lay back in convulsions of laughter. When he could speak again he said, "Jeez Rolly!" as he wiped tears from his eyes. "Have you ever heard yourself telling that joker up there all about it?" and again started laughing.

I reached out to take the fresh beer that he offered and much to my own amazement I didn't swear or call Jim any more names. I was just too damned dry and only interested in quenching my raging thirst. One thing that I've got to say, it was probably the sweetest beer I have ever tasted. With a nearly empty bottle in my hand I began to make threats. Jim was saying nothing, just a big wide grin on his dial.

I threatened him, "Just you wait boy, for when I do get my revenge, it'll be good! You just don't know what you've let yourself in for do you?"

Jim held up his hand in a mute protest. "One thing for sure Rolly, if I hadn't hidden the beer under these trees in the shade, it would've been as warm as hell by now and I know how you hate warm booze. So don't be too tough on a fella please?"

There was no doubt about it, the cool beer was like the nectar of the Gods. All the pig fern pollen had been rinsed from my mouth and throat. On emptying the dregs I reached for a second bottle, smiling slyly with the thoughts of how I was going to get my revenge.

"Yes, Jim, it is a nice cool drop and I don't like warm beer. But just you wait. I can tell you it's far too late to try getting back into my good books! Boy am I out to get my own back, and in mighty big chunks at that, you wait and see."

Still grinning like an ape, Jim replied, "Fair enough, Rolly. But it was worth it, you should've seen the look on your moosh when you burst through the scrub!" Again he rocked with mirth.

This time I had to join in as, I think I had a pretty good idea of how I'd looked. If anyone had seen us, they would've reckoned that we were a couple of nut cases and no doubt about that!

By the time I'd knocked back a second bottle I'd nutted out what I thought was a pretty good way to get my own back and my plan was going to start right now.

"Jim, I'm afraid that nature's callin' me this time. Don't happen to have any of that paper left over do you?"

I knew damned well that he wouldn't make things any easier for me by admitting that he did have, and I started to make my way back to the car.

"Nope, I must've used the lot," and he had the cheek to laugh some more.

"Okay Jim, no worries. I'll just get some more from the car." So now the boot is definitely on the other foot, I sniggered to myself as I ambled back through the scrub. As soon as I opened the driver's door, I reached up under the dashboard and flicked the isolating switch to off. No power, no go and who was going to have to push start? Oh lucky Jim, how I envy him! I also reached over and turned the ignition key to the on position. After all, he was a bloody mechanic, and I had to make sure that it all looked legit. As I entered the scrub on the other side of the old bomb, I called back, "Hey, Jim, the flies are hovering around this pork like vultures, we'd better get it home and into the safe before they blow it all!"

From in the scrub Jim agreed, "Be right there!"

Beauty! The trap had been set. Got ya mate! It was already going to plan. So it was my turn to head into the bush where I took my time, and when I arrived back at the car, Jim had got everything loaded up, the pork in the boot and Gray on the back seat.

Grinning to myself at thought of what lay in store for Jim, jeez it was now all on!

Hands on his hips Jim greeted me with, "What took you so long? I had to struggle to get the pork into the boot by myself." And the sweat was pouring off him, but Jim was playing right into my hands well and truly!

"One thing though, Rolly, I knew you hadn't died yet, because all the flies were still hanging around here, although some of them took off in a hurry. Must've been something that attracted them away from here!"

As per usual Jim was getting his usual dig in. I didn't say a thing, just grinned and climbed in behind the wheel, shutting the door, looking at him.

He then came out with, "Hey, mate, I'm sorry but I've got some bad news for you, you've left the ignition switched on and the battery is as flat as a pancake. And that's not all, I can't find the damn crank handle to kick it over with so the only thing to do is push start the old bomb or get a tow!"

I put a shocked look on my dummy. "Jim, you're joking. We're at least a mile away from the road as it is."

I turned the key off and on a few times and pushed the starter button but it was dead as a mackerel!

"You're right, Jim, just how I could do something like that? Buggered if I know."

I kept a straight face but inside I was having a huge laugh. And that horrible nasty fella inside of me was fair bustin' and in order to hide my feelings I frowned deeply "Damn and blast, I'm sure that it was switched off before we began hunting this morning. You're sure you're not pulling my leg again, because if you are…" I left my words hanging in the air.

"Look, Rolly, I've had my bit of fun and I certainly wouldn't sabotage this old girl, and definitely not this far back from the road. Besides, I'll be the one who is gunna be doing the pushing to get the old thing started. Look, there's a bit of a slope down there and then a little rise and a bit more of a slope. If she starts it'll be just great, but if not, one of us is goin' to have a long walk back to the main road for help!"

Jim went behind the car. "Are you ready? Ignition on, clutch in and don't forget, leave her in second while I begin to push, then drop the clutch like a hot spud when she's rolling! Okay?"

With Jim pushing his guts out we went down the slope, I dropped the clutch and she slowly ground to a stop! I snickered to meself, oh, how could I be such a rotten mate? I called out, "Well, Jim, it's not far, only just a short push to the top of this little hump then we can try again."

Up we slowly went, I could hear Jim blowing like an old draught horse. At the top of the hump I stopped to give him a breather until he called out, "Okay, Rolly, same again? Let's go!"

And the whole process was repeated until we came to a stop again. Jim came round the car and looked in the window, the sweat was pouring out of him and in between gasps, he panted out, "That's the end of that, looks like I'll have to start walkin' out to the road in the hopes that someone will be able to giv'us a tow."

I let him walk about twenty paces or so and called out, "Hey, Jim, I just remembered, I think the crank handle is under the back seat!"

"Are you sure?" He started back towards me as I got out and reached behind the back seat. Lo and behold, there was the handle. I waved it at him and walked around to the front of the car, where I stood all smiles.

Jim reached out, grabbing the crank handle, saying, "I'm the mechanic and have heaps more experience at cranking than you. I'll do it!"

He fitted the handle into the hole in the bumper and then in under the radiator and onto the crankshaft dog, ready for cranking. "Ya ready? I'll have this motor ticking over in no time at all!"

Seated back behind the wheel I thought to myself, that's what you think? Boy, I'm a real horrible mate all right. Then barely able to contain my mirth, I nodded. Around and around Jim wound the crank until he was absolutely stuffed. Once again, he gasped for air as he tried to get his breath back and with beads of sweat pouring out of him he came around to the window. "Jeez," he gasped, "I'm fair knackered, she's as dead as a door nail. I'll start walking towards the road in the hopes of getting a tow or someone to give us some assistance!"

Again, I let him walk ten paces or so then flicking the isolation switch to on, got out and called after him.

"Look, Jim, it all depends on how you hold your mouth." I reached down, gave the crank a quick yank and she was purring like a contented cat. Jim's mouth dropped open like a coalscuttle. I quickly grabbed the crank handle and shoved it under the front seat of the car, and now it was my turn to laugh. The look on Jim's face was priceless, but I made sure that I got into the driver's seat post haste.

Then Jim started laughing, because he knew he'd been taken to the cleaners. And my revenge was sweet as! "Bloody hell, Rolly, you certainly got your own back all right. One thing for sure, I won't ever try to put another one over you again. As for that bloody isolating switch, I'd completely forgotten about it. You're a cunning bugger all right!"

He then stuck out his hand. We both smiled as we shook hands.

"Truce?" he enquired.

"Truce," I agreed.

We both laughed, our friendship all the stronger for our leg pulling.

And so ended our first real taste of successful pig hunting. We were well and truly hooked on our great day out!

So was Franno, when we turned up with his half of the pork. There's no doubt about it, one good turn sure deserves another and week or so later we received a nice surprise of quite a few packets of delicious wild pork, bacon and sausages in return. Boy it sure was fantastic eating!

CHAPTER NINE

TO HELL WITH IT, LET'S GO FOR A BEER

For the next few weeks, work dragged on in much the same mundane way as usual. That was, until a couple of the guys, both of different origins, didn't see eye to eye. One of them had a sense of humour and the other had very little and was very quick to rise to the bait.

The first was Burt, a little short-arsed bloke who stood all of five foot nothing. He was a real character, who didn't seem to give a damn about anything except enjoying life, and never let anything get under his skin. In fact once, after we'd been told to dig up the same pipe for the fourth time in a row just because some bloody idiot in the drawing office hadn't done his calculations correctly, Burt calmed me down when I was about to hang a bunch of fives on this bright bastard. This bloody illegitimate glow-worm, who not only made some real bad boo-boos, and wouldn't accept the fact that he'd gotten it all wrong, always blamed everyone but himself.

"Rolly, we both know that he's a bloody idiot and a liar so don't let it get to ya. He'll get his come-uppance some day. Just remember, if they tell us a dozen times over to dig it up and do it again, they're paying us and the money will keep on rolling in. Another thing is, as long as we're doing this job, we're not doing something a damn sight worse. So c'mon mate, let's get our heads down and into it again."

I thought about his words of wisdom, they made good sense. I looked at Burt, nodding my head. "Thanks, Burt you're dead right."

Then we were back into it, bum up, head down.

Now this Burt was a great one for taking people off. His imitating of different people was so humorous that he often had us all in fits of laughter. During the latter part of the week, near the end of our lunch break, he started to do an impersonation of the site manager, who was also the engineer on the job. Hank, the redheaded Dutchman, was as large as Burt was small, well over the six-foot mark. So Burt made up for lost height by crouching on a chair, making as though he was squinting through an imaginary theodolite. He signalled violently with his arms, yelling and in general giving a good display of the performance that usually took place when Hank was on the job!

"Oop a beet, a little to zee right. No, no, to zee left a beet, holdsit steadys, oop a beet, oop a beet more!" All the time, signalling frantically with his arms, he never did things by halves.

"Okays, mark it dere. Rights, we'z betta checks it? Haf yous got it on zee mark? Whats are yous doings? Hold it on zee marks!"

By this stage he was, as per usual, getting more and more worked up, and the hotter he got, the more his English deteriorated. Then he cupped his hand to his ear to 'hear' the reply. Talk about a pantomime!

"Yous tellings mes it's ons zee marks? Votta yous tryinks to doos, makings mes a bigs lottsa ofs fools ins fronts ofs allaones?"

We were splitting our sides at Burt's antics, when in stormed the Dutchman, his face the colour of his hair - a bright red. By the looks of it, he must've heard every word Burt had uttered. A tense silence engulfed the lunchroom. The Dutchman just stood and glared at little Burt, who was still perched on the chair. Then, without

82

uttering another word, and almost frothing at the mouth, he spun round on his heel and stomped out the door.

Burt only took a second to regain his composure and reacted accordingly. "Boy oh boy, if looks could kill I'd be dead and buried that's for sure!" the little Canadian remarked at the Dutchman's rapid departure.

This brought another burst of laughter from the guys which no doubt rang in the redhead's ears.

From that time on, it was noted that Burt copped all the really shitty jobs, but Burt wasn't in the least bit perturbed. He was only on a working holiday anyway and didn't give a damn when he moved on, or what sort of work he did.

Then he must've decided to have a shot at giving the square head a run for his money. So on the next payday when the gong rang for payout, Burt made sure that he was the frontrunner in the queue. The paymaster set up his table with time sheets and the pay packets. And as per usual, the red headed Dutchman stood beside him to keep his eye on the proceedings so he could deal with any irregularities on the spot. Little Burt started to sign for his dough, then looking up at the Dutchman, stopped signing and stepped over in front of Hank. He reached out and up as high as he could, making out he was trying to brush something away from the engineer's shoulders. The square head took a quick step back, his hands out, "Hey, what's yous doings huh? Vot yous oopts too?"

We all watched totally spellbound in the silence that followed. Not a soul moved, all eyes were focused on Burt as he replied casually, in a very off hand manner, "Oh, I wouldn't let it worry you, if I were you. It's not much, just a handful of small flies hanging around your head and shoulders - I just thought that I would do you a favour an' chase them away."

Spluttering a bit, the engineer bellowed out, "Vot yous means small mans, vats yous oopts toos?" His face was getting redder and redder by the moment.

But Burt just smiled up at him for a second or two and slowly replied.

"Well, for a little joker like me, it's easy to explain. Y'know those little blue flies? The ones that hang around bad smells, toilets and things! By gosh, they're persistent aren't they? There's some more of them!" Burt then rapidly leapt forward, as though to brush them away.

The Dutchman, his face now the colour of cooked beetroot, took another quickstep backwards, away from Bert's up-flung arm.

"I see's no flies, yous taka da pess outas mes?"

Burt replied quietly, "Nope, I'm not fooling, but there's a few more of them. Stand still will ya' while I chase 'em away. Wonder what makes them hang around you like that?"

The Dutchman, with hands spread out in defence, was really on the boil and the back foot!

"Yous stays aways froms mees, yous leetles mans. You tinks I's a chithouse, that's vots yous sayings huh?" He stood there shaking, almost frothing at the mouth, his complexion nearly as red as his hair!

Burt just stood there quietly for a moment, and then slowly dragged out his reply.

"No, no, no, you've got it all wrong, I think you're a real nice guy! But you just can't fool those bloody flies, can you?"

We all watched with bated breath, transfixed for some twenty seconds or so while the Dutchman stood shaking with rage, his bottom jaw swinging in the breeze. Not a sound came from his wide-open mouth.

Then much to our astonishment, Burt spoke again, topping it off by saying. "If I was you, I'd close your mouth or you might just wind up swallowing one of them little blue flies!"

The Dutchman's mouth obeyed the command and slammed shut like a trapdoor. Everyone roared with laughter, there was no way we could hold it back any more!

Giving Burt a wide berth, the Dutchman stamped around to the pay clerk. He must've strained his lungs screeching out, "Gives hims his days, he finished, he goes, he goes!"

Then turning back to Burt with both arms outstretched, he pointed towards the gates roaring, "You tinks yous cana taka da mecky out da mees, yous calls me da chithouse. Yous nos dos its agains! Now's yous goes outova gates always. Yous fired!"

Burt looked up at the Dutchman's deep purple complexion, smiled placidly, and retorted, "Jeepers, look at all the flies around here will ya! You can bet your sweet life on it, I'm off just as soon as I get my money!"

This was too much for the square head, and he retired rapidly to the sanctuary of his office. Burt finished signing for his pay and then as he walked past us, offered. "Any of you guys feel like a beer? If so I'll see you down at the pub!"

Jim licked his lips and looked questioningly at me, "Well, what about it, Rolly? Don't ya reckon a few cold ones 'd hit the spot? Better than slaving our guts out an' diggin' at this bloody place anyway!"

I looked Jim square in the eye, and the thought of a cool beer was all I needed. "Yeah, a cool beer is better than working in this dump. Let's have the rest of the day off. There's only one small problem though, we just might get the order of the boot too. Burt has put the square head in a real bad mood, but then again, what's wrong with the idea of propping the bar up and havin' a bit of the week out hunting. If he does give us our marching orders, we can tell him where he can stick his job. I for one would much prefer to get back driving earth moving machinery, and another thing, the pay's a bloody sight better than the money we get around here!"

Jim grinned from ear to ear and yelled after him, "Hey, Burt, line us up a couple of jugs will ya? We'll be with ya as soon as we've changed our mocka!"

Jim and I changed and were on our way towards where I'd parked the old bomb. When a bellow came from behind, we turned enquiringly. 'Here goes', I thought to myself.

"Hey yous twos! Where yous twos ofts to?"

We looked at the square head and you could see that he was still simmering away.

"Hold onto your hat, Jim," I said. Then I yelled back, "We're not feelin' too good. In fact, we're pretty crook, so we're just heading on our way to get some medicine to put things right!"

No doubt about it, we had certainly upset the apple cart too. He fair roared as he strode towards us.

"Yous a liars. I sees yous talks to little mans, I knows yous goings to hotel!"

I thought to myself, well, there's no use mucking around. I'd had more than a gutsful, anyway definitely a time to head for newer pastures. Waiting until he was a short way off, I let rip.

"Listen you bloody square head, we don't like you or your job. So put that in your pipe and smoke it, we've had an absolute gutful. It's no bloody wonder, as you've been an inconsiderate moaning foreigner ever since we started on day one. So now you can take this job and shove it!"

With that I glared at him, and once again, he was bellowing, his complexion changing from white to a deep purple.

"Yous goes outa da gates, yous nots comes backs in's here's for ever! Yous sacked!"

Rounding on his heel, our bloody ex-boss headed back toward his office. Well with me being me and Jim being Jim, we couldn't resist having the last word.

"Watch out for those bloody flies!"

With that we were into the old bomb and off to the pub. Arriving there, we walked into the bar where Burt was lining up a couple of jugs. When we'd knocked back a couple of quick ones to kill the thirst, told him our tale of how we'd got fired and were also now in the ranks of the unemployed. After much leg pulling and joshing about the three of us getting the boot, we continued our session for the rest of the afternoon.

About the time the clock showed five, we were interrupted in our drinking, and to our astonishment, it was the pay clerk. We looked at him, wondering why he was there. He'd had very little to do with us apart from when he'd dished out the pays. He then handed us an envelope each.

"This is your final pay, included is forty hours in lieu of notice, plus holiday pay!"

Both Jim and I were amazed as we'd discussed the holiday pay on our way to the pub and had decided that it wouldn't have been worth the trouble of picking it up, it was only a few bob. But this put a new light on it all. Money to burn! A very nice hand out, thank you. We offered the pay clerk a beer for his trouble, but he declined and was on his way.

When he'd left, Burt commented, "The only reason that I took the mickey out of the square head was that I knew if I was able to get him wild enough, I'd be fired on the spot, hence forty hours pay in lieu of notice for sweet bugger all. It's not often in my life that I've got something for nothing, so I'll gladly accept any donations for the cause. But one thing I didn't anticipate was you two getting the same deal!"

There was no getting away from it and we all agreed it was certainly better than a kick in the bum!

All this reminded Burt about a guy he'd shared a room in a boarding house with. So he related the yarn to us.

"This Aussie joker, although he'd never had any more experience as a barman other than putting a spigot into a nine gallon keg at a do on a Saturday night, had the cheek to apply for a job in a pub as an experienced barman. Well, he was as full of it as Barney's bull an' had slung a great line of how he'd been a barman in the Chevron in Sydney, and he ended up with the job. Anyway, he'd only been on the job for about three hours handing out a lot of free beers to everyone, including me! The proprietor was as happy as hell at the thought of the way this joker could drum up trade, things were looking good. That was until he went to help out in the bar himself. Not a lot of money had come across the bar, and the till had only a little more money in it than it'd had when the bar had opened that morning. Realising that his prize barman was taking him to the cleaners, the owner sacked him on the spot. Anyway, this Aussie had thought that this was fair game, gaining plenty of instant friends and free booze for himself. It just goes to show how sometimes a little bit of bull goes a long way.

Due to a shortage of barmen at the time, the Aussie was able to do this a few more times, especially because he was such a good talker, and I for one didn't mind a few free ales. Eventually all good things must come to an end, sooner or later. The word must've got around the pubs and one of the owners had a natter with the cops, because a couple of plain clothes dicks turned up at our room in the boarding house, informing the Aussie that his days of giving free beer were over. When he'd packed his one and only suitcase, they drove him to the bus depot, made him buy a ticket on the first available bus that was heading up north, and warned him that if he ever turned up in this neck of the woods they'd run him in on some charge or another and make sure that he'd spend quite a bit of time in the pokey!

As it turned out I bumped into him eighteen months or so later in another boozer a bit further up the country and much to my amazement, he was dressed up to the nines. Evidently he'd up and got hitched to some sheila who had pots of gold. Anyway, he was just rolling in it, and another thing, he seemed to be well known and respected wherever he went. Y'know it just goes to show, these women always seem to fall for the joker with the biggest line of bull. I met her a short while later and she certainly didn't seem to be a pushover to me, and was definitely no dumb blonde."

Jim piped up. "With all this talk about free booze, I'll go and refill our jugs."

When he returned with the jugs and filled our glasses, Jim said, "Talking about beer, pubs n' things, I remembered about a couple of guys I knew. They were a real hard case pair and were relating this yarn to us in the pub about working part time for an extra bit of pocket money at a public hospital..."

They were there five nights a week from six until midnight with their main jobs as orderlies and cleaners taking them to all parts of the hospital, including the morgue. Now for the first few times they were both pretty uncertain about being around this part of the hospital, but after a while they no longer found the area quite so creepy. It even had its advantages, one being that it was a good place to have a smoke on the sly, as usually they were involved with wheeling in the unfortunates anyway. While sneaking in a smoke one night, they could hear exuberant voices coming from outside the hospital. It was common knowledge that the local sports ground fronted onto the morgue. A couple of drunken-sounding guys full of dutch courage were egging each other on to climb up onto a fairly low ledge that ran along the front of the building and have a look into the morgue. Now Wally was always on the lookout for the opportunity to pull someone's leg.

"Hey, Brian, we might get the chance to give these fellas a bit of a fright. Hop onto that trolley and I'll cover you up with a sheet and then when you hear me click my fingers, slowly sit up and give a moan like a spook!"

With Brian on the trolley and covered by the white sheet, Wally hid in the shadows so he couldn't be seen. They waited as the voices outside continued to laugh and crack jokes about the morgue and what was inside. Then one of them said that the ledge was a bit on the high side, and if his mate could give him a leg up he'd be able to reach down and pull him up too. After a bit of grunting and cursing, the first joker was up on the ledge, shortly followed by his mate. Then they were both looking in through the open window, when one excitedly called out.

"Hey, look over there under that light, there's a stiff covered by a sheet!"

After a couple of seconds came a nervous laugh, and his mate spoke up. "Gosh, it's nothing to be scared of, is it?"

There was a drunken sort of a giggle, as his off-sider added. "Look, you can even see it's got shoes on. Do you reckon they'd fit me?"

At this Wally clicked his fingers and Brian started to slowly sit up, letting out slow ghostly sounds. "Oooooooww ooooooww!" The eerie sound floated through the air. The two onlookers were rooted to the spot, then one of them managed to stammer out, "LLLLllook, the bloody thing is sitting up! Bugger this, let's get the hell out of here!"

On hearing the sound of bodies hitting the ground and the pandemonium of two high-pitched voices mixed up with rapidly receding footsteps, Brian and Wally were left in fits. In fact, they reckoned that they were close to dying from laughter, and so were the rest of us who were listening to the tale.

As it happened Brian and Wally had only just finished relating this tale a couple of days after it had happened.

Suddenly right out of the blue, two complete strangers who'd been having a drink on a nearby leaner arrived at our table with a couple of jugs each. They placed them down on the table in front of Wally and Brian, while we all looked in amazement until Wally, who was the first to gather his wits, queried them suspiciously. "Who are you two? What are these jugs for?"

We all waited expectantly.

One of the two guys stated, "Well it's like this, we couldn't help but overhear you two jokers telling about what happened up at the hospital morgue and how you put the wind up a couple of half-cut nosey parkers, who'd had more than a skin full. And to cut the story short, we're the two fellas that you scared the living daylights out of, and you've got no idea what it's like to be on the receiving end of something like that! When it happened we were so shaken up that we considered giving up the booze for good and becoming members of A.A. But it's lucky for us that we didn't give it away, otherwise we'd have never heard the full story! I can tell you that it certainly put the wind up us!"

At that point everyone roared their heads off again at hearing the story from the receiving end, and shared the jugs all round!

It had been an enjoyable day for Jim, Burt and myself, plenty of yarns, laughter and the inevitable beers but it was getting late in the day and Burt said it was time for him to make tracks. He was heading south early the next day, so we shook hands in farewell.

"Well, Rolly, Jim, it's been great to have a few beers with you guys and I'm hoping that I'll bump into yous again some day. So until then, keep your eyes peeled, I might just be leaning on the bar nursing a cold one. Catchya." And he headed for the bar exit.

"Hey Burt," Jim called as he went to walk out through the doors. "Don't be too rough on those square heads, giv'em a bit of a break will ya?"

Quick as a flash Burt retorted, "Vat you thinks huh! You stinks mes somes kindsa toilets is dats vots you stinks?"

He waved and was on his way.

Just as Jim and I were about to shoot for home, having drained the dregs from the bottom of our glasses, Curly beckoned us toward the bar.

"Look, you two, I couldn't help but overhear earlier that you're thinkin' about doing a bit of hunting tomorrow, and it also happens to be one of my days off. So what about coming and doing a bit of pig hunting with me? Ya see, a cocky mate of mine asked me if I knew of anyone with good pig dogs that didn't worry sheep. He's having a fair bit of trouble with a couple of rogue pigs on his boundary that've turned cannibal and are killing and eating the newborn lambs. Reckons his lambing percentage will all be to hell and gone if he doesn't do something about it pretty quick!"

I looked at Jim, and we both nodded in agreement. This was something that we couldn't turn down!

"You bet, Curly, That'll be just great, thanks for the offer!"

"Fair enough, fellas, but one thing, do you reckon that you can trust that kuri of yours to not worry sheep?" he asked with a serious look on his face.

Even though I was dead keen to get out hunting, it was something that I didn't have a clue about. "To be honest with you Curl we've never had him near enough to any sheep to answer that one, but he's pretty obedient. Doesn't chase anything other than pigs and deer as far as we know, so what do you think? After all, you're the joker we're going with."

Curly looked at us and slowly nodding his head, decided. "Sounds as though he could be okay, and we should be able to keep an eye on him. So what say you two jokers meet me here outside the pub at five in the morning with your gear and your kuri?"

"Outside of here at five it is then, we'll be here with bells on!" I replied eagerly.

"Beaut," replied Curly. "We'll leave your bomb here and make our way out in my jalopy. It's not too far out to the farm, just off the Old Coach road, and by taking my old girl, it's got plenty of room for the three of us and the dogs." With those parting words he moved quickly along the bar to serve some customers who were shouting good-naturedly that if he didn't shake a leg and fill their glasses, they'd die of thirst.

As we left the bar Jim exclaimed, "What a little humdinger, I don't think there's anything I'm gunna enjoy more than the thought of goin' out hunting especially while everyone else is havin' to go to work!"

Then he was silent, frowning, as the wheels turned over in his mind. "Hey, Rolly, I sure hope Gray doesn't worry sheep like he does pigs!"

Looking at Jim I was pretty thoughtful about it myself and nodded in agreement. "I'm with you there, mate, suppose we'll just have to see what the 'morrow brings. So let's keep on moving homewards and worry about that later on. Right now, all that I'm looking forward to is a good feed at home and an early start tomorrow!

CHAPTER TEN

CRICKEY! JUST WHAT'S AROUND?

Early next morning just before five, Jim and I were sitting in the car outside the pub having a quiet smoke, waiting for Curly to turn up, when two cops in a prowl car pulled up beside us.

"What are you two jokers hangin' around here for at this time of the morning? If it's a beer you're after, you've got a long wait ahead," rattled out the cop sitting in the driver's seat.

I was deep in thought miles away, caught completely on the wrong foot, so it was Jim who was quick off the mark.

"Hell's bells, Rolly, caught in the act of casin' the joint, an' even before we managed to get inside. Okay, we surrender - you've just caught us in the act of tossin' up about which will give us the most enjoyment, knocking off the safe or breaking into the public bar and drinking some free booze."

The cops didn't know what to make of Jim's reply as he kept a straight face. But before they'd had time to make up their minds, a Land Rover pulled to a stop behind us, we were saved by the bell, so to speak. A voice that we recognised as Curly's called out.

"Hey Jim, Rolly, are these two coppers worrying you? If so, I might just be havin' me some early morning exercise."

Both cops laughed and the driver replied. "Good God, how come you're out of bed so early Curl'? Didn't wet it, did ya? Or did the missus smack your hand?"

The next thing, Curly was standing beside us grinning at the cops, threatening. "One more squeak out of of you two blokes and you'll have to call out the rest of the force to protect you!"

"Yes sir!" answered the cop in the passenger seat as he gave a mock salute. "We'll beat it before you get too stroppy to do us any harm!"

Then with a wink towards Jim and me, the cop continued. "Keep an eye on him, boys, he's got a real bad habit of putting other peoples' teeth in his big mouth!"

With this remark the two cops and Curly broke into loud spontaneous laughter. Then with a wave to us, the driver of the prowl car dropped the clutch and planted his foot flat to the boards. They took off like a bat out'a hell, doing a big wheely, showering Curly, who was standing unprotected, with bits of gravel and clouds of dust. When the dust had settled and Curly had stopped calling the two cops nasty names, he wiped his eyes.

"Boy, just keep watching for when I eventually catch up with those two buggers!"

Jim and I looked at each other as though to say, what's up?

Curly, still with a big smile on his face, turned to us. "You jokers all set to go?"

Jim nodded, "Yep, Curly, ready and raring to set off!"

With a jerk of his head towards the Land Rover, Curly said, "Right, toss ya rifle and kuri into the back and then leap in the front with me. Don't worry about my two mutts, they're all noise when it comes to other dogs.

Rolly, I don't see a mag for your rifle, haven't left it behind have ya?"

Patting my pocket, I said, "In here, Curly. As far as safety goes, I have no worries about something going haywire as long as it's stashed in my pocket. A number of fellas have pointed out to me that people do strange things with guns, an empty rifle is a safe one, so the mag's in my pocket!"

We walked to the back and opened the Land Rover up, to be greeted by Curly's dogs snarling at Gray, who much to our surprise, jumped in and brushed past without showing the least bit of interest in either of them. On seeing Gray's look of total disdain, they shut up and wagged their tails in greeting. Curly was dead right, they were all wind.

"Where's your rifle, Curly?" I asked, seeing no sign of another rifle.

"I don't bother with one, Rolly. I use a ten-four Kea gun with solid lead instead of birdshot, you'll see it under the dashboard when you get into the front."

As we climbed in, Curly pointed to it. "Ideal for putting an end to a pig at close range, but not so very accurate at anything over ten feet. But it certainly does the trick all right, and another thing, it's light and short. With me being a lazy bugger, I always take the easy way out. Well, now we're all set, so let's make tracks."

After a couple of miles down the road I could see Jim was up to his old tricks. He just had to ask Curly about his copper mate's remarks.

"What's the score about you and how you go about wearing other people's teeth, Curly?"

Curly gave a bit of a chortle, grinned and replied. "Trust those two bloody cops, they always have to get a shot in. Who wants enemies when you can have mates like that? Can't keep their big traps shut! Y'see it goes like this…

The three of us went over to see a shield game and as per usual, once the game was over, we dropped into a pub to argue the pros and cons as to why, where and how the game had gone. Plus this pub always put on a hell of a good counter meal, so with the inner man more than satisfied, we left the pub for a mate of mine's place. Jeff's a cocky who is a great lover of rugby and there was the added attraction of having some fresh venison on hand for his mates and the fact that he lived right on the main road. One could hardly drive past without calling in could they?

We arrived at Jeff's place to find the place chocka block. He was throwing a party just for the hell of it, with the main topic being the day's rugby game and the great try that Bunny had scored at the last minute enabling us to retain the shield by one point. Well, I for one was having a great time of it, meeting and drinking with old friends from all points of the compass. Not only that, I had made the bad mistake of mixing my drinks, but I think what really got me going was a couple of glasses of pretty potent home brew. All of a sudden the room began to spin, and having been in this state before, I knew that it wouldn't be too long before I puked. Somehow I managed to stagger outside, making it to Jeff's longdrop. Jeez I was as crook as a dog and must've flaked for a while too.

When I came to, I found that I'd lost my teeth and in the state I was in, I realised that they were no doubt deep down the black hole of Calcutta. I sort of staggered back into the house and related my tale of woe to my two mates, who didn't offer me any sympathy whatsoever. In fact, the bloody ratbags thought it was a hell of a joke with them swearing black and blue that if they were me, and ever lucky enough to get the teeth back, they wouldn't wear them, even if they were the last pair of teeth on earth. Not after where they'd been! Seeing I wasn't getting any change out of those two buggers, I got hold of Jeff, who dug up a torch and off we went outside. Well, talk about a bit of luck. When the light filled the longdrop, there were my teeth lying on the floor. They hadn't taken a dive down the black hole after all!

I said to Jeff. "Whew, that's a bit of luck, if they hadn't been on the floor, I'da been havin' to fork out quite a few bob to have new ones made!"

"Yep, you can say that again Curl, the old dunny is built over a tomo, it's at least a good fifteen feet deep and y'd never in a month of Sundays have gotten them back. It sure has been your lucky day all right and it would've been a pretty high price to pay for a day out with the boys. Now hop back inside, clean 'em up and plonk them back in your moosh. You sound a bit like Donald Duck without them!"

On the way back through the house to the bathroom, everyone gave me heaps, about me calling for Herb and losing my chompers. But it was those two copper mates of mine that started everyone off by askin' me in loud voices and really rubbing it in.

"Curl, did ya find ya teeth all right? Did you need a fishing rod?"

In the bathroom I rinsed out my mouth and scrubbed the teeth with disinfectant and a nailbrush. Then giving the teeth a final rinse, I tried to put them in my mouth, but the bloody things just wouldn't fit. I checked them over and there didn't seem anything wrong with 'em, and tried them again but they still didn't fit. It had me absolutely stuffed. I walked out to the lounge and waved my teeth at Jeff. He grinned at me and called out, just when everyone had shut up.

"What's up with the teeth Curl, you not like the taste very much?" Then everyone burst into laughter including my so-called friends. I can tell you, it's a wonder they didn't lift the roof off the house! When the mirth eventually quietened down, I said disgustedly, "It's not the taste, it's just that the damned things won't fit, buggered if I know why, they bloody well fitted before!"

This led to another bout of rafter-lifting laughter. The humour of the situation even got to me and I had to smile too. Then Jeff reached into his top pocket and handed over a pair of teeth wrapped in plastic. "It so happens that I have a spare pair of my old choppers. Try these for size, it might be your lucky day!"

I took them from him somewhat dubiously, unwrapped them and tried them and they fitted perfectly. I was amazed, and. then the penny began to drop. Everybody bloody near split their sides again and when the laughter died down, I spluttered "Where in the hell did you get these from? They fit spot on, they must be mine!"

Again the room rocked with mirth. I could see that I'd been taken for a ride all right!

Grinning from ear to ear, Jeff replied, "Yep Curl it's a bit of a yarn and this is how it happened! Ya see, I was on my way out to the old dunny myself when you came out mumbling something about losing your teeth down the black hole of Calcutta. You didn't even see me as I stepped to one side and it wasn't until you'd gone back into the house that I'd managed to make head or tail of what you'd been on about. Striking a match gave me enough light and I spotted your chompers on the floor.

Well, this was a golden chance and I couldn't let an opportunity like this slip by could I? It was revenge time and I was going to make the most of it!"

Again everybody roared, so that is how the story of my teeth has been ever since.

Jeff then said "So now I'll just take you back to that time when you guys carried me back to the scratcher absolutely legless one night and you knew that we'd all need a reviver to put us right in the morning. The first thing I can remember when I came to was you saying, "C'mon you old bugger, rise and shine, it's time to head back down to the pub for a hair of the dog that bit you last night, so you'd better rattle your dags or we'll be late!" I can't say I was too keen on the idea, but I thought it might just put a bit of life back into me. At the time I remember vaguely thinking, why's Curly so keen to get to the pub? Anyway, we headed down to the pub, walked into the bar and bumped into about two dozen of our old cronies from the night before. All there for the same reason, I thought, to have a reviver as we'd really been whooping it up at the Rugby club reunion. Lots of fun, and no doubt it would continue when we'd gotten our second wind. We waited at the bar for the first beers to be served, and then Curly, you and your damned loud voice said, "Jeff, can you loan me a few bob until we get home? I seem to have forgotten my wallet!"

Even as I was getting my wallet out to pay for the first round of drinks, you said in an even louder voice, "c'mon Scrooge Mc Duck, don't take all day about it, we all know that it's probably the first time you've opened it for years!"

With all the fellas in the bar looking my way, I pulled open the zip fastener of my wallet and out came moths galore. Heaps of the buggers, Jeez, the laughter that erupted and continued on as I emptied everything out onto the bar. More and more of the moths fluttered out and right off I knew I'd been stitched up all right! You guys must've spent ages catchin' the moths and stuffing my wallet with them!"

When everybody had stopped splitting their sides, Jeff continued with his story. "I tell you, the burst of laughter that shook the place, you've just got no idea. It was a wonder that it didn't register on that thingummyjig, the seismograph in Wellington. Now, getting back to the story of your teeth Curl', I picked up your teeth and shot into the shed to where there was an old set on the ledge. Where they'd come from I haven't a clue. But they were here when I bought the place, and you all know me, I never throw out anything that could be useful!"

Another burst of laughter poured forth and when the mob had settled down again, Jeff resumed his story. "I rinsed them under the tap and gave them a quick wipe, took them out and put the old teeth on the floor in the dunny and rushed back inside passing the word around!"

Curly finished the story by, saying. "So at last that bugger Jeff'd managed to even the score!

When Jim and I had stopped laughing, Curly continued. "So now you have the full story, and you can see it's been a standing joke between me and my two copper mates for a heck of a while now!"

For a short time, none of us said anything as we were all preoccupied with our own thoughts, until I finally chipped into the silence. "One thing for sure Curly, it wouldn't be a good idea to try to put one over you, you've sure got some real hard case mates!"

Curly chortled. "Yeah, but good guys to have on your side in a tight spot. Anyway it won't be long now

102

before we arrive at Charlie's farm. Don't worry about Charlie being a bit abrupt with ya, it's not that he doesn't like people, it's just that he gets the stutters real bad at times and as a result says as little as possible. Another thing, he's got three nice looking daughters, in their late teens to mid twenties, so you'd better be a bit cagey in that direction. They tell me he's pretty slick on the clay birds with his twelve gauge. Just jokin'!"

Curly stopped talkin' as he slowed and turned up a gravel drive that led up and beyond a cattle-stop to a house tucked in amongst some trees. He drew to a stop near the house, where a girl opened a window, poked her head out, then pointed across the paddocks. "Hi, Curly, Dad's already gone over to the western boundary. He said for you to meet him over there but don't forget to close the gates after you. You know what he's like, always saying it's hard enough to get a good breed of lamb at the best of times without letting the rams into the wrong paddock!"

Curly replied, "Thanks, Carol. We'll get on our way, see you later."

Carol waved and we were on our way towards the first gate. There were quite a few of them and by the time we'd gotten through the last gate, heading for someone leaning on a strainer staring into the scrub, we were pretty close to the boundary.

Jim who'd taken the seat next to the door complained bitterly. "Hell, there must be ten or more bloody gates at the least that I've opened and shut. It's no wonder we got the message about the damned things. I bags the centre seat on the way back, reckon I've done my fair share as it is!"

Curly laughed. "You should be on ya Pat Malone when it's blowing up here. That would really give you

103

something to moan about. Ya stop the car, get out, open the gate, get back in the car, drive on through, but just before ya get right through, the bloody gate is caught by a gust of wind and to stop it making a bloody great dent in the panel work, you dive out to grab it. If you're lucky enough to stop the gate, you then have to find something to prop it open with, and then get back in again and drive through, get out and shut it behind you. And another thing is, it's twice as bad if it's raining cats and dogs!" In a taunting manner he said, "Now, if it was like that today, then you could really say you were hard done by!"

Drawing to a stop, Curly leaned out his driver's window. "G'day Charlie, how'd it go with the lambs last night?"

Taking a deep breath, Charlie stammered out a reply. "Gggggggooday, Ccccurly, I thththink I lo lost ssss damn it seven mmmm-more tto thth-the b-b-blighters."

"That's no good, Charlie," Curly commiserated. Then as we walked around the front of the Land Rover Curly introduced us.

"Like ya to meet a couple of mates of mine, Jim and Rolly. They reckon they own a champion pig dog."

Charlie nodded his head to our greetings and shook hands with us. Then switching his attention back to Curly, he said. "I hhhope yyyou hahahahaha damn it have aaa bbbit ooooof llllllll damn it ...luck. It's nnnno ggggood bubuyin' tttotpp nnnotcha rrrrr... damnit it.. rams, ttto hahahaha...damnit it.. thththth..the ppp..pigs knknkn..knocking   thththth..the   llllllll..damnit lalala...lambing pppp..percentage aaaall ttttt..damnit it..to hhhhh..hell!"

Curly held out his hands.

"Okay Charlie, we'll see what we can do about it for you, and give it our best shot."

Curly walked to the rear of the Land Rover to let the dogs out. While we were getting our gear ready, he was buckling on his homemade holster that held his Kea gun.

I watched Gray carefully to make sure he didn't head in the direction of a small mob of ewes with lambs feeding fifty yards or so away. I breathed a sigh of relief as he didn't even look at the sheep, but walked over to a fencepost to do what all dogs must do. Then lifting his muzzle to the air, I could see he had winded something, and immediately he scrambled through the fence into the scrubby secondary bush and disappeared from sight. Curly's two dogs wandered down the fence-line a short distance then returned, showing no interest in anything except staying near us.

Curly looked around enquiringly. "Where's that kuri of yours, Rolly? These two mutts of mine aren't showing any interest in the scrub at all, though admittedly the wind's blowing in the wrong direction. Reckon we should make our way up to the top of that ridge so that the wind is more or less in our faces. It might give the dogs a better chance of picking up a pig."

I answered Curl's query about Gray. "The last I saw of him was when he dived through the fence. Do you think we should give him another few minutes or so, just in case he's lucky enough to latch onto something?"

After waiting for another five minutes we slowly started making our way up the ridge, parallel to the fence. I guess we'd covered near enough to a hundred yards when we were pulled up short by Gray's bark. It sounded like he was onto something all right!

"You beaut! No doubt about that kuri of yours, Rolly, he's onto something!" With that Curly's dogs energetically dived through the fence and disappeared in

105

the direction of Gray's barking. Jim was first over the fence, I handed him my rifle and began getting over myself. Once over, he passed the rifle back to me and we were hot on Curly's heels. Then we heard Curly's dogs join in with Gray, and the noise certainly got the adrenalin going! Then without warning, the barking ceased altogether. We stopped in our tracks listening, but couldn't hear anything from the dogs or the pig. We waited.

"Blast, that damned pig must've broken on them," Curly muttered. He'd no sooner stopped speaking when the pig started squealing loudly, roughly in the same spot where the dogs had first been bailing. He called out in encouragement. "You little bottlers, hold on, hold on you kuris, we're coming." And we were on the trail again with Curly in the lead by about two yards and I was amazed at how fast a guy of his size was able to make his way through this dense scrubby bush. I was having a struggle keeping up, and that was even with using the track that Curly was creating. Man, he was like a human bulldozer. The pig was squealing non-stop, those dogs were certainly giving it a hard time. The nearer we got to the pig, the denser the scrub was, until we finally reached a flattened and rooted up area. Curly, being the first there, saw the hindquarters sticking out of the dense scrub, reached over, grabbed the tail, a leg, then very quickly and confidently threw the pig on its back, despite the dogs hanging on from all sides. It was then only a matter of seconds before Curly had thrust his knife deep into the chest cavity and the pig ceased its frantic screaming and struggling. It was all over and boy was our adrenalin flowing!

Regaining our breath we stood around staring at the pig. It was a boar, probably weighing about eighty pounds.

Jim commented to Curly, "Well, what do you think of Gray now? I reckon he's a gun pig dog!"

Curly nodded his head in agreement. "If it wasn't an out and out fluke, I'd say he's a little bloody beaut all right. Those two mutts of mine didn't have a inkling that there was even a pig around!"

Looking around at his dogs Curly commented. "Now where is that Gray anyway? Look at those two mutts of mine, looking well pleased with themselves, and I haven't seen Gray since we made the kill. Surely he can't be on the go again?"

Jim, always the one to have something to say, answered in a nonchalant manner. "Oh, I expect he's just about ready to grab another pig by now!"

As though to prove a point, Gray started to bark again bailing, this time a bit closer to us from where he'd latched onto the first boar. Curly's dogs took to their scrapers towards Gray's bark. Shortly after they all held back bailing, rather than going in for the hold. Once again, it was all on and somehow I was the one leading the chase. It was no easier than the first scramble through this dense, gut-busting stuff. I led the way, arriving at the pig first, and I was amazed. Bloody hell! No wonder they'd only bailed. The boar's beady eyes were glaring at the dogs, his tusks were chomping away in anger. He was a bloody monster, big enough to be the daddy of them all. I had to admit, I was not the very happiest of fellas, but I had to do something about it, and quick at that. Seeing as I couldn't get in closer, or behind him, as he was backed into a deep washout that was surrounded by a mixture of interwoven broom and dense manuka, I couldn't get a clear shot. So the only alternative was to get down into the washout and shoot, and without hitting one of the dogs in the process.

Scrambling down into the washout about twenty feet behind the dogs, I took several steps forward, raised the rifle to my shoulder and called to the dogs, hoping they would move back a bit and allow me a clearer shot. They shifted back slightly, and the boar, given a fraction more room to move in, started coming rapidly in my direction. Hastily I sighted and fired.

"Peeyow!" The projectile ricocheted off the thick shield that covered the boar's shoulders. I'd been told that the boar's hide on its neck and shoulders was really thick and tough, just like armour plating, and up 'til then I'd just thought that it was all a load of bull. Not any more! In one hell of a hurry - jeez he was getting mighty close - frantically I worked the bolt, ejecting the spent shell, slammed another round up the spout. I sighted and fired in one movement with the boar looming huge in the sights, even though I hadn't really had time to aim carefully. Luckily the shot was on target, right between the eyes. The huge pig dropped barely two feet in front of me. The three dogs were on it in seconds and they weren't letting it go, even after the animal was clearly dead! Boy, I can tell you, for a few seconds it had been all touch and go, I was shaking in my boots. Greatly moved and had just about filled my pants!

"Thank God I managed to get a direct hit, boy was I all set to take to my scrapers!" I muttered aloud for my own peace of mind, as I wiped the mixture of hot and cold sweat from my brow.

"You can say that again," said Curly, "and you weren't the only one who was about to leave the scene in

108

a hurry!" In fact, I hadn't realised he was there too. Spinning around I faced him.

"I'll tell you something, Rolly, that's the biggest pig I've seen in all the years that I've been hunting, and man I've seen some bloody whoppers. But the thing that really had me worried was that this was his only means of escape. If I were you, in future I'd keep it in mind about not getting between a pig and its only way out. He could've make mincemeat out'a ya!"

Stepping past me to have an even closer look at the boar, Curly gazed at in awe. "Just take a gander at those tusks, will ya? Can just imagine the mess they'd made of you if the second shot hadn't been right between his eyes?"

It was then that a feeling of trepidation again came over me. Whew, I'd been lucky!

"You're right, Curly. I was damned near filling my pants when the first shot didn't do the trick and I didn't think I had a snowball's chance in hell of getting the next shot in. I'll definitely be giving more thought as to where I'll be in respect to the pig's escape route from now on! I'm in full agreement with you about those tusks, just look at the size of them. They would have made one hell of a mess. A guy's lucky not to be auditioning for harp practice with St Peter, or singing solo in his choir."

For once, Jim didn't have much to say. We stood about taking a good look at the scene. That was until without warning a chorus of barks broke into our thoughts.

Jim reacted fastest and was first out of the washout. This time the barking was a little further away, quickly followed by the pig's frantic squealing as the dogs went in on the hold!

"Sounds as though they've latched onto a sow this time," was Curly's grunted comment as we attempted to follow the track that Jim was bashing through the scrub. There was no time left for talking, and I had to admit by now, I was getting a bit on the knackered side. The squealing came to a piercing crescendo then slowly diminished. In the silence that followed, I heard Curly say to Jim, "That bloody Gray is a real champ, but for God's sake don't let him take off after another pig. I don't know about you guys, but I'm absolutely buggered! Besides we've still got to lug these three porkers back out to the fence. And in this rough stuff it's going to be no joke believe you me!"

By then at last, finally, I'd caught up with them and managed to gasp out, "I'll second that, you guys!"

I then heaped praise on Gray. "You're a bloody little bottler aren't you? Come here boy!"

When he joined me I lavished more praise on him. His tail was going like hell as he took it all in, lapping it up. Then he contentedly lay in against the base of some shadowy manuka bushes, only too happy to have a breather as well.

He wasn't the only one, and as we crouched around the pig I noticed that Curly had been right. It was a nice fat sow. So my knowledge of pig hunting had increased greatly, in just the one day.

Curly, who had watched Jim knifing the pig, said, "Jim, you did a nice job on that pig. Your knife went straight into the heart. If you can always do as good as that you will never have any problems, and it's real quick for the pig too. Not a slow, painful death."

Jim just nodded and I could see he was more than chuffed with Curly's remark. By now we'd all rolled a

110

smoke. On looking at Jim I could see he was as stuffed as I was.

"Ya know something," Curly said. "There's no getting away from the fact that Gray sure is a bonza dog all right. Three pigs in next to no time, and what's more he's got brains too! Did ya see the way he was staying neither too close, nor too far back, while those two stupid mutts of mine looked like they wanted to go in and hold that big boar. If they'd gone in on him, I reckon that all I'd be taking home would've been a couple of ripped up, or dead dogs to boot. Another thing that I like about Gray is his strong bark. He really lets you know it. That type of bark seems to carry for miles and miles. Every time he lets rip it's a monty, and in fact, I'd lay odds of a hundred to one, that you'll always get the pig he's got bailed."

"I only hope that he doesn't bark until the next time I have the opportunity of going out hunting again with you two. I wouldn't say I'm stuffed, but I'm not too far away from it!"

These were words of praise indeed, and I'm pretty sure Jim reached for his tobacco again for the same reason that I did, to help hide the smug smiles on our faces. I was more than happy to agree with Curly's remarks.

"Yep, Curl', he's a purler dog all right, and not only that, he's setting a pretty steep yardstick in makin' Jim and me keep up with him. F'r instance, look at the size of him compared to me, a grown man who's also got the use of a rifle for protection, with my knees knocking together at the sight of that boar. But not Gray, he's in boots and all, bailing on his tod until your two dogs gave him a hand. One thing for sure, and if I was Gray, especially if I'da come across that particular boar, I would've left him well alone. It's sure been a wonderful stroke of good luck to have found Gray in the first place."

Jim nodded happily then added, "I've never ever had a dog in all of my life, or been pig hunting until Gray led us into it. He's tops in my books, a real bobby dazzler!"

I'd been thinking about the size of the boar, when it suddenly occurred to me that we would have to put in a real effort to carry that big boar out to the fence.

"Curly, even with the three of us, it's, gunna be one hell of a struggle to lug that big old man boar back out to the Land Rover!"

Curly smiled. "Ya know, there's more than one way of skinning the proverbial cat, Rolly. An' goin' from what old Charlie told me on the blower the other night, that monster of a boar is the one who's been puckaruing his fences. And not to mention knocking off his lambs as well. I bet ya, he'll be absolutely chuffed and I reckon be more than happy to bring his horse in to carry that big mother out. So we won't have to break our backs doing it! Anyway, what's the betting that this sow has been at the lambs too? He pointed towards the sow's head. "See there? Looks like a few strands of wool caught in between her teeth. Now Jim, seeing you were the one that stuck her, what say you open her up so we can have a gander at what she's been getting stuck into?"

Jim stood up, removed his knife from the sheath and was about to start cutting, when he turned back to Curly with a puzzled look. "I know that Rolly and I are basic newcomers to this game, but shouldn't we singe it before gutting it?"

Curly replied. "Nah, it's hardly worth the trouble. This sow and the old big man boar look as tough as old boots anyway, so what d'ya say we flog 'em off to that game meat company? Give us a few bob to line our pockets with, or beer money, whatever? Anyway, the meat dealers won't buy them if the heads have been removed, or if they've been singed. Another thing is, just think of what a hell of a job it'd be like trying to singe 'em all? Real hard yakker at that! But that first smaller boar is in real good nick, it'll be the one to singe and it oughta be more than enough tucker for the four of us. What's say you and Rolly take one side and I'll share the other with Charlie. I'm sure he'll be pleased as punch with some fresh wild pork, and another thing I reckon is that you'll always be able to come back onto his farm hunting for pigs and deer, whenever you like. Especially after a successful day like this. What do you say?"

Curly was waiting for our response, but unbeknown to us, Gray had slipped quietly away and was at it again, bailing, letting us all know that our day of pig hunting wasn't over yet! Curly's two dogs had taken off like rockets to join Gray. This time Gray was a fair way off and it took us a good ten minutes of hard yakker to get there. The dogs had latched onto another nice sized pig, another fat sow of about ninety-five pounds. It was quickly dispatched and I made another great fuss of Gray. Then using half of a bootlace, I tied him up to a small bush. Enough was enough, though there was probably no need to, as the dogs looked pretty well tuckered out anyway. By now all of us had had more than our fair share of hunting for the day.

Grinning across at us Curly stated, "Without a doubt, you guys, this is the best day's hunting that I've ever had in all my life. Take a gander at my watch will ya? It's only just after nine, barely two hours and a bit later with already four pigs in the bag. Man, this sure is great going!"

We all enjoyed a good breather and after a couple of smokes, took it in turns to carry this pig out to the fence line. Even in relays it took us close on half an hour to lug it there. By then, the sun was well up and did the sweat begin to pour out from us!

Waiting for us at the Land Rover was Charlie. He looked at the pig, and then at the three of us.

Curly began with a smile a mile wide, we could see that he was on cloud nine, and blurted out,

"Told ya we'd do our damndest for ya Charlie, there's one to start with!"

Charlie eyes lit up and he enquired eagerly, "Hhhhhhow mmmmmany dddid yyu gget?"

"Only four of the buggers," Curly replied, exultingly, "but best of all, it sure looks like we've nailed the one that has been knocking off your lambs. One thing though, we could do with your horse to help bring them out of this rough stuff. It's damned hard yakka humping them out on our backs!"

Charlie stared incredulously at Curly. "Fffff four oooof thththth.damnit the fffflippin' ththings aaaand ttthe kkkk killer?" Old Charlie stammered out, his eyes sparkling like diamonds, his grin spreading from ear to ear. He was one happy fella all right.

In no time at all he was up and into the saddle, cantering down the paddock to where he opened a locked gate that got him into the dense scrubby bush and back to us. While we were waiting, we'd had time for a puff on a smoke as well as a short welcome breather.

"Now there's a happy fella for you," Curly remarked. "But just wait until he sees the size of that big boar. He'll be lost for words!"

Jim and I could see it and that's for sure. We made certain that the three dogs were well tied up under some

114

shade, as there was no way at all that we wanted to tackle another pig today!

We led Charlie and the horse through the bush and scrub to where Gray had latched onto the second pig. When Charlie spotted the old man boar his eyes nearly popped out of his head. He turned to the three of us and shook our hands emphatically and tried to express himself.

"Ccccccccripes, iiit llllo..looks aaas bbbb..damnit… bbig aaaas aaa ffffflamin' elelelphant, thththose kkkkuri mmmmust bbbe ch…champions. Thththis iiiis ththth.. damnit…the bbbigest wwwwild ppig I…Ive eeever sss… seen!"

"You can say that again Charlie!" Jim replied.

All I can say is, thank goodness Charlie didn't repeat it, but the look in his eyes said it all.

Even with the four of us to drag the boar from the washout to where there was enough room to open it up it was a fair bit of a struggle. In a matter of minutes with Curly welding the knife, there was the final positive proof. The mangled remains of Charlie's lambs, not a very pleasant sight, in fact it was pretty gruesome. But one thing for sure, that cannibal boar couldn't cause any further destruction to the new born lambs!

With one hell of a struggle we manhandled the now much lighter gutted boar up onto the horse and across its back. Once Charlie had it lashed on securely he and Jim headed back to the fence line, while Curly and I made our way to where we'd knocked off the sow. That was only after we'd done a fair bit of scouting around to find it.

Out came the knife, and after opening up the guts, there in the sow was again more ample evidence, remains of chewed up lambs. But at least there were now two less of the damned killers around!

As we waited for Charlie and Jim to arrive back with the horse, we decided it was time to roll a smoke, relax and enjoy a well-earned breather. Curly and I were about to get the makings out for another smoke when we were interrupted by a shout.

"Where are you guys? Rolly? Curly?" It was Jim, and they'd evidently lost track of where the pig was too.

"Over here, over here," Curly replied.

Jim came back quickly with, "Here, there and everywhere, same as Old MacDonald's Farm eh?"

No doubt about it, Jim was rarely lost for words at the best of times, even if sometimes they were pretty corny. In about another ten minutes or so we could hear them, so we gave another yell just to let them know they were on the right track. When they finally joined us Curly pointed out to Charlie and Jim the remains of the lambs that had been in the pig's gut, and did Charlie let rip. He really went to town!

"Llllloook aaaa..damnit..at thhththe fffflamin' cccccanibal," and pointing an accusing finger at the dead sow, he stammered on, "Yyyyyyou wwwwon't bbbe eeeeating mmmmy llllll.. damnit.. lambs aaaaanymore, yyyyou bbbbbbloody mmmmurderer, nnnnow thththat yyyou've dididi..damnit..dddone yyyyyour chchchips."

No doubt about it, he was pretty well wound up, and later on Curly commented that was the most that he'd ever heard Charlie say in one go!

Our next move was to lash the sow onto the horse and make our way to where Gray had first latched onto the fat, well-conditioned boar. We didn't gut this one, as we wanted to singe it and keep it for our own tucker. With this soon lashed on the back of the horse with the sow we were more than happy to let the horse do all the hard work of carrying its load out to the Land Rover. By the time we'd climbed over the fence and unloaded the pigs off the horse, we were all just about stuffed!

Somehow, Curly did a magician's trick, and appeared with half a dozen bottles of Waikato. I didn't usually drink Waikato and it wasn't all that cold, but I certainly wasn't going to look a gift horse like this in the mouth, and much to my surprise it tasted like nectar of the Gods. I could feel it rinsing the dust from the back of my throat and in a word it was 'ambrosia'.

Then who do you think had to say something? You guessed it, Jim! "You know something, Curly? I always considered that to drink Waikato was like drinking swamp water and the fella who drank it had something wrong with his taste buds, but boy, is this good!"

Curly came straight back with a retort. "I don't know how you guys from up north can drink that bloody sweet fizzy stuff! To me it's just like lolly water, and anyway people who drink it can crap through the eye of a needle at forty paces. This is a real man's beer!" he laughed.

At that we all laughed and I for one didn't comment or stop drinking. It was only once the beer had been consumed and the flies had started to home in on us and we began the great Aussie salute, that we agreed it was time to make tracks. We loaded the pigs into the Land Rover, but there was a fair bit of grunting when it came to getting the old man boar in the back, it was damned heavy. Once we'd got the dogs loaded we were on our way.

It was then that I realised that we weren't following the same track back as when we'd came in. It seemed to lead in a different direction. Charlie was on his horse, and he wasn't following us either, so my curiosity was aroused.

"Hey, Curly, how come we're taking off in this direction? It's not the way we came in, is it?"

He chuckled. "I haven't been entirely honest with you guys, it's just that Charlie's got his own little thermal area so I thought you two might enjoy the pleasant surprise of removing the bristles and hair by scalding the pig in a real hot thermal pool. A damned sight easier than singeing and it also turns out a much cleaner job at that. Plus, if you feel like it, you can have a dip in another hot pool that always seems to be just the right temperature for a good soak. And not only that, it's a real good time to clean off the sweat, blood and guts. But best of all, it eases all the aches and pains, as well as helping to soothe any scratches from fighting your way through the underbrush. Then it just happens that Charlie's got a few half gallon flagons in his fridge, so how about that for a way to cap off a real fab' day's pig hunting?"

Well, that sure didn't take any thinking about.

"You can say that again!" Jim was up to his usual tricks.

I chipped in. "Sounds bloody great to me, Curl'!"

Not long after this, we crested a ridge and could see down into a valley that seemed to me to cover quite a large area, far more than Curly had hinted at.

Pulling to a stop next to a steaming hot pool we hauled out the nice-sized boar that we were going to keep for meat, and it didn't take a great deal of time to scald the pig. In fact it looked as though it had come straight from the meat works. A real clean job at that!

"This sure is a very nice porker," Curly commented, "it'll make real good eating. So how do you guys feel about us leaving it overnight in Charlie's meat

118

safe to harden up before we break it down? It'll be perfect eating by then!"

Jim and I were more than happy with that idea, so it was out with the guts, and off with the head, and back into the Rover with it. Then we continued down the track to a smaller, cooler pool and it was off with clobber, and easing our scratched sweaty bodies slowly into the thermal water. There was no doubt about it, the scratches certainly stung a bit as we slowly immersed ourselves, but it was most certainly soothing as my body acclimatised to the temperature. Curly and Jim were just like me, lying back soaking it up, it was fantastic and we were all sighing in satisfaction!

After a while, Curly interrupted the silence that was only broken by the effervescent bubbling around us.

"Hey you two, don't forget there's a flagon or two waiting back at the farmhouse and I wouldn't put it past old Charlie to start getting stuck into them before we arrive there."

That was it, A into G, clothes on and into the Rover for our return to Charlie's. This time it was up to me to open and shut the gates and it always seemed like there was 'just one more to go'. At last we made it through the final gate, and rolled to a stop beside an implement shed that had a big meat safe attached. Charlie came over and opened it as we carried the pig, and hung it onto a set of gimbals connected to a roof beam.

Curly said to Charlie, "A quarter of that is yours. Hope you've got enough room for your share in the freezer when we break it down tomorrow or the day after?"

Charlie nodded, giving him the thumbs up. He was chuffed all right, more than pleased with the outcome. We moved outside, with Charlie closing the door behind us. He pointed to the house. "Ggggotta aaa bbbeer aaaawaiting!"

At the back door we removed our boots and entered the kitchen where with a flourish Charlie opened a big fridge displaying not just one flagon, not two, but about half a dozen of 'em. Jim and I looked at each other. The only place I had ever seen more beer at one time was in the cool room at the pub. Charlie dragged a couple of flagons out and set them on the table, while Curly reached into a cupboard and got out the handles. Charlie motioned towards the now opened flagons and Curly, with his practiced hand, filled the handles and in no time at all, we all touched glasses.

"Thththanks yyyyy..damnit..you chchchaps ffffor ggggetting thththe ppppigs. Iiiiiit's aaaa rrrrelief. Bbbbut iiiit ttttook yyi' aaa..damnit..llllong ttttime tttto ggget hhhhh..damnit..here. IIIII nnnnearly ddddied offfff thththirst wwwaiting ffffor yyyous tttto ggget hhhere." he stammered, his face wreathed in smiles.

Curly jokingly rose to the bait. "Don't hand us that line of bull, you old coot, you've probably sunk a flagon while we were getting here!"

"Dddddon't cccall mmme ooooo..damnit...old, ooooor IIIII'll ppput yyyou oooover mmmmy knnnnee iiin aaaa mmminute!" he tossed back at Curly and winked at Jim and me.

I could see that they both enjoyed havin' each other on, then just as we'd emptied our handles, it was our turn to cop a bit of light-hearted flak. Curly, knowing damned well that Jim and I would never part with Gray, said tauntingly, "How much do ya want for that Gray mutt of yours? Not much of a pig dog is he? So I'll tell ya what, seein' as he's as useless as tits on a bull, I'd be prepared to take him off your hands for nothin! Save ya the cost and the trouble of feeding him!" A big grin spread all over his face.

Before either Jim or I were able to react to Curly's remarks, Charlie rose to his feet and called out to a whiskered old joker who had just stepped in through the back door. "Ggggood day Aaaarch, iiiit's dadadadamit, ggggood tttto ssssee yyyy..damnit..you!"

The two men shook hands and you could see the affection and the respect they held for each other. Charlie then turned to us and waved in our direction.

"Hhhhhere, mmmeet thhhththe chch... damnit ...champ ppppp..damnit..pig hhh hunters, Rrrrolly, Jjjjjim, aaaand sososo..damnit..son-in-law Curly!"

My ears pricked up. So Curl's the son-in-law? So that's why he'd been giving Charlie such a hard time, and hence the knowledge about Charlie's daughters. That bloody Curly was married to one of them. I wondered what else Curly was keeping under his hat. He's a shrewd bugger all right, I thought as I decided I'd better keep on my toes whenever I was around Curly.

Then shaking hands with us, Archie said gravely. "How are ya young fellas? Nice load of pigs you've got out there in the Land Rover. Being lambing time an' all, have you been havin' bother with pigs, Charlie?"

And before Charlie had time to even get out a stutter, Arch continued, "Of the three dogs out there, I'd say off-hand the grey mastiff whippet cross was the pick of them. They always seem to have it over the other breeds, got good ears, nose and big feet on him. There wouldn't be many kuri that would be able to foot it with him either!"

"Well, Archie," Curly replied, "you know your dogs all right, he's a real humdinger finder and holder. If it hadn't been for that Gray, I don't think we'd have cottoned onto one pig, let alone four of the buggers and all in a very short time at that, it took us all our time to catch up. Every time we'd knock a pig off he was onto another and thank goodness he was tied up after the fourth pig, otherwise we'd still be sticking the bloody things. He belongs to Rolly here, and with your appraisal of Gray, you've just mucked up a good offer I made for him! Now Rolly, this here's my last offer, how's three dozen Waikato sound?" Followed by a big wink in Jim's and my direction.

At all the praise being lavished on Gray, my head and chest felt as though they were ten times bigger than normal. Trying to act modestly, I blurted out with a big grin all over my face. "Come off it, Curl, you wouldn't get to buy his collar for that. Anyway, when you get right down to it, there's no way that we'll ever part with him, he's just too good a mate!"

Curly, being Curly, had the last say. Looking at Jim and me, he said, "In all seriousness you two, if you ever have to part with Gray, I'd like to be the one to offer him a good home, so just keep my words in mind, okay?" We could tell by Curly's manner that he really meant it.

Then Charlie reached into the fridge, grabbed a couple more flagons and filled up our handles again. The conversation went on from Gray and pig hunting to deer stalking, to fishing, and then it was all about Charlie and Archie's younger days when they were gallivanting around the countryside, doing whatever made them a few bob and enough to keep the wolf from the door.

Charlie nudged Archie and with a bit of a grin on his face, said. "Ttttthose bbbbbbbloody rats!"

They both laughed then. Archie replied, "Yup, I always have a grin to myself when I think of that trip." He launched into telling us the yarn…

Had bugger-all money in those days and we'd been offered a job of shearing down near Gisborne so we took it.

Well, we were lucky enough to get a lift to just past Waikari, and from then on it was all shank's pony. It took us a couple of days of enjoyable walking, during which time we passed through Waikaremoana. Lucky for us the weather had been fine and the country was just great; beaut scenery, with heaps of native birds, kereru, bellbirds, tui, and at one stage we thought we heard the haunting melodic call of the kokako. Not absolutely sure it was, but we definitely did hear kiwi along with the morepork calling after dark!

It was on the second night, well past Waikaremoana, probably five hours' comfortable walk from there, that we found an old roadman's hut, a bit dilapidated and ramshackle, but at least we had a roof over our heads if it decided to rain. This was great until just after dusk, when heaps of rats started running all over the place havin' a go at our bags. They could probably smell food, but they were fresh out of luck 'cause we'd finished off the last we'd had anyway. It wasn't so bad, the fact that they were running around, but what got us worried was a couple of 'em had come sniffin' around our ears. I don't think they would've hurt us, but at that point we had a bright idea. Catch one in a sack and attach a ferret bell around its neck. Just in case you don't know, it's a bell that we used ta hang around the ferret's neck before we let it go down the rabbit's burrow so we'd be able to keep track of it. Because sometimes if it killed a rabbit down there we'd know by the tinkling of the bell where to dig to get the ferret out. Also at times, they came out another entrance, so the bell at least gave us a chance to catch the ferret as well.

123

Anyway, we let the rat go and it was the tinkling of the bell that no doubt had the rats wondering what in the hell was going on and they took to their scrapers, leaving us in peace and giving us reasonable night's sleep. The only annoying thing was the loss was one ferret bell, but we reckoned it was worth a good night's sleep!

About a month later we'd finished up the shearing job we'd gone there to do and on our return trip we spent another night at the old roadman's hut, and believe it or not, heard the bell still tinkling away!

Next morning we were on our way, and it was a rough old day, windy as hell and raining cats and dogs. Seein' as we had a few bob in the kitty we decided to spend the night at the Waikarimoana hotel. After we'd had dinner and sat back with the owner, enjoying the warmth from the open fire an' havin' a good old chinwag, there was a loud thumping on the door.

When the owner opened it, two Maori fellas rushed in. All they had on was boots, longs and shirts! I'm telling you, they were both thoroughly drenched to the skin, but under their normal tans they were as white as any pakeha around. They hurried in, getting as far away from the door as they could. It took them about five minutes to get their breath back, and when they did, the owner who evidently knew them, asked, "Where have you two jokers come from in such a hurry? The Johns aren't after you are they?"

They both shook their heads vigorously before replying, "No, no boss, not the police!" while casting several anxious looks over their shoulders at the closed door. Then with the proprietor still not getting a satisfactory answer, he asked again. "Well, whereabouts have you jokers come from?"

Taking another look at the door, one of them took a deep breath, and responded, "Taratapai way, boss." And they both visibly shook.

The proprietor queried again. "Well, why didn't you's stop over at the old roadman's hut at the Mokau Flats until tomorrow? The rain might've eased up by then and saved you's from getting half drowned anyway."

Looking over their shoulders as though they expected someone or something to join them, the spokesman said half a dozen words in Maori, and then in English.

"We did, boss. We was staying there, but when it got dark," he paused, his teeth chattering in fear. "Then the kehua started ringing the bell!"

At this old Charlie and me clicked on to what had happened and we only just managed to keep straight faces and no more.

The proprietor prompted, "Kehua, that means ghost doesn't it? What bells are you talkin' about? Ain't no bells round there!"

Still saying nothing, both of them nodded in reply. The proprietor looked at them more questioningly. "Aw, come off it you two, this is probably some cock and bull yarn that you've cooked up to get a free night's accommodation out of me! Even I know it's at least four hours' hard tramping from that hut to here, and according to the time you reckoned you left the hut, it's taken you's about half that amount of time to get here, and in the dark too. Tell ya what, you've had your joke and it's worth a couple of cups of hot tea on a horrible night like tonight, and while I'm makin' the brew, you'd better hop outside and get your gear before it gets any wetter from the rain or blown away with this wind.

At the mention of having to go outside they were both visibly shaken and hung onto the end of the mantelpiece for grim death. They weren't budging. The talkative one spoke up, nearly pleading. "No boss, not outside. Our gear's still in the hut at Mokai Flats!"

At this stage old Chas here and myself was just about ready to burst, so we made a beeline out of there and off to bed!"

In turn we were all in fits of laughter and when we'd all quietened down, Archie wound up the story.

"Ya know, it didn't take long before the old roadman's hut at Mokau Flats got a name for being haunted. As a result of us knowing the full story about the bell, we had the hut all to ourselves on the odd occasion that we passed through!"

There was no doubt about it old Archie could spin a great tale all right. But after we'd stopped laughing I had to feel sorry for those two Maori fellas and I wondered how I'd have reacted in the same circumstances.

For a while we chewed the fat on all sorts of topics while the cool beers flowed down easy, and once again, it was old Charlie who prodded Archie to tell the tale about how they had been in uniform in W.W.2. Between them they'd managed to wangle their way into the same Signal Corps and then had been shipped out to some islands in the Pacific. You could see that Archie really enjoyed reminiscing and entertaining us...

The first thing that you learn in the army, or any of the armed forces for that matter, is that you never volunteer for anything, no way, no how. Anyway, there were four of us, Charlie, me and two other blokes who were lumbered with the damned job of diggin' a latrine for a bunch of WAAFS who were due to fly in on a DC 3 troop transporter. According to the sergeant in charge, they'd be staying on the island for a couple of days and then be on their way. For some reason or another, our C.O. wanted this hole dug a damned sight deeper than the usual six-footer. I can tell you, in the tropics it was a hot, humid and sweaty bugger of a job, taking a lot of hard yakka, but we reckoned that it was for a worthwhile cause, as maybe we'd get to see these women and possibly even meet up with them.

Little did we know that wasn't to be. Somewhere along the way someone had gotten the bright idea of havin' a bit of fun with these women. Good clean fun, mind you. So we installed a small loudspeaker down on one side of the hole; it was sort of borrowed from a wrecked liberty ship on the edge of a reef about a stone's throw from the shore. With this all set up we connected up the wires and made sure they were covered and couldn't be seen. From there we ran the wires into a grove of palm trees to a microphone, then tested it and all was A-okay. It was then just a matter of reporting back to the sergeant, who had the C.O. check it all out and give his stamp of approval.

All we had to do then was hide in among the palms, waiting for the plane to land. No doubt the WAAFS would have been in the air for a fair old while. No toilets in those transport aircraft, so as soon as it had landed, they were directed straight to the new dunny and began lining up, they must've been bursting. The first one entered, as we watched and waited, well hidden in the palms, and after about ten seconds the guy on the microphone uttered the amazing words!

"Jeez, can't you sheilas wait until we finish diggin' this bloody hole?"

There was a scream, followed by a bang as the dunny door flew violently open! Boy, she came out of there like the shot out of a gun, as fast as that champion horse Cardigan Bay, with her panties around her ankles, just like hobbles on a trotter. Boy, she could sure move. I can still remember it just like it was yesterday!

Old Archie had us in fits again and when we stopped laughing, he said that wasn't the end of the story. "So we got to see and meet the WAAFS, after all, and we also personally had to apologise to them all. After this we were sent in disgrace to another tiny little godforsaken atoll to guard it. What in the hell from? It could only have been from the bloody mosquitoes and they were there in the thousands, they didn't give us any peace day or night and we were still there when the Japs surrendered on VJ day!"

Curly had just begun refilling our handles, and it looked like Archie was about to regale us with another story, when in walked one of Charlie's daughters, loaded down with groceries. She said her hellos to Curly, her Dad and Archie. Then Curly introduced her to Jim and myself as Nancy. She stood looking somewhat sourly, I thought, at the group of us, and burst out. "So it's the same old story is it? How many did you get? And it's not the flagons that I'm talking about. It's those bloody pigs that have been killing off those poor little lambs that I want to know about. None, I suppose?" She stood stock still, looking rather disapprovingly at us.

I tried to fathom out as to how or why she was getting stuck into us all like this. It had me stumped. Then before anyone could say anything, she was at it again, hands on her hips. "So, there'll be more lambs dead and missing in the morning and all that you pack of hobos are doing about it is sitting in here on your big ends knocking back the booze? I expect that's all you're any damn good for anyway."

I thought to myself, is she fair dinkum?

Curly stepped quickly into the breach, winking at us.

"Nancy, you're absolutely dead right, all us men are good for is drinking and yakking. We didn't stand a dog's chance and those pigs are just like the women around here, too quick off the mark with their words, they simply talked us out of catching them!" He was grinning at Nancy like a Cheshire cat.

For a few seconds, a very few seconds, Nancy was stumped and had no reply. Then the colour in her face heightened, she couldn't see that Curly was just having her on. Then she let him have it with both barrels.

"I'm amazed at you of all people, Curly, and I've a good mind to get on the blower to my sister who, just in case you've forgotten, is your wife!"

Then the penny dropped, he was up to his old tricks as always, pulling legs. Curly took advantage of her hesitation.

"Listen Miss fancy pants, you are forever getting off the mark too quick, isn't she Charlie?"

Old Charlie grinned widely and nodded in agreement before pointing out the window towards the Land Rover. It all came out later on that Nancy was always over-defensive with anything to do with her father, the farm, and especially the beer.

"Gggggggo aaaan' hhhhhave aaaa lllllook."

She headed outside towards the Land Rover and it was only a few minutes before she rejoined us, a little crestfallen, and apologetic. Then seeing she wouldn't be getting much change out of us, she gave up the ghost, disappearing into another part of the house. But you can't keep a good woman down can you? She quickly returned with a camera, a pleasant smile and asking if we wouldn't mind having a few pictures taken of us, the dogs, and the pigs. Just goes to show a woman's smile is pretty hard to resist. We all agreed and traipsed outside.

She couldn't hide her astonishment when she saw the size of old man boar. "Gosh, he's a real monster isn't he?"

Curly replied. "Yep, and your Dad reckons he's the one responsible for damaging the fences, plus him and the sow there were both responsible for the lamb losses. We found definite proof of their cannibalism!"

Nancy used up all the film in the camera so she could get them developed the next day, then again was just not able to let things lie as she gave Curl' a bit more stick. "You've never done as well as this before. How come?"

Curly smiled, and raised his eyebrows. "All the credit goes to that dog of Rolly's! Gray's a great finder, bailer and holder, he was onto them like a demon and they weren't out an' out flukes either. We didn't begin hunting until about sixish and in next to no time we had four pigs. I'm telling you, not only were my mutts stuffed, the three of us jokers were too. Even had to tie that Gray up to make sure he didn't latch onto any more pigs, hence the celebratory drinks!"

I had to smile at Curly, he was a shrewd bugger all right, and it wasn't wasted on Nancy either, but it was just like water off a duck's back with her reply.

"You're just a big-head, but one thing though, it's great that those poor little lambs are going to be much safer now!"

Then old Charlie began to stutter. "Ddddddon't fofofoforget thththth.damnit that tttthe bbbbeer iiiiiis nnnnnot gggggetting aaaaa..damnit.. any cocococooler!"

He didn't have to say any more and in no time at all, the pigs were all loaded back into the Rover and we adjourned inside making sure that the beer remained cold. A short while later Curly got on the blower and rang the game meat buyer, arranging with him for us to sell him the pigs.

Well not too long after this we'd just about knocked off all the beer when Curly reminded us. "Hey you guys, it's time we made tracks. That buyer is waiting for us to take those pigs in!"

We'd drained Charlie's flagons anyway, so were making ready to leave when Charlie spoke up. "Nnnnnnanc' IIII'll hhhhhave ttto gggo tttt..damnit..town ttto rrrrr...damnit..fffil mmme jjjars aaan IIIII'm gggggg..damnit...going tttto hhave aaaa ffffew bbbbeers wwwwith thththe bbbbb..damnit..boys aaaas wwwwell."

"Now Dad, don't you think you've had enough beers as it is? Remember what happened last time you and Archie had a session. When you got home, you forgot to pull the handbrake on in the truck and it rolled back down the drive, flattened the chook house, and sent chooks in all directions including a few that we had to cook. Not only that, they went off the lay for weeks and we had hardly any fresh eggs for ages! And don't forget who had to tow the damned truck out of the duck pond in the morning."

Nancy stood, hands on her hips, looking askance at him.

"Iiiiiiit wwwwon't hhhhappen aaaagain. IIIIII've mmmmmoved thththe chchchchook hhhhhouse."

131

We couldn't resist it, Charlie had a great piece of logic there and we all cracked up!

Nancy had to laugh as well for a short while, then she started up again, "Oh Dad, you're the limit. This time why don't you and Archie leave your truck here and when you're ready to come home, either ring me or get a lift home. I'll even drop you off at the pub and bring your jars home for you. Curly, will you make sure that Dad doesn't do anything too stupid? I'll get Maggie to put a bee in your bonnet if you don't!"

She was certainly like a mother hen when it came to her father. Charlie nodded his head in agreement.

Curly then chipped in. "Fair enough Nancy, but you just remember one thing, he's over twenty one!" Followed by big grin. "And he can be as stubborn as his eldest daughter when push comes to shove!"

We said goodbye to Nancy and arranged to meet Charlie and Archie at the pub. On our way back into town, I asked about Nancy and her over-protectiveness.

"What's up with your sister-in-law? She's pretty quick off the mark, isn't she?"

"It's like this," Curly replied. "Her mum, Charlie's wife, was killed along with their six-month old-son. Anyway the other driver was high on something. A witness estimated the speed was well into the eighty mph mark and going like a bat out of hell. The only sign of any braking was by Anne, so ever since then, Nancy has been like a mother to her sisters, as well as taking care of the running of the house as you have seen. She can certainly be a bit overbearing at times, but deep down she has a heart of gold. Also as you have seen, she's a bit overprotective towards Charlie. According to the family it was the shock of the double tragedy that caused him to start stuttering. I couldn't ask for a better father-in-law.

So let's get onto another topic, like the selling of these pigs to the buyer. We'd better keep an eye on him, some of the rumours floating around about him aren't too complimentary!"

Twenty minutes later we were in the process of lifting the pigs out of the Rover and hanging them on the scales. Even we were amazed at the weight with the old man boar, by far the heaviest, at two hundred and sixty five pounds, that was gutted. Man, what a bloody monster, no wonder it had taken some lifting. Nothing happened to make us suspicious of the buyer's actions, so as soon as he'd handed over the cheque, Curly dropped us back at our car, and arranged to meet us at the pub about half an hour later. This gave us time to head home to drop off Gray and grab a quick change of clothing.

CHAPTER ELEVEN

THE EASIEST PIG EVER

At home, we gave Gray a big, meaty beef bone. He'd really earned it. Talk about a dog with two tails! You could see his huge grin. A final quick clean up for ourselves, and we decided to walk to the pub. No worries about being caught D.I.C.

We walked into the bar a short time after Curly, who had already cashed the cheque and divvied it up three ways. A nice reward of beer money, thank you very much!

When Charlie and Archie turned up, we offered some of the cash to Charlie but he wouldn't take a penny of it. He was only to thankful to have gotten rid of the lamb-killing menace.

Not too long after this Eddie, a good friend of Curl's, joined us for a beer and, after introductions all round, Curly enquired, "So what've you been up to lately Eddie? Anything worthwhile that we should know about?"

Eddie grinned ruefully and proceeded to relate his tale. "Well, you could say I had a bit of luck the other day, the easiest pig I've ever caught. But it didn't all go as good as I'd wished it could have!"

"How come, what's the story? We're all ears." Curly's curiosity was awakened as well as our own interest…

Okay. Well as you know Curl', my place backs onto a Lands and Survey farm and stretches way back up to the forestry reserve. Y'see I was mowin' the back lawn yesterday when my missus came skittlin' around the corner like a sprinter over the last ten yards. She was closely followed by the kids, and called out to me over the noise of the mower motor.

"Eddie, Eddie, there's a wild pig running down the road!"

At first I thought that the kids and mum were tryin' to pull my leg a bit. You never know what they'll do for a bit of fun."

"A what?" I replied with a grin. I was willing to play their game.

"There's a wild pig and it's running down the road!"

And they all pointed toward the front of the house. So, a little bit wary of what was up, I switched off the mower and jogged around the front and there, as large as life, trotting quite unconcernedly toward the scrubby gully at the end of the road, was a bloody wild pig. Thoughts flashed through my mind as I wondered how it had gotten this far into town without being scared off? Must've come across the farm from the reserve, it certainly wasn't a domestic pig anyway. Boy oh boy, this'll be the easiest bit of pork that I've ever latched onto.

Rushing around into the back of the shed I found my sheath knife, but the kids had been using it trying to carve shapes out of pumice and it would've taken ten minutes to get it sharp again and by that time the pig could've been long gone! I thought about using the slasher or axe, but then remembered that I'd loaned them to you Curl'! As for Mum's carving knife, it was such a

135

bendy thing that it wouldn't be of any use at all. So it came down to one thing. The old Lee Enfield was the only option open to me! I wasn't overly keen as I didn't like the idea of using it in town, but I couldn't let an easy bit of pork slip through my fingers like that so I was prepared to take the risk. Climbing onto a saw stool I unlocked the gun box that was bolted to the rafters and dragged out the carrying case containing Old Faithful. It was a three o three that I'd bowled quite a few animals with. Quickly I checked that there was nothing up the spout, like a mason bee nest. Clean as a whistle! So I placed five rounds in the mag and clipped it home.

I told the missus to make sure the kids stayed home then hotfooted it down the edge of the road on the pumice verge, following up the tracks the pig had left in the dust. I saw where it had entered the patchy scrub and spotted the pig almost at once. The fact that it didn't take to its scrapers gave me a nagging doubt as to whether or not someone owned it. So I did a half circle around it scanning it carefully, but with no sign of a rope mark around its neck, no earmarks, nothing to show that it belonged to someone, I raised the rifle to my shoulder, squeezed the trigger and bang it was in the bag, shot through the head. Throwing it across my back I carried it home, as happy as a sand boy. Hell man, only one hundred yards from my front gate! This was the easiest bit of hunting I'd ever done! Just wait 'til the boys in the pub heard about this one, they'd never believe it!

It took me quite a while to sharpen the knife and get a good edge on it. Then I tossed the pig into the back of the van, drove to the hot water outlet from the geothermal bores, scalded and scraped the bristles and hair off, then dressed it out. On arriving back home I left the pig hanging from the rafters in the garage to cool down, letting the meat set firmer so that it was easier to cut up. I had once made the mistake of not letting it cool down before it went into the fridge. It sweated and went off. I sure wasn't going to let that happen again.

I was relaxing after my hard work, enjoying a well earned beer, when the missus saw three Maori chaps talking to our kids a short way down the road. The kids nodded their heads and pointed to the house and then this trio began walking up the drive. I waited until they were halfway up drive then went out to see what they wanted.

"G'day. What can I do you for you chaps?"

One of them replied, "G'day, you the fella that shot our pig? Those kids said you did and there's a blood trail leading here!"

"Yeah, I shot a pig, but it was wild, not a domestic one!" I was pretty blunt about it.

"Well, it happens to be ours. We've had him in a pen fattening him up for a long time now, but somehow he got out."

Then it hit me. 'So that accounts for why the pig wasn't too perturbed about me', I thought to myself. But there was no way that I was going to give this pig away, especially not after all the trouble of scalding and dressing it out. Anyway it might not even be theirs. They could've have heard about it and just been tryin' to con me out of it. I wasn't going to give in that easy!

"Can you prove it's yours?"

In a gruff, menacing manner that made my hackles rise, the spokesman bluntly stated, "You'll just have to take our word for it, won't you now?"

I thought to myself, two people can play at this game.

"Look, mate, I put more than enough work into dressing it, and I'm quite willing to go halves, if you can definitely prove it was yours. I can't be any fairer than that, can I?"

The quick reply came back quickly, but still with lots of menace. "We don't think that it's fair at all. We've been feeding it for about twelve months now, ever since we caught it as a sucker off Sandfly Knob. We know that it belongs to us, and we reckon we'll take the lot!"

This made my blood begin to boil and my dander was well and truly up! "If that's the way you want to go, you can forget about even half and that's final!" I was getting pretty hot under the collar.

"Okay mate! Seein' as you won't give us our pig back, we'll be givin' the coppers a call!"

The three of them then began making their way back down the drive. I decided to have the last word.

"You do that. But don't forget that possession is nine tenths of the law!"

Well, that's that, they won't be bothering me again, were my thoughts as I returned to finish my glass of beer.

About an hour later, there was a knock on the door and there stood a cop. After much discussion, even though the cop was sympathetic, he said that if they didn't get the pig back they could force him to bring a charge against me for discharging a firearm inside the town limits. So now he's taken the bloody pig to them. Wouldn't it brass ya off! If I'd only had a good sharp knife, they wouldn't have had a leg to stand on and I'd still have a chunk of pork hangin' in the shed!

We all agreed that it was a bit of a bugger about what had happened. So after Jim and I had a quiet chat on the side we reckoned we could easily part with a bit of the pork that was hanging in Charlie's meat safe. We decided that a quarter was more than enough for Jim and me. So getting Eddie off to one side, we offered to share a quarter of the pig hanging in Charlie's meat safe. Initially Eddie looked a bit taken aback, but then realised that we were dinkum. He smiled gratefully. "Thanks, you guys. That's real decent of you. My faith in human nature is growing by the minute!"

We then approached Curly. "Do you mind if we go out tomorrow and pick up our half of the pork from Charlie's and give a chunk to Eddie's family?"

Curly had overheard what we'd suggested to Eddie and was all for it. "Go for it you guys; that's real decent of you both!"

It certainly put a grin back on Eddie's dummy and gave us both a nice feeling of satisfaction.

Just then Archie, who'd been called to the phone by a barman, returned saying he was sorry but there was a slight change of plans and he wouldn't be staying at Charlie's tonight. Something about another old mate who had been rushed into hospital, and needed someone to do the milking and run his small dairy farm for a couple of weeks. Shaking hands all round he wished us all the best with our hunting then departed.

This reminded Curly about his promise to Nancy about getting Charlie home in one piece. Luckily enough, another patron of the pub who'd only had a few beers was going right past Charlie's front gate. So we handed Charlie, along with his jars, to this good Samaritan seeing him on his way home. We'd also made arrangements for Jim to go out the following day to collect our share of the pork.

Then it was back into the bar! We were certainly making a day of it, until at the closing of the bar Curly suggested, "What about dropping around to my house for a feed?" As we'd eaten nothing much since early that morning, I can tell you that it didn't take any arm-twisting at all, we agreed. So it was off to Curly's for a binder.

We eventually arrived at Curly's where he whispered, "Now you guys try not to make too much noise, or we'll be waking the missus or the kids!"

We were doin' pretty well until we stepped onto the back porch and then in the dark, and with my big number elevens, I had the rotten luck to stand on the cat's tail. I lost my balance, and it seemed like ages before I could lift my boot off its tail! And there's no doubt about it, the joker that reckoned he could do an imitation of the bagpipes by tucking a cat under his arm and nipping its tail between his teeth was dead right - it certainly screeched making one hell of a racket. There's only one thing that joker forgot to mention; the scratch marks and the agony of torn skin and wounds to my shin and ankle made me realise that a man would've needed a suit of armour for protection at the same time!

Curly muttered, "What the hell are ya tryin' to do to the bloody cat? You're makin' enough noise to wake the dead!"

He carefully opened the back door and poked his head in, then beckoned us in after him. "All right you jokers, the coast is clear. C'mon in!"

He'd no sooner stepped in and switched on the light than there was an almighty crash. What a bloody shock! Bits of a big vase shattered all over the place as it was smashed over his head. Assuming that it was Curly's wife, and that she was not in such a welcoming mood after all, Jim and I didn't hang around to get a second helping - we took to our scrapers, not bothering even to open the gate. We both cleared the front fence with heaps to spare. All the way home we discussed what had happened to Curly, and why.

It certainly didn't take very long to get home where we threw together a quick feed and at last hit the scratcher.

CHAPTER TWELVE

BUCK FEVER

The following morning I awoke remarkably early. My head was as clear as a bell. It was right on sparrow-fart and as I lay there I recalled how the guys had talked about an old, disused road that went through a large patch of dense, second-growth native bush. The only reason the old pumice road was still there was the fact that a row of power poles ran parallel for about eight miles or so and it was used for the odd bit of maintenance.

On getting up I ate a quick bite of breakfast, then decided to go out and have a poke around. You never know, I just might be lucky enough to score an easy deer! With Jim still being out to the count, it was a matter of letting sleeping dogs lie. So I left a note on the fridge for him as to where I was going hunting and roughly what time I should be getting back.

Outside Gray spotted me carrying the rifle. He was as keen as mustard, but my feeling was that he could do with a breather after yesterday's successful hunt, so I left him chained at home and looking a bit peeved off.

On reaching the old disused road I parked the car out of sight well off the road in a small clearing in the scrub. Then it was just a matter of following the pumice road on foot. Finally, after about two hours or so without seeing anything apart from the odd rabbit track on the pumice surface, I decided to retrace my footsteps. The secondary growth and thick scrub was just too dense to bash through anyway.

After some twenty minutes walking on the return trip I came across fresh deer tracks crossing the old road and they certainly hadn't been there on my walk out. My heart rate lifted. I kept moving as quietly as possible for the next little while, all ears and eyes, but to no avail. The deer was probably long gone. But deep within me were feelings of intense excitement and anticipation.

Not too long after this, I was alerted even more by the sound of rapid movement in the scrub, about fifty yards ahead and off to the side. I was on full alert, easing a shell into the breech, leaving the bolt half-cocked. Moving along the edge of the road as stealthily and as silently as possible, I had the rifle at the ready and pointing towards the sounds ahead. I could see a brownish, indistinct shape from time to time as it wended through the dense undergrowth. It looked like a deer and sounded like a stag - possibly its antlers rattling against some pieces of the dried tea tree! Sliding the bolt full home I sighted on these slight movements. No! No! I couldn't identify my target as yet! Just wasn't able to see it clearly enough. My heart was thumping frantically. All my senses were at their highest pitch, with the adrenalin really running wildly throughout my body. Just wait, I told myself, remember the golden rule; you must identify your target. Anyway, I might lose it in the bush if it was only wounded. Taking the rifle from my shoulder, I continued tracking as quickly and silently as possible along the edge of the old road to try for a more open shot. Not yet able to see the animal clearly enough I decided to wait, just hoping, nay willing, for a better sighting of the animal before it caught my scent. All the time, with the tension building, I continued following its progress through the scrubby stuff, with my mind going nineteen to the dozen. I thought of Jim and how he would've

143

wished he'd been out hunting with me rather than having a sleep in. Then the deer appeared to be making a move in the direction of a slightly clearer section of the bush. Just think, it was as good as good as in the pot! Now c'mon you little beaut, move out into the open. My imagination was running wild with thoughts of fresh venison and fried onions for lunch. Hell! It must've gotten a whiff of me, because it started moving more rapidly. Sighting where I felt it would appear on the edge of the scrub, I was all set to pull the trigger. Another couple of paces and I'd be able to let rip! Ready. I tensed myself, the adrenalin surging wildly through my body. A little more tension on the trigger and with the first pressure on the trigger, I was ready, so keen to down this animal the excitement was nearly unbearable! My heart hammered wildly, come on you bugger!

Then, aghast, I couldn't believe my eyes! My mind frantically tried to realise what I saw. No, no, no, it can't be! Don't pull the trigger! Bloody hell! It's a joker with a slasher on his shoulder! The shock of it really hit home to me. The deer that I had been about to shoot was a man! Thank God I hadn't pulled the trigger. The feeling of tension was immense. What a relief it was that this joker wasn't coming towards me or looking my way. Jeez he'd probably have died from fright! As it was I'd bloody nearly crapped myself!

I watched frozen to the spot until he'd walked away from me, out of sight around a bend. It took all of my willpower to eject the shell out of the breech. I sagged back exhausted against the bank. Propping the rifle beside me, I dragged out my tobacco, barely able to stop my hands from shaking as I tried to roll a smoke.

"Whew! Rolly boy!" I barely managed to utter. Wild thoughts raced frantically through my mind at one hundred miles an hour; 'what if you'd up and shot him, killing or wounding him?' All different sorts of pictures flooded through my mind. None of them made a pretty sight!

By the time I'd finished my second smoke the nerves had settled down somewhat so, slowly rising to my feet, I shouldered the rifle and continued walking on in a very sober manner back towards the car.

Coming around a bend half a mile or so further on, I stumbled onto a group of guys who were sitting around having their smoko. One was the guy that I'd had in my sights. There was no way I could avoid them. I didn't want to, but stopped and forced myself to speak to them and found out they were cutting down all the scrub that grew under the power wires running parallel, about a couple of chain back from the road. Little did they know what had almost happened further down the road, even today I consider myself very lucky to have had the most important lesson and rule of shooting rammed down my throat so completely. The memory still sends a cramping in my guts!

You must identify your target clearly, before firing! One thing for sure, in the future I would always take Gray with me when I was out hunting. His actions would have alerted me that something was not as it should have been.

Arriving home, I was met by Jim and Gray. At least Gray didn't seem as uptight as I was, making a big fuss over me, but then again he might just been putting the hard word on me for another feed!

"How'd the hunt go, Rolly?" asked Jim.

I looked at him, replying slowly and emphatically, "Not much, just some deer sign that was fresh, but apart from that there was nothing much to speak of. I don't think it would be worth going back to that spot again."

I thought to myself 'I'll tell Jim about the so-called deer some other time.' I was still a bit shaken!

"By the way, Curly called in earlier," Jim then informed me. "He looked a bit battered around the ears and had a number of bits of sticking plaster adorning his dial. He apologised for the reception we received at his place last night. Somehow, he'd forgotten that his eldest nipper was taking part in a school play. Reckons he's going to make it all up to them by taking the family for a day out. Said he'd be grateful if I could pick up the pork for him and Eddie, as well as ours. So if it's okay with you, Rolly, could I borrow your car? Or do you want to come out too?" He looked at me expectantly.

I shook my head. "She'll be right. You go for it. The keys are still in the ignition."

"Thanks, Rolly, I'll see you when I get back. Just imagine it, more roast pork for dinner tonight! I can't wait."

After he'd taken off, I cleaned my rifle and located a cold beer in the fridge. Jeez it went down well! I was thinking to myself that Jim was pretty keen to get back out to Charlie's and wondered how he'd get on with Nancy. Accordin' to Curly, she was holding a candle for some guy in Pommie land who was away on his big OE. Anyway, as far as I was concerned he was welcome to her, she was a bit too bossy for my liking, and pretty fiery at that!

When Jim returned it was late in the day. He walked into the house and there was a real lift in his step. His cheeks were glowing and his face was lit up like he'd won first prize in a raffle.

146

"How'd it go? Did you get lucky or something?" I tossed at him. But Jim completely ignored my pointed remark.

"Guess who jacked himself up a date with the best bundle of curves and good looks that I've ever laid eyes on?"

I looked at him and then taunted happily, "Well just who do you think you're kidding? Who in the hell would want to go out with a bloody scruff like you anyway? As for a bundle of curves, that Nancy is built like an underfed heifer, more bones than meat!"

He beamed at me good-naturedly and taunted happily, "Well, Rolly, you'll just have to wait and see won't you? Besides, you're a scruffy looking bugger yourself. Anyway, on my way back from Charlie's I thought about it and I've decided that it was time to begin looking for a set of wheels myself. Reckon that I've got enough dough stashed away for a second hand Land Rover, as long as it's in reasonable nick. Be great for hunting in, huh?"

"Sure, sure," I agreed. "It'd be terrific as a hunting wagon, far better than my old bomb. And as for something for doing a bit of tomcatting in, I reckon there are far more comfortable vehicles around. Anyway now that you've roused my curiosity, where are you takin' that bossy boots, Nancy? Or maybe she's draggin' you out? An goin' by that soppy look on your dummy, could you be thinking of a quick elopement?"

Jim took no notice of my dig. He looked me in the eye. "Well, just for starters, mister know-it-all, it's not that bossy old Nancy, it's her sister Jenny. What a dish. You'll be green with envy when you see her!"

I could just about see Jim's mind drift off into the clouds. He had got it bad all right. "So Jim, hello, hello,

I'm over here." I thought to myself old Cupid has been busy with his bow and arrow hasn't he? "All right, Romeo, come on back to ground level and finish off your fairy tale."

"Huh," he replied as it took him several more seconds, but he landed safely. "I'm taking her out to the stock cars next week."

Boy, he had it bad all right. It was a bloody transformation and a half. I tried to bring him to his senses. "Have you lost your marbles or something? It's twenty odd miles if it's an inch; and double that there and back. Whew, you have got it bad!"

I stared at him in astonishment as he continued.

"Tell you what, Rolly, it'll be a real good night out. Even going early so we can have a fancy meal at one of those licensed joints and then, after the stock cars, call in for a nice cup of coffee to cap it all off."

I watched as his mind slipped into neutral and again the alarm bells were ringing. Was there some way that I could get him back to earth gently?

"Hell's bells, Jim it's gunna cost you heaps for this date and she'll probably never go out with you again. Just weigh it all up; a new jalopy, a pricey meal with the trimmings. All this just for a bit of skirt? Talk about going out on a limb!"

Jim's face was brimming with confidence. He then proceeded to set me back on my heels.

"She's not like that, and talking of dates, you wouldn't like for me to jack up one for you with old 'bossy' would you?" and he started to hum the tune 'Jealousy!'

I looked at him to see if he was dinkum or not and there was no doubt about it. He was! I quickly got out,

148

"No way boy. You've really flipped your lid, haven't you?"

With a big smirk he elaborated. "Well, that's too bad because Nancy wants you to take her and make up a foursome. So, on your behalf mister, I stated that you'd be only too happy to make up the party!"

It was just as well that Jim departed on his way to the throne room or he might've needed the services of a member of the St. John's! Not really, but it just goes to show what the green-eyed monster can do to the thinking of a good keen man!

Half-pie serious, half-pie joking, I retorted through the closed door. "Bloody hell, man, how come you included me in this deal? One thing that I definitely know for sure, is I don't need enemies when I've got a friend like you!"

All I got for my trouble was a muffled laugh from behind the door. He knew that I'd be there, even if was only for moral support. A friend indeed!

CHAPTER THIRTEEN

THE SEARCH FOR JIM'S SET OF WHEELS

As we were still out of work, the hunt for Jim's Land Rover was all on. Here there and everywhere. Someone had once said to me that some of these car dealers were pretty sharp; sharks, maybe even bloody man-eaters at that. A couple of them that we'd found seemed to be reasonably honest and straightforward, and a pleasure to deal with.

The first shark we struck in the search for Jim's heap had two Rovers in his yard. One of them was a real clapped-out looking machine; bloody hell it was rough. It had been nearly flogged to death, and it was a wonder that it had been driven in the gate, let alone out it. Its stable mate was a bit tidier-looking all round, and appeared as though someone had at least taken the trouble to give it a coat of paint. This was a possibility for us.

The dealer who spoke to us gave a great spiel. "Not a thing wrong with it. Good for at least another twenty thousand miles before you'd need to put a spanner to it, in fact, the original owner said that it's never had a tool on it! The keys are in the ignition; so why not go ahead, be my guests and take it for a spin around the block. Okay?" It started reasonably well, so we drove out of the yard and down the road. Well, the dealer had been right about one thing, it'd definitely had not had a spanner put to it. The diff growled like a hungry lion and the gearbox grumbled in a real heartbreaking way. You didn't have to change gear as it leapt from gear to gear all by itself. We pulled into a side street and Jim revved her up. Man, if we'd offered it to the military they could've used it as a very effective smokescreen, and hidden a bloody naval destroyer behind it. This was too much for us and over the racket it was making, Jim yelled, "Let's get this bucket of bolts back to the dealer before it drops most of its innards on the road behind us, hell it's a bloody shocker!"

I couldn't have agreed more. The dealer on our return even had the cheek to ask us just what we thought of it. Needless to say he, wasn't very happy about the pointed six-letter reply he received!

Another car dealer's yard we called into had a Land Rover that was a bit rough as far as the body went, but the rest; good rubber, transmission and motor. It seemed to be in pretty good nick all round. It was well worth a thorough inspection and we went over it with a fine-toothcomb, definitely nothing wrong with it that we could see. Jim decided to offer the dealer a lot less than the asking price. Eventually, after a fair bit of to'ing and fro'ing, the dealer agreed to Jim's terms. They shook on it; a done deal as they say.

Then it was off to the bank so that Jim could draw out his dough, but owing to some sort of a mix up in accounts it took Jim about two hours to organise his money. On returning to the dealer, I was just admiring the Rover while Jim was in the office handling the paperwork. Glancing at the spare wheel, I thought to myself, 'I'm sure the spare had a good tread on it when we first examined it.' But now there was little or none, it was just about bald. What in the heck? I'd better mention it to Jim so I walked over to the office and poked my head in the door.

"Hey Jim, hold your horses for a sec' and come out here will ya', I think that there's something that you better cast your eyes over!"

Jim was a bit annoyed at being interrupted at first, but he soon changed his tune when I pointed out the nearly bald spare.

"Take a gander at it. I'm bloody sure it had a good tread when we first looked at it."

"Crikey, Rolly, you're dead right, it's bloody near smooth!"

Now that our suspicions were aroused we walked around scrutinizing everything thoroughly, and you wouldn't read about it, the two rear tyres had been changed too, hardly any tread on them either. I could see Jim's blood was coming to the boil pretty quickly!

"Thanks, Rolly, it looks like this joker thinks that he's gonna put a smart one over us. We'd better take an even a closer look at everything else. On further inspection we could also tell, just by looking at the terminals, that the battery had also been changed. We both looked at each other.

"Bloody hell, what does this idiot take us for? Talk about this being the last straw!"

Jim was about to storm back into the office when, all smiles, the dealer came out. "Something wrong, boys?" he asked smoothly.

Jim saw red! "Something wrong? You've got a bloody cheek, what do you take us for, a couple of country bumpkins from the sticks? The spare has been swapped along with the two rear tyres. The battery has been changed and you've probably even got a couple of handfuls of ground rubber in the gear box and diff to quieten down the whines!"

Jim was really fuming by now. "You know what you can do with this deal don't ya? You can stick it right up your chuff where it'll hurt you most. Types like you are nothing more than an insult to a man's intelligence. I've a good mind to call into the cop shop and report you!"

Jim was well and truly fired up as he continued. "Ya know something, if it wasn't for the fact that the stuff you're made of stinks and splatters, I'd thump you good and proper!"

The dealer at this stage was beginning to edge back towards the safety of his office, but said rudely, "Why didn't you say that you didn't want it in the first place?" And stepped back into his office quickly closing the door behind him!

I grabbed Jim by the shoulder before he had a go at kicking the door down. "C'mon mate, we've wasted more than enough time and words on this bloody no-hoper. Let's get the hell outta here. Leave him to stew in his own juice."

Although Jim was well and truly wound up, he could see that there was nothing more to be gained by hanging around any longer.

"You're right, Rolly, let's get the hell away from here!"

Turning on his heel, Jim stormed away in the direction of my old bomb with me close behind and it wasn't too long after that we found a pub and called in for a few cool beers. How someone could behave in such an underhand manner and still run a car yard like this had us both baffled. To say that we'd nearly been taken for a ride was an understatement and as there appeared to be no other suitable wagons around for Jim, we turned for home, somewhat the wiser. But no closer to finding a suitable Land Rover.

It was just after we stopped for a feed of fish and chips, and were eating them beside a stream, when Jim brought to my notice an advertisement on the newspaper wrapping under 'Vehicles for Sale'.

"Look, Rolly, a Land Rover for sale and, better still, it's on our way home near The Old Coach road!"

I looked at the ad. "Just as well we stopped for a feed. Now there's a bit of luck for you, and look at the date, it's only last week's paper. Right, as soon as we've finished our chips we'll make tracks and have a look at it."

Another fifteen minutes or so further on, we turned up a short driveway and there parked on the front lawn of a farmhouse was the Rover and a For Sale sign. We pulled up beside it, to be greeted by a big dog. He was telling us as to who was the boss in no uncertain terms! Then from somewhere out of sight came a loud whistle. The kuri shut up immediately and, with his tail between legs, disappeared behind the house at a great rate of knots. We got out of the car at the same time as the owner turned up.

"Hi, you guys interested in the Rover?"

We both said yes, then introduced ourselves and shook hands. He explained that he'd been forced to sell it as he'd also sold the farm. Then he told us all about the Rover in general, showing us receipts for any work that it had needed. His main reason for selling was because the wife had stated, emphatically, that it was not going to be parked outside their new house at Papamoa Beach. A real pity as he'd owned the Rover from brand new and it was just like losing an old friend.

He insisted that we take it for a run, first of all up a steep track that ran across the back of his farm, and then out onto the tar-sealed road. We did, and it was great in every way; it didn't burn oil, no unusual vibrations and no whines. Another thing, it had new rubber all round. This was a good one all right! We were both more than impressed with its performance and to cut a long story short, as Jim had the cash in hand, he was able to cut the price back to the bone. And so Jim had his Land Rover. The cocky even insisted that it was filled with gas from the tank beside the cowshed. What a change it was to deal with someone open, honest and who wasn't out to rip you off.

So, that was how Jim got his set of wheels and boy was he tickled pink. Like a dog with two tails, a huge grin spread right across his face.

We were up first thing the following morning, more to try out Jim's Rover than to go for a hunt. It performed exceptionally well, impressing us both. In fact, we wound up deep back in the bush, as far as it was possible to go on four wheels. There we had a bit of a hunt and even though there was plenty of fresh deer sign, we didn't manage to score anything to fill the pot. Although yours truly did miss a simple shot of about forty yards, but them's the breaks; not everything goes according to plan. After giving it up as a dead loss for the day, we returned to the Rover and followed the track until we drove out onto the road.

Another fifteen minutes or so later we were hailed by a couple of guys at the side of the road. Jim pulled to a halt beside them. The younger of them smiled in relief and said, "Thanks for stopping, you guys. We're stuck about a hundred yards back up the track. Do you think you'd be able to give us a short tow? Just enough to let us

155

get moving again will be all that it'll need. We'd be most grateful if you could?"

I smiled and nodded in reply as Jim got in a quick word. "No worries, we should have you out in two ticks. Is there enough room for me to turn around in there?"

The spokesman said, "Yes there's a ton of room to turn around. Thanks you guys, it's real decent of you. We'll walk in ahead. I've already got a tow rope all set up so we're ready to hook straight onto your tow ball."

With that Jim turned around onto the rough track and followed them to the utility, which was right up to its chassis in a swampy patch. They were certainly bogged all right - not a hope in hell of getting out without our assistance! With just a little bit of effort Jim was soon in position for the tow. I hopped out and connected up the rope and called, "she's all set Jim!"

With that the younger fella slid in behind the wheel of the utility and started up, and when ready he gave the thumbs up. In gear, with the motor running for Jim to tow, he slipped the Land Rover into low ratio four-wheel drive and with hardly any effort at all revved lightly and both of them were well out of the quagmire onto the firm part of the track. I couldn't help but see the huge smile of satisfaction on Jim's dummy; he was over the moon all right, as was the owner of the utility!

As the ute was being pulled out I noticed on the back tray was a dog box and on top of it was a decent-sized boar that looked in damned good nick.

"That boar's in bloody good nick," I commented to the older guy. "Did it put up much of scrap when you latched onto it?"

"You're right. It's in good condition. You should have been up there on top of the mountain up when we nailed it. Talk about laugh!"

156

The younger one said, "Dad, are you trying to put my weights up?" And then laughingly reached into the back of his ute where he dragged out half a dozen bottles of Waikato. My eyes lit up!

"Take these beers," he said, "maybe it will at least say thanks for getting us out of that swampy stuff. And by the way I'm Barry and this is my Dad, Claude."

Jim reached out and taking the Waikato said, "Well it's no good leaving the tops on, is it? We might as well have drink or two and relax for a while as we celebrate getting you guys out! Fair enough!"

With that we all started chewing the fat in general. When Jim and I admired the boar, I prompted Claude about his son's remark about putting his weights up.

They both laughed. Then Claude, grinning at us, said, "Barry and I haven't had the chance to get out hunting for a couple of months. When I was at the local rubbish dump that blue merle there was getting stuck into some offcuts of smelly, flyblown meat. When I looked at it more closely, I thought to myself that it had all the looks of a good pig dog. I managed to get a leash around it then took it home, so this was really a trial to see if it was up to scratch or not. I guess only time will tell, maybe not!"

We settled back to hear the story…

Well before first light this morning we started heading to the top of the mountain up there, and the higher we got up the more the mist and fog thickened; it was a real eerie place. Anyway we decided to wait until it lifted a bit and have a yak and a smoke amidst some trees with rotting branches festooned with swathes of moss. While hunkering down, hoping for a break in the weather. Barry's dog headed off nosing around, doing its thing with us waiting in anticipation for this blue merle to show some interest too. But no, all it did was to cringe up against me and shiver. Could it be going to turn out another useless mutt, a real no-hoper? Then shortly after this, as the watery sun began to breaking through the mist, Barry's mutt started to bail like hell. In a rush we were off at the run towards the bark and this bloody blue merle stayed right in behind me. I wasn't sure why, maybe it was deaf? Well we came to an area, a hollow of about twenty yards by ten. The whole of it was covered with a lawn like fine grass. Unusual at this high altitude, it was probably being kept neatly trimmed down by the rabbits and deer. Barry's dog was bailing flat out keeping the boar pinned in the one spot and still this bloody blue mutt stayed right behind me giving all the signs of being absolutely shit scared. Barry quickly summed it all up and decided to put a shot into the pig, especially as the blue mutt wasn't going in to give a hand with the pig. I watched as he quickly raised the rifle, sighted and fired but all that happened was that the boar just stood there with his dog going in on the hold. Barry handed me the rifle, drew his knife and strode down the slope but, without warning, his feet shot out from under him and he landed flat on his arse and started sliding rapidly on what we later found out was greasy papa covered with a thin slippery layer of clay and grass. I can tell you, even if he wanted to stop, there was not a chance. He slid straight in under, right between the boar's front and back legs! There was not a bloody thing that I could do to help him out. Luckily he was still holding the knife, but there he was flat on his back struggling to hold onto the backbone and at the same trying to stab up into the front of the boar's chest! Then, surprisingly enough, and without any warning, this blue dog rushed in to get a hold. But instead of grabbing the boar it latched onto Barry's knife hand! All the time I was trying to scramble across this treacherously slippery slope to help out. Now I've heard some pretty horrible swearing and abuse in my time, but Barry was fair letting rip, and then bugger me the mutt surprisingly released its grip of Barry's hand and shot back to cower behind me. Jeez what a bloody useless animal! But I can tell you, I didn't have time to think about putting a bullet into it. I was too damned worried at Barry's dangerous predicament.

Then much to my dismay I watched as the boar fell in a heap on top of Barry, trapping his legs, and boy, was my heart in my mouth. Then somehow I managed to get beside Barry without going arse over kite myself and between the two of us managed to roll the boar away.

Luckily for us, when he'd fired the shot the projectile had hit the thick shield on the shoulder and ricocheted forward, breaking the boar's jaw in two places, otherwise it could've ripped Barry to hell. A pretty close call all around we reckoned.

Eventually when we'd both had a couple of smokes and our hearts had stopped racing, we were more thankful for small mercies. But as for this bloody blue merle, I've got a good mind to take it back to the rubbish dump where I found it in the first place. It's not even worth wasting a round of ammo on it!

Jim and I were only too happy to raise our bottles to Barry and his old man in a toast to lady luck but I was also thinking second thoughts as to what I might've have done to the useless mutt, especially as I had complete trust in Gray. There wasn't a single doubt in my mind.

Then having knocked the last two tops off the Waikato we shared them around. It had sure been quite a tale that we'd heard. I thought to myself just how lucky Barry had been not to get all ripped to hell.

"Well Barry, one thing for sure, I'd be getting myself a ticket in the next Lotto draw, eh? What do you reckon Jim?"

"Bloody lucky all right," he replied whole heartedly, "I would've been crapping myself. And now that you've told us roughly where you've been hunting, is there much sign up around there? Rolly here has got a dammed good finder-holder, do you reckon that it would it is worthwhile to climb up and hunt up there?"

Barry seemed more than happy at Jim's asking. "Yeah, why don't you guys go for it? I probably only come pig hunting over this way a couple of times a year because it's a fair old trek for us. We do most of our hunting in the Tauranga district. As for pigs there wasn't what you'd call a lot of sign about, so this one was probably a fluke. It'll certainly be no skin off our noses, you guys. Go for it!"

With that Barry and his old man said that they'd better be making tracks as they had a couple of hours of driving before they arrived home.

Having seen them on their way, we happily headed homewards ourselves. Surprisingly enough, Jim didn't have much to say about how well the Rover had performed, but his big grin of contentment said it all.

CHAPTER FOURTEEN

ANOTHER HUNTING LESSON

The next day, as we'd been doing a bit of necessary work around the cottage and had worked up a bit of a thirst, we made a beeline for the pub and a few welcome cold beers.

On strolling into the bar, we were confronted by Curly's face; not the prettiest at the best of times, but looking a bit more dog-eared than usual, with patches of sticking plaster and the odd scratch thrown in.

Jim and I looked at each other, trying hard not to grin too much, but throwing in the odd wry comment. We couldn't resist having a dig at Curly. Yeah, we're great mates all right!

Curly filled our jugs and patiently waited until we'd stopped giving him a hard time. Then he pointed to me. "You, you bloody great fairy-footed ape, if you hadn't tried to dance the light fantastic on the cat's tail, none of this would've happened. And that bloody vase, it was one that we'd been given for a wedding present. My missus thought that I was trying to kick the cat to death, that was why she up and clobbered me!"

He then winked at Jim, and continued, "When she heard what had really happened all was well. So, put it this way, at the moment I can't put a foot wrong. But Rolly boy you'd better watch out. Is she after your blood!" He chortled. "Nah, forget all that, just a little family tiff between me and the missus, it's all over and done with now. Thank goodness!"

By then, he'd poured himself a small beer and joined us.

"Anyways, here's to more good days out pig hunting. And another thing, they tell me you two Romeos are off to do a bit of tomcatting around? A little word of warning for you Jim, you'd better watch yourself, that Jenny's got a punch like the kick of a mule!"

Followed by another wink and a look of 'okay I'm pulling your leg well and truly'. "But as for you, Rolly, I'm amazed, I thought that wild horses couldn't drag you out with Nancy?"

As I replied to Curly's gibe, I gave Jim a hard poke in the ribs. "Yeah, it just goes to show how far a fella will go to help a mate out, doesn't it!"

Curly was about to say something else, but was called away to answer the phone. Arriving back shortly after he'd hung up, he was waving a piece of paper in his hand.

"That was an old farming mate of Charlie's on the phone. Anyway he's been havin' the devil's own job with a pig getting at his lambs as well. Evidently, Charlie's been doin' a fair bit of crowing around the district about how Gray got stuck into the pigs. And as much as I'd like to have a lash at this pig, or pigs, I haven't got a chance of getting any time off at the moment. We're one barman short as it is, bugger it all! So if you jokers are interested, this is his phone number and John is a real decent bloke they tell me. Boy, just what I wouldn't do for another day out with the dogs! Bugger it all, especially if it's as good as it was at Charlie's!" He sighed with exasperation.

162

Jim and I looked at one another and nodded, we were in boots and all, didn't have to be asked twice did we?

"You betcha, Curl!"

I was as keen as mustard and I could see that Jim was all for it too. Curly handed across the paper commenting on the contents.

"One thing though, if ya haven't ridden a nag yet, you'll have to learn pretty quick or there'll be a helluva long walk on Shank's pony for you both!"

Jim couldn't get it in quick enough. "That's all right, Curl; and another thing, I'm now the proud owner of a Land Rover myself, bought it the day before yesterday, not as late a model as yours, but it's in bloody good nick all the same!"

Curly raised his eyebrows. "A Rover, ya say? Good on you, they're worth their weight in gold for what you'll be using it for. When you've got time, bring the Rover around home, I'd like to take a good look at it. Another good thing is that it doesn't matter if it's got scratches or mud all over it - nobody takes any notice at all! Not like an ordinary car that belongs to someone we know. No rust either with its alloy body."

Curly nodded at me, and winked to Jim.

"Anyway, gettin' back to John and his problem of the wild pigs. The Rover will only get you up halfway to the boundary because the country is full of windfalls and real steep-sided gullies. About as crappy a type of place as you're ever likely to hunt in. Another thing, be careful, there's heaps of tomos around there, fall down one of them and it will take them days to find you. Listen to me, I'm not joking, some of them are bloody deep. I've also saved the best bit for last, he's willing to pay ten quid for every pig you get, plus you can do whatever you like with them, good deal eh!"

Both Jim and I were keen as mustard to give it a go.

"Thanks Curl. We'll get in touch with him as soon as we arrive home and if lady luck is good to us, we'll be dropping off some fresh pork for you too!"

As soon as we'd walked in the door we were on the blower to John the farmer, and it was soon all jacked up for us to come out early the following morning. Boy, were we looking forward to it all.

We drove out in the pitch black of the pre-dawn and on our arrival just after first light, we met up with John and introduced ourselves. He then led us around the back of an implement shed to some dog kennels that housed a couple of his working dogs, plus another. He pointed to it. "See that brindle bitch there? Found her hanging around the house a couple of weeks back and thought that I might be able to use her on the pigs myself, but things just haven't worked out the way I'd like. And seeing nobody's placed an advert in the local rag or even enquired about her, would you guys like to take her with you? She might be all right on the pigs, but she's sure no damned good on stock. Just another hungry kuri to feed as far as I'm concerned. Anyway, you guys can think it over and let me know later on if you like."

Jim and I nodded in agreement and I replied "Thanks John, we'll give her a run with Gray today an' see what sort of stuff she's made of. So now we'd better just duck back and collect our gear and get Gray out of the Rover."

"Good one, I'll meet you both on the other side of that shelter belt over there in about five minutes, okay?"

He pointed to the row of trees about fifty yards away and we made our way back to the Rover to collect

Gray. He was his usual exuberant self, all over us as though we'd been gone for months, especially when he saw us belting our knives on. I slung the rifle over my shoulder, with Gray watching our every move like a hawk.

Then we headed off to the hedge line to meet up with John, and on rounding the end of the shelter belt, we spotted him standing beside three tethered and saddled horses, along with the bitch that was tied on with a length of bailing twine. So Curly was right, we were going to be on horseback for the first time in our lives. Now this was going to make a difference for Jim and me, but not in the way that we would have bargained for. When we were nearer, Gray wandered over to the bitch; there was no growling, just some raised hackles, and after a bit of doing what all dogs do, they quickly settled down and all was well.

"So, this is the champion Gray? I'm looking forward to seeing him in action, and if he's half as good as what Charlie reckons, should be just desserts for those damned pigs. As for the bitch here, it'll be interesting to see exactly how she shapes up too. Now, about these horses - have you guys ever ridden before?"

"Nope, not me," I replied pensively.

"Nor me," echoed Jim.

John grinned. "Well, you'd both better be a bit cagey, they could be a bit stroppy, y'know, they haven't been ridden for a while, they might be full of beans!"

He paused then, with a twinkle in his eye. What was he leading up to? Something was going on here and I wasn't the least bit reassured by the twinkle.

"Thanks very much for the word of warning, but the only thing I've ever ridden in my life was a rocking horse and I reckon it was more than enough trouble handling that. For me, I reckon I'd be a damned sight safer if I kept both of my feet on the ground. What do you think, Jim?"

John grinned, then laughed. "All right you jokers, I've had my bit of fun. That bloody Curly put me up to it, he's always out to have someone on, so you can get your own back on him some time in the future. Anyway, they're as quiet as a couple of church mice, really!"

And so it proved to be; even so, Jim and I were still a bit apprehensive. That was until we'd got over the unnerving part of actually climbing into the saddle. Boy, it seemed like one helluva long way to the ground from up there, but in a short while we started to relax and somewhat tentatively enjoyed the ride, along with the high panoramic views afforded from the saddle. As we rode across the farm, John pointed out to us where the first attacks on his lambs had occurred.

"All that was left was the pelts, as clean as a whistle, couldn't have done a cleaner job with a skinning knife, bugger it all. Don't know how many, or if there's more than the one pig that's doin' the damage, but as far as I'm concerned any pigs you get around here are killers. I've seen them getting into anything that was dead and rotten, so it wouldn't pay for a man to die in the bush, because as soon as ya got a bit on the ripe side, there'd be little left to pick up except scattered bones. Nice thought eh?"

After another twenty minutes or so, we came to a fence that needed re-straining as the wires were pretty loose, with the battens lying at all angles. John showed us where a big pig had pushed its way under it, and even to Jim and me, the tracks it had made in the mud were huge. Another large boar maybe?

There was no sign of Gray anywhere and he'd been gone for a while now. We sat still for some time, listening. I noticed that the insides of my thighs were becoming a bit tight and tender. You're able to cover a lot of ground on horseback, and perhaps there would be a price to pay, but so far it was certainly a damned sight easier than walking!

I'd noticed as we'd ridden through this mixture of roughish steep-sided gullies that Curly had been right, it was pretty tough country at that.

John said, "If you follow this fence about ten chains, there's a gate that you can get through, but normally I go on foot as it's nearly too damn rough even for the horse, also it seems a bad place for tomos. So remember, no matter what you do, keep your eyes peeled and stick to the tracks the stock have pushed through the scrub and you should have no worries!"

Deciding to stretch my legs, I dismounted and began rolling myself a smoke. It became noticeable to me as soon as I was on the ground that my legs were starting to feel a bit on the fatigued side. Hmmm, perhaps there's more to riding a horse than I had first thought. Finishing rolling my smoke, I wondered where Gray had got to. What's he up to? So far we hadn't seen hide nor hair of him. Then it was as though he'd received a telepathic message.

"Woof, woof," followed by a short silence, then the frantic squealing of a pig as Gray went in for the hold. I called out in excitement, "Good on you, Gray, I'm on my way!"

I took off through the fence in the direction of the squealing pig. At the same time, John must've released the bitch because she shot past me like a rocket. I was thinking, 'That's a good thing, at least she's keen to get

167

to the squeal, might be promising, maybe she's gunna turn out all right after all.' As per usual, it was an exciting madcap scramble through the undergrowth, but I also kept in mind John's warning about the possibility of hidden tomos.

The squealing from the pig was a lot louder now, not far to go. Breaking out into a smallish grassy clearing, I could see Gray latched hard onto an ear and the bitch hanging grimly onto the other ear of a good-sized pig of about the eighty pounds mark. It took only a few minutes before my knife was in and, with a quick thrust up into the chest cavity, the sow ceased squealing and kicked her last.

As soon as the struggles ceased, the dogs released their hold. I patted both of them and lavished on heaps of praise, boy did they lap it up. Although I noticed Gray kept on making a point of getting in between the bitch and me. Perhaps she was going to turn out to be a holder? But this was very early days yet, and she still had to show her true colours. At a call from Jim, I stopped my musing.

"Hey, Rolly, where are you?"

"Over here, Jim, over here," I yelled, shaking a tall thin tree to give him something to focus on.

"Righto, gotcha, we're on our way!"

I could hear them pushing through the undergrowth towards me and then several minutes later, Jim and John were standing looking at and discussing the pig. So, now all we had to do was to carry the pig out to where the horses were. It was the first one in the bag for today, so to speak. The carry out wasn't too tough, especially with the three of us taking turns out to where we dropped the pig in a clump of fern up against the fence.

We were getting ready to remount our horses when John beckoned to us and said, "Come on over here, I've got something of interest to show you guys."

We followed on foot for about thirty-five yards or so to where he stopped and pointed over a clump of broom and pig fern about three feet high. Then he cautiously pulled it apart, exposing to our view a deep tomo about a metre and a half across. If someone had been bashing his way through the scrub it would have been invisible until you were damn near into it. John then picked up a chunk of pumice and dropped it in and it took a few seconds before it hit the bottom. I guess it reinforced to us just how careful one would have to be.

"Not the sort of place you'd really want to visit, eh! I stumbled across it by luck, or really by the smell if the truth be known. I realised that something was dead and followed my nose. All that's left in there now is a pile of bones and," he said with resignation, "all in all about seven hundred pounds of prime beef gone west, so to speak!"

"Well, I sure as hell am glad I'm not down there!" muttered Jim.

"Nor me," I echoed somewhat thoughtfully, thinking that John certainly had got the message across very well indeed.

Then we returned to our horses and mounted them, and over the next three hours or so covered a fair bit more ground, much more than we would've by walking. And from then on the bitch didn't need to be tied with the bailing twine, she just kept following behind us. Of Gray, the only time we'd see him was whenever we stopped and listened, hoping to hear his bark. Like always, whenever we took a breather he'd just arrive back, look us over and then move off again as soon as we did.

By now, my legs were becoming uncomfortably tight up the insides of my thighs and maybe just a little more tender elsewhere. So much for the joys of my first shot at horseback riding, but it did have one big advantage though - you could see a lot more of the countryside from up here, there was no doubt about that!

Following another break and a smoke and a bit of a natter, I mentioned to John and Jim that maybe we might have a bit more luck on the return trek as now we'd be facing into a slight head wind, giving the dogs a better chance of latching onto another pig.

All the same, Gray still didn't come across anything of interest until we were nearing the spot where John had suspected the pig of killing the lambs first up. This area we'd moved into was slightly more open, with quite a number of ewes with lambs at foot scattered about. But still, there was nothing up as far as we could tell, so it looked like we'd done our chips for the day.

Then everything changed and suddenly we were on high alert. Gray was on the go again.

"Woof, woof!" followed by the glimpse of a damned big pig and was he going for it, flat out about 100 yards away, directly into a dense patch of real rough stuff - an interlaced mixture of blackberry, ferns and thick manuka. The bitch had picked up on Gray's bark and she'd taken off in that direction as well. We followed suit and headed towards where we'd last seen the boar. We all reined to a halt, waiting expectantly for more action, but to no avail, nothing out of the ordinary was occurring. Eventually, after about half an hour or so with us being on tenterhooks, Gray eventually turned up, his tongue hanging out. He was panting deeply, and was followed a couple of minutes later by the bitch. Luckily there was a cattle trough fairly close by and they both leapt in to cool off and drink their fill.

At this point we all decided to call it a day, and after a bit of a detour collected the pig that we'd caught earlier in the day and continued on the trek back to the Rover.

We decided to start the following day's hunt by returning to the same spot that the wild boar had been frequenting, arriving as close to first light as possible. The theory being, that the early bird gets the worm or, in this case, the pig. Also, seeing that there was really nowhere suitable at home for us to keep the bitch at the moment, John suggested that we leave her here until we'd knocked up something better to keep her in. But in the meantime, he said it was no bother for him to look after her.

Although we'd covered a lot of ground on our first day's horse riding, it wasn't the most enjoyable, and we were both feeling the effects of all those hours in the saddle. We took the golden opportunity of going for a soak in the local public hot pools and boy it was pure bliss all right, relieving the tension and strains, a real enjoyable, relaxing time all round.

We also called into the game meat buyer, receiving more than enough cash in hand to buy a few cold beers and a big feed of fish and chips. Gray thought that this was just great, especially when we shared some with him. What a way to end a great day's hunting, well fed and tired out, and more than ready for a good night's sleep!

Early the following morning we drove out to John's farm; it was before daybreak, with the hint of a frost in the air and a thin covering of white on the ground.

Once again, John was there with the horses saddled ready.

"Morning you guys, how's the aches and pains from your ride yesterday?"

I had to be a little bit honest, and with wry grin replied, "Just a bit on the stiff side, but after we'd had a decent soak in the hot pools on the way home last night it did us both the world of good and now we're dead keen, raring to give that big bugger of a boar a run for his money!"

John smiled and nodded in agreement then replied, "Yeah, that'd be great if we can get him. He's certainly a big bugger all right and probably as cunning as a cartload of monkeys with it. I'll go and get the bitch out if ya like."

We let Gray out of the Rover and Jim shouldered the rifle. He was going to have the job this time around, I'd had more than enough of it yesterday, he was welcome to it! Then the bitch that John had released came rushing over to us, looking as eager as hell. We mounted up and began riding off in the direction of where we'd seen the big boar the previous day. The sun was just coming over the horizon, warming not only our fingers, but slowly dissipating the light frost off the ground in thin wisps of ghostly vapour.

I couldn't help myself. "Ya know something you guys, who'd want to be dead on a day like this? What a great morning!"

Jim, who was slightly out in front at this stage, was as keen as hell, but we were both thinking ahead on tenterhooks of anticipation. Then, without warning, Gray let rip. He started to bail in one of the many deep scrubby gullies that wound through this part of the farm. The bitch took off in the direction of Gray's bark and we all trotted our horses after her, the excitement and adrenalin lifting us; our blood was certainly pumping, it was all on, our anticipation was buzzing!

Near as we could tell to where Gray had been bailing the pig we all reined in, listening intently, eager for more continued action. Worse luck there was nothing to be heard, or to be seen - no dogs, no pig!

We waited expectantly until again our adrenalin began pumping at the crash of breaking branches. Something, presumably the boar, was smashing its way through some scrub in a gully off to our right, followed by a 'yip' of a dog. As Gray never made a noise unless bailing, it must be the bitch adding more to the thrill of the chase. There was the continuous sound of a body crashing through the undergrowth on the far side of this densely wooded hollow, followed somewhat unexpectedly by the metallic snick of the bolt as Jim pushed home a round into the breech of the rifle. It was cocked ready for shooting. More crashing was followed by the appearance of the pig! Yes, he certainly looked like the boar we'd seen on the previous day, he was like greased lightning as he shot out of the gully. Boy, he was pulling out all the stops, and certainly wasn't hanging around, he was heading for the same dense patch of scrubby stuff and blackberry that he'd made for yesterday. He no doubt knew that once he got in there, the dogs didn't have a hope in hell of stopping him. A couple of yards behind the boar was Gray, with the bitch a close second. Then, to my astonishment, I watched Jim raising the rifle to his shoulder. Thankfully the dogs were not in his line of sight, but surely he didn't think he was going to bowl the pig? Bloody hell, it was moving at speed, and at that distance? It was like everything was in slow motion. I watched as Jim raised the rifle and firmly held it to his shoulder, with my immediate thoughts being, 'Hell surely not, and on horseback at that?' The next thing was the crack of the rifle! I didn't have time to see if he'd hit the pig or not, I was far too busy trying to hang on for dear life, with my mount and all three horses prancing around in all directions. Jeez it was touch and go for me as I tried to remain in the saddle. But I caught a glimpse of Jim; he'd certainly left the saddle in a hurry, the rifle flying in one direction and him over the other side of the horse. John and I were lucky to have remained in our saddles. But as for Jim, he was sitting on the ground swearing and rubbing his shoulder. Concernedly I managed to somehow scramble down from the saddle, no mean feat for a greenhorn like me. More than a little worried as I came to a crouch beside him, I anxiously asked, "Jim, are you okay?"

He looked at me with a wry grin as he rubbed his shoulder. "I think so, mate, but that is the first and most definitely the last time I'll ever fire a rifle while I'm sitting on the back of a horse! Never, ever again!"

Then John, whose horse had bolted away a fair distance, came riding back jubilantly, excitedly waving a hand. "What a shot! What a shot! Where'd ya learn to shoot like that? It was the most amazing bit of shooting and a moving target at that, the pig was going like the clappers. One hundred and fifty yards at least. Jeez that sure was some shooting!"

Jim looked up at John and I could see even he was amazed as well. "I bowled it? You're joking aren't you? What else can I say except, I guess wonders will never cease, aye!"

John grinned down at him. "Don't be so bloody modest, come on, let's ride over and you can take a gander yourself, that pig went down like a ton of bricks and one thing's for sure, the bloody thing's not going to get up and run again!"

Jim was still massaging his shoulder as he rose gingerly to his feet. "Thanks all the same, John, but I think it might be a damned sight safer for me to walk over there. Ya never know, this horse might still resent me for firing a shot and I'm not at all keen on the sudden stop at the bottom of another assisted swallow dive!"

I picked up the rifle and the three of us made our way across to where the pig finished up. He was a bloody big boar all right, with Jim's shot hitting just behind the shoulder, dropping him cold. Even if it had've been a fluke it would have taken a shot of exceptional accuracy to equal it!

After quite a lot of discussion, and after we'd rolled ourselves a smoke, then came the post-mortem revealing the gruesome evidence, remains of lambs; something that we'd rather not have seen, but it was very satisfying to know that this killer had met his Waterloo.

John was over the moon and boy, was he chuffed! "Got him, this is the end for you, you bloody lamb killer. You've gotten your just desserts at last, so now there'll be no more sleepless nights for me, worrying about how many more ewes will be bleating for their missing lambs in the morning! Man, what a relief and thank goodness that it's all over and done with."

After we'd all had a breather we lifted the boar and lashed it across John's horse. Even though he was more than happy to keep hunting with us, he really wanted to get stuck into a few jobs that had been neglected due to his continual vigilance against the lamb killing menace.

"So, what's your plan of action now?" John queried.

"What do you reckon, Jim? How's the shoulder feel now? Do you want to have a bit more of a scout around or head off for home?"

Jim shook his head. "Nah, Rolly, I'm in pretty good shape really. The shoulder is a bit on the tender side, but nothin' to moan about, so let's keep going, as there's plenty of hours left in the day yet."

John looked at both of us. "Well, if that's the case, and as you guys have a fair idea on the layout of the farm, what say I leave you both to it, and in the meantime I'll take this big bugger back to your Rover? You've taken one helluva load off my mind, so thanks very much! Also, now I'll be able to catch up on some of the jobs that I've been putting to one side. That is, if you guys don't mind?"

Jim and I could see that John had more things on his plate and we agreed with him. As he walked away leading his horse by the reins, John called back to us. "Don't forget there'll be some cold beers waiting in the fridge when you get back to the house!"

"Thanks, John, we'll certainly be looking forward to them, catch ya later!" I answered happily.

With that, we both swung ourselves up and into the saddles. Jim winced a little as he put some strain onto his shoulder, but I could see that there was no way he was going to give in to it, at least not for a while anyway.

I was now carrying the rifle. That was after I'd checked it out, and luckily nothing seemed astray with it; no dirt up the end of the spout. Everything appeared to be in good A1 working order. So we moved off, basically letting the horses find their own way in and out of the scrub, and from time to time we stopped, enjoying a smoke and chewing the fat in general. But all the time we were listening hopefully for the sound of dogs bailing, or a pig squealing.

"Ya know, Rolly, I've been watching the bitch, she seems to be getting pretty keen and wasn't all that far behind Gray when he was after the boar; it looks like she might make the grade after all."

"Agreed Jim, it looks like we've got the job of making another dog run all right. Although we could probably put her in with Gray for a couple of days, or maybe even chain her up in some way if need be."

Finishing our smokes, we moved off again. And though we caught glimpses from time to time, or heard the dogs making their way through the undergrowth, they didn't latch onto any more pigs. So it looked like we'd be going home with only just the big boar for today's effort.

Finally we decided to call it a day and began making our way back in the general direction of the Rover. As we got closer to the main paddocks, the bush, fern and scrub was a lot more open, thinning out a fair bit. This was ideal, as we often caught sight of the dogs working together and boy, they sure were covering a lot of ground.

Then suddenly we were alert. We watched the bitch come to an abrupt stop and begin sniffing the air as if she'd winded something, then she took off at speed across a jumbled pile of partially burnt trees and branches, disappearing beyond the brow of a hill down into a scrubby-looking gully. This was followed some few seconds later by her excited barking. It was all on again as Gray shot past us like a bat out of hell. I was a lot closer to the action than Jim, and leapt out of the saddle at the sound of a pig frantically squealing. Good, they were in and holding, so I probably wouldn't need the rifle. I hurriedly leant it against a stump. The heart thumping excitement was all on in the thrill of the chase. Being so close to the dogs, I was there in next to no time. Unsheathing the knife, I drove it up into the sow's chest putting an end to its struggles, and another nice pig was all ours. I lavished praise and patted the dogs and on looking at them more closely, it appeared to me that Gray was pretty brassed off at being beaten to the pig by the bitch. But I was more than happy with the outcome.

A short while later Jim joined me and we decided that as it was in such good nick we'd take the pig to the thermal bore outflow for scalding; it sure looked like it would make nice eating. Another bonus was that there was very little carrying as we had a horse to do all the hard yakka for us.

After lashing the pig across the saddle we resumed our trip back towards the Rover. All that time Jim and I were discussing the bitch and her possible future.

"Hey, Rolly, did you see the way she latched onto that sow? Head up. Off like a rocket and in on the bale and then as soon as Gray arrived, going in holding. It certainly looks like we've fluked it again, another good all round pig dog, what do ya think?"

"It certainly looks like it Jim, and possibly a good one at that. Seeing as we're going to keep her I guess we'd better give her a name of some sort, though what she's answered to in the past is anyone's guess."

About another hundred yards on Jim suggested, "Hey, Rolly, maybe we should try a whole range of names to see if she reacts to them in any way?"

As we rode on we tried calling her all sorts of names, but in the end I gave this up, as she would only come to my whistle anyway. Later on I heard Jim call again, "Speckle, here Speckle. Look at that Rolly!" He was excited.

I watched as she pricked up her ears and trotted over to him whining.

"Rolly, I was looking at the little spots on the bitch, so it made me think of specks, and so 'Speckle! And it seemed to work!"

So Speckle she became.

On arriving back at the Land Rover we loaded the sow in the back with the boar and then tied the dogs up under the trees in the shade. After giving them a drink of water, we joined John on his back porch, where he'd already lined up a couple of cold ones. Boy, did they slide down easily, they barely touched the sides.

We discussed the pig hunting over the last two days and explained to John how we'd come to find out the name that Speckle was now answering to. John repeated his thanks at how we'd gotten rid of the lamb-killing boar and with that, he handed over an envelope that contained a note expressing his thanks and a cheque for sixty quid. We tried to give it back, but he wouldn't have a penny of it and was most adamant that we keep the lot!

As the beer flowed, more and more diverse topics were covered. Then grinning from ear to ear John asked if we'd noticed the new bridge just down the road a bit that was almost in its final stages of construction. We told him we had spotted it and waited curiously. Giving us another amused grin, John started to tell us about it all…

Ya see, I was on my way to town a couple of weeks back and there had been a bit of a hold up at the temporary bridge that had been erected while the old one was being replaced. Anyway, the contractor in charge of the job was having a go at talking some sense into a truck driver and as I was waiting I couldn't help but overhear what was being said.

"Listen mate, you must be blind if you didn't see the big sign back there at the turn off. It's about the same size as your truck! 'All heavy duty vehicles are to take the alternative detour as the bridge is under reconstruction'."

The driver responded, you could see by his manner that he was reluctant to turn and go back. "But this is only a little truck boss, and it's only got a small tray. All she carries is a ton of cement and three yards of builder's mix, that's not very heavy is it now? C'mon, giv'us a fair go, let me cross it, I've got a job to do, ya know."

The bridging contractor frowned and scratched his head in disbelief.

"Let you go over? Just take a look at your tare weight, even without your load on, the truck's close on five tons. All up loaded you'll come out close to carrying ten tons or more, and that's damn near double what the temporary bridge is ever meant to carry and that's the reason for the detour sign!"

The driver poked his head out of the window and looked down at the tare weight printed on the side of the fuel tank and pointed to it.

"Hmm, only four tons, eight hundred and fifty pounds tare, that's not five ton weight is it? So, I'll be able to cross, won't I boss?" he asked eagerly, and slipped the fully laden truck into gear in anticipation of crossing.

The contractor's mouth gaped wide and you could just imagine what was going through his mind! Annoyed, he emphasised, "You don't get the picture do you? Your truck and load is at least five ton over the limit of what this bridge is capable of carrying!" With the contractor

180

standing there, he was absolutely flabbergasted, just about speechless.

The driver wasn't. "I know that, boss, but don't forget this cab is very light, doesn't weigh much, and it's only made of aluminium!" Trying to make his point, the driver slapped his hand on the outside of the door!

We almost split our sides and when we stopped laughing, John continued with his yarn.

At this point the contractor had taken about all he could tolerate from the truck driver. He didn't mince his words. "Listen, mate, I've had more than enough of you and your bloody crap. So now, if you don't back up, turn around and piss off, I'm going to tell the driver on the bulldozer over there to come across here and use his machine to push you back up the road to the metal pit and bury you and your bloody truck!"

With that he waved his arms and beckoned the bully driver towards him. The driver immediately gave it full revs and began rolling forward in low ratio, with his smile a mile wide, and a fanatical gleam in his eyes!

The truck driver's eyes were just about hanging out on stalks. He rapidly crashed the gears into reverse, dropped the clutch, and the truck flew lurching back, with the driver spinning the wheel frantically, just about causing the load of cement to fly off the top of the builder's mix! Then he rapidly departed back down the road in a cloud of dust. He certainly wasn't prepared to push his luck any further!

At this time the bridge building crew all broke out into raucous laughter, then they signalled John to come on through.

As I was driving past the boss man, he called out, "Sorry about the hold up John, but at least that bloody idiot of a driver and all his mates will know from now on to not try coming up this road until this new bridge is up and running. All I can say is that some blokes are as dense as pig shit!"

He then mimicked the driver, "The cab's only made of aluminium!" Again the whole crew bloody near pissed themselves!

Jim and I certainly enjoyed John's yarn and the next thing you know he was into another one. Then while getting a few more cold beers out, he also brought out a photograph album and showed us a picture of him and another joker holding up a big fish. And even we could see that it was a beaut, a monster snapper.

"See that, it's the biggest snapper I've ever caught, and the guy helping me to hold it up is a great fishing mate of mine. It weighed all of twenty-eight and a half pounds, but there's a bit of a twist to the tale associated with it, and I'll show you what it is when I've told the yarn…"

My mate and I, every time things were a bit slack on our farms, were always going out fishing on the Waitemata harbour in a boat called the 'Florence Kennedy.' She's an old ex-Navy Fairmile that always rolled its guts out and that's on a dead flat calm day too. Anyway, this particular trip out in the gulf it was a pretty rough sort of day and with the big seas and the rolling, by the time we'd reached the fishing grounds out past Rakino Island, my old mate Trev was feeling crook and pretty green around the gills! We'd no sooner gotten our lines down when Trev spewed, bringing everything up!

Talk about burley, he was really feeding the fishes all right. Then as he straightened up, he turned to me, pointing to his mouth, mumbling ruefully. "Bugger it all John, my teeth have gone over the side, I've lost them. Bugger, bugger, blast and damn!"

I commiserated with him and then concentrated on my own line and about five minutes later, I felt my line give a twitch and it started to run through my fingers. I muttered to Trev.

"Whatever I have got hooked up, it's real big, a bloody stingray maybe?" Trev, who by now was taking a bit more of an interest in things, watched me. After a while I managed to slow down whatever it was, and then I could feel by the steady thump, thump, that it was a snapper and a good sized one at that! It took me about fifteen minutes to get it up to the boat and I couldn't believe my eyes! A bloody great monster of a snapper, the biggest I'd ever seen! The skipper of the boat came over with a gaff, so it only took a jiffy and it was flapping its last and was safely in the bag. We all tried fishing for a while longer but then the weather really began to pack a sad and the skipper said we had better call it a day, it was just too rough for any more fishing.

On the way back into the ferry buildings, along with all those who had been lucky enough to catch something, we were gutting and filleting the fish. And then a real humorous thought came to me. I had the chance to have my mate Trev on a bit, and pull his leg. Smiling to myself I slyly removed my own false teeth from my mouth and secreted them deep inside the guts of this monster snapper. Then I called to him loudly so that all the other fishermen could hear and watch the ensuing bit of leg pulling.

"Hey Trev, you're never going to believe this, but look what's inside this snapper's gut!"

I slowly reached in and pulled out the teeth from inside the gut cavity and boy they were smothered with blood and guts. I waved them in front of him. "Look, I just don't believe it, here are your bloody teeth, it's true, literally, Trev!"

He looked at me, shaking his head. "You're having me on! You're pulling my tit!" Trev was staring at the teeth in amazement and disbelief.

"No, I'm definitely not having you on Trev." So I handed the teeth over to him. "See, all they need is a good wash and they'll be just like new. Here, take them!"

As I handed them over, all the time I was trying to keep a straight face but inside, boy, was I cracking up! And was I going to give him heaps, when he found that they didn't fit, and he finally realised they were mine. I watched every move as he washed and rinsed the teeth clean, looked them over carefully then he tried them in. After making a face, he pulled them out of his mouth. "The bloody things don't seem to fit any more, buggered if I know why." He then tried putting them back in his mouth again.

I waited and watched as he removed them again and boy was I having trouble trying to not give the game away! I was all ready to give him heaps, when the penny finally dropped, and he realised that they weren't his teeth at all. He looked at them carefully again and turning them over in his hands several times he stated most emphatically.

"One thing for sure John, they don't fit and they're definitely not mine!"

And before I could say or do anything, he flung them out over the rail and into the deep water. I watched

184

them disappear down into the depths with shock and amazement. So that was that and now my bloody teeth were gone too!

Jim and I split our sides.

Then John said, with a great deal of irony in his voice, "Of course, the joke had backfired on me completely and it certainly gave all the fishos on the boat a damned good laugh. But it was my mate Trev who laughed loudest! There's no doubt about that saying, 'he who laughs last, laughs longest!'

"So now, if you two take a closer look at this picture of us holding this monstrous snapper, you'll see that there's a couple of real gummy toothless wonders smiling back!"

There was no doubt about it, John had a great way of telling a story. Then after he'd turned over a couple more pages of the photograph album he showed us a picture of a relation of his on a nice tidy looking yacht.

"That's Chris who owns the boat and the guy beside him is a yachty mate. I think his name was Peter. Anyway, that flag that they are showing is the emblem of the Arid Island Yacht Club. Well, the Yacht Club doesn't really exist officially, but once a year there's a group of old yachties who sail out to Arid Island, which is about two miles on the other side of Great Barrier, which is about forty miles north east of Auckland on the outer reaches of the Hauraki Gulf. So, once a year these fellas get together to have their Annual General Meeting. Which is really, in all honesty, just a lot of fun, because the higher the sun goes over the yardarm, the more rum is consumed and accordingly the stories and yarns just keep getting more and more preposterous!

Anyway, this is how it all started...

The family that farms the island and its eight thousand acres or so were all pretty keen on fishing, and most times they had to launch their boat on the one and only beach that is usually accessible. Well, after a good day's fishing they got back to the beach just as the weather was beginning to deteriorate badly, and with the boat laden with fish at that. It was manoeuvred onto the trailer, and they began to drag it up on the beach through the soft sand. They weren't quite up to the high tide mark when without warning the big shackle attaching the trailer to the tractor broke. Even though they tried all sorts of methods to get the trailer and boat off the beach, nothing was suitable or strong enough to do the job. Also, there was the added worry about the rising tide, as the building waves kept coming in, rolling from the north.

As the wind was rising, so were the seas and they were quite capable of destroying both the boat and the trailer, so there was a fair bit of urgency in getting a replacement shackle organised. In desperation it was arranged for it to come all the way from Auckland, some forty miles as the crow flies. The only contact was by radio to Great Barrier Island and then relayed by telephone to Auckland. As I said, there was the rising tide and the weather was really packing up, so after a couple of urgent phone calls a shackle was arranged, but they still had to get it out to Arid Island.

There was only one way of getting the shackle out there in time to stop a catastrophe happening, and that was by aeroplane, it was Fred Ladd's amphibian.

Now Fred was quite a character and a real decent bloke who would always go out of his way if he could to help anyone in need, even to the point of dropping the most recent newspapers for free as he flew over their

186

isolated homes. He also took on emergency flights, using his amphibian as an air ambulance, landing it on the water, taxiing up onto the beach, collecting the patient, then back into the water and taking off back to Auckland.

By the time Fred had reached Arid Island with the shackle, the weather had really packed it in and the wind was fair howling. He couldn't think of landing, even if it had been to save someone's life. Now Fred had been out and about on the Island on many occasions and knew it well, so he contacted the homestead by V H F radio and it was arranged for him to drop the shackle in a sack into the bull paddock near the house. Now, in the paddock were a number of bulls and Fred, being Fred, thought it might just add a bit of zest by dropping it in right amongst the bulls. What a sense of humour! So Fred lined up the bulls and zeroed in towards the mob, reached out of the window and let the sack go; with that he was on his way as the weather was really closing in quickly. Visibility was becoming marginal. Fred hightailed it back to the big smoke of Auckland, and, with some difficulty, put the amphibian down into Mechanics Bay. With everything marginal it was a relief to run his amphibian up the ramp to safety and lash it down.

The next day he was just in the process of doing some paperwork when there was a call into the office. Fred answered, to hear a voice he knew quite well on the other end.

"Arid Island calling. Thanks for the shackle Fred, you saved the day and as it was just by the skin of our teeth that we managed to drag the boat off the beach in time. Another half-hour and the waves would've battered the boat to pieces and even so, she was half full of water. So that is really great, thanks very much for the shackle, it certainly saved our bacon. Also, I wondered if you would like to drop in home the next time you're out this way, as we've got a bit of prime beef to spare."

Fred said thanks, he'd be only too happy to take them up on the offer next time he was out that way.

"There is just one last thing, Fred, your aim with the bloody shackle was spot on. It was only last week the scow unloaded some stock for me that we'd been waiting for ages for, one of them being a champion bull for breeding and in absolutely prime condition. He was going to do wonders to the quality of my herd. The only trouble is," and there was a pregnant pause, "you were too much of a dead-eye dick, the shackle you dropped copped the animal right between the horns! You've killed my bloody prize bull!"

So, to this day, once a year a group of yachties get together for the Arid Island Yacht Club AGM. There are no minutes of the meeting recorded, the least said about elected officers the better, as the Yacht Club doesn't officially exist, but the members keep coming back each year. Anyway, back to the picture and the official yacht pennant that they are holding. It shows a bull lying flat on its back, legs straight up, as dead as a doornail! The stories, tales and lies told out there at the AGM just keep on growing, and some are even getting to the legendary stage.

There's no doubt about it, John could relate some great tales, and the beer was getting more and more enjoyable. But the day was getting on, and we still had to drive home. In reality, neither Jim or I were in a fit state to drive, but somehow we made it home under our own steam, though probably more by sheer luck than good management!

So it was the next day before we took out the last pig that we'd caught at John's to the outflow from the bore field and boy, was it nice to get our teeth into some more real good wild pork! Also we dropped off a leg of pork at Curly's. After all you've gotta look after your mates don't you? Also, we wanted to do a bit of a skite and some stirring at the same time, it all goes with a nice cool beer!

CHAPTER FIFTEEN

JIM'S NEW RIFLE

Jim had been keeping his ear to the ground and his eyes peeled for a rifle of his own for some time now, and it was several days later that we bumped into Curly at the pub. After the usual pleasantries, Curly spoke quietly and pointed out a joker down at the far end of the bar. He was drinking with the flies, all on his tod, and he didn't look very happy at all.

"Jim, are you still in the market for a rifle?" Curly enquired.

He nodded enthusiastically. "Sure am if it's any damn good; do you happen to know what type and calibre it is?"

Curly raised his eyebrows in thought. "If I remember rightly, it's a three-o-eight. And another thing is that the poor bugger's on the bones of his backside!" He again pointed to the joker down the bar. "So you might even be able to pick it up at a real good price. As I said, the poor bugger's flat broke, hasn't got a bean to his name and just wants enough dough to get him back up north somewhere. What do you think?"

Jim was summing this guy up as we quietly supped away at our beers, then came to a decision.

"I'll go and have a chat with him. Curly, pour us out another jug, will ya?"

Then, armed with the jug and his glass, Jim headed towards the lone drinker where he introduced himself and, after they'd consumed most of the jug, the two of them made their way out of the door towards the car park. Curiosity got the better of me and I wandered over to the window, where I watched the owner of the rifle reach into the back of his utility, retrieving a bag that clearly held a rifle. When it was removed from the carry bag, I could see it was equipped with a scope and, going by the way the owner looked at and handled the rifle, it was his pride and joy. He carefully passed it over to Jim who, after turning it over several times, sighted through the scope. After a few questions they both got into the utility and drove off in the direction of the rifle range at the old quarry.

Some three quarters of an hour later they returned to the car park where Jim got out of the ute and reached in to shake hands with the driver, who carefully handed across the rifle, then with a short wave departed from the car park.

As Jim walked, carrying the rifle, towards the pub entrance, he spotted me and made hand signs asking if he could use the car to take the rifle home. I gave him the thumbs up and he was off towards home. In ten minutes he was back at the bar shouting a round of beers, smiling widely and looking as pleased as punch! He quickly told us what he'd paid for the rifle and thirty rounds of ammo.

Curly interjected. "It's a bloody gift at that price, worth at least double the amount you've just paid for it! A damned good deal all right, hell, I should've bought the bloody thing myself and not have told you about it!"

Jim retorted, "Stiff cheese, Curl, it's finders keepers now y'know. And another thing, talk about being bloody accurate! I hit the target three times out of three and it was no bigger than the end of a pony beer glass at seventy yards. I'm really itching to get out and have a go at a deer with it!"

The smile was spread right across his dummy; it was like all of his Christmases had come at once!

After several more beers, we were joined by old Charley and his farmer mate John who again expounded to one and all about the fantastic shot that had dropped the lamb-killing boar in its tracks. And like magic the distance was doubled; according to John, the shot was at the extreme range, and it couldn't have been an inch under three hundred yards! So what had started out to be a quiet drink or two gradually escalated into a happy hour or two, with lots of oddball yarns and tales, including some that stretched the truth a bit! John was again in his element telling them.

Looking at Jim and me he asked, "Do you guys remember me telling you about a fella Peter and the Arid Island yacht club? Well, he dropped into home for a night as he passed through and as per usual we talked the leg off an iron pot. And he was in full swing again, telling me about the owner of the farm there and how two of his teenage boys were right into their pig hunting, what they were getting up to." He paused to swig his beer…

Anyway, the dogs latched onto a mob of pigs and they succeeded in knifing a very nice well-conditioned sow. After they had carried this pig up hill and down for a while they'd decided to do things the easy way. As the beach was directly beneath them down a steep drop of about fifty feet, why not let it fall? It would be so much easier to just collect it there after a relatively short walk from the foreshore. Luckily they were carrying a short length of rope that they soon attached to the pig and dropped it slowly to save the meat from getting too bruised.

Then they had to rush off hastily as the dogs were bailing another pig. They both took off and in the madhouse that ensued, they caught a pair of young suckers, a live one each. For some time now they'd been hoping to get hold of one to fatten and now that they had two, this was all the better! They had a fair distance to carry them back to the tractor, with the little buggers wriggling, struggling and squealing!

After a while they had to stop for a breather and, in an attempt to stop the suckers struggling and escaping, they tied them together to a small stump by using two dog collars plus a short piece of bailing twine. But, as it then happened, the dogs were again on the go and latched onto another pig. So, leaving the suckers tied there, they were trying to catch up. But worse luck, this pig kept breaking away time after time, until somehow it completely eluded the dogs and they had to return empty handed to collect the suckers. After climbing up several steep pinches both the boys were buggered.

After the hot sweaty return trip they found, much to their dismay, that the tethered suckers had broken free. They had taken to their scrapers, and the dogs were completely knackered. All the boys saw was one last glimpse of the suckers, still with the tied collars attached, away in the distance disappearing over a far ridge.

Even with the dogs being sent after the suckers, they couldn't catch up. Anyway the dogs were so buggered that they were unable or weren't interested and returned to the young hunters, their tongues hanging out almost dragging on the ground. After they disappointedly returned to the tractor they drove down onto the beach to collect their first pig of the day along with the rope they'd dropped down. But it was a mystery. Nothing, not a sign of that pig, it wasn't there! Even though they were vigilant in their searching, they ended up empty handed, with nothing except the chunk of rope they'd used. So despondently and empty-handed, it was off home to relate their woes to their dad, telling him all about the useless day's endeavours.

Anyway a couple of days later, their dad was on the VHF radio, arranging for bits and pieces to be delivered from Great Barrier Island. And as he was chatting idly he was asked how did his boys' hunting go the other day? So he explained how they'd missed out and were still mystified about the pig on the beach and how the suckers had escaped, over the ridge.

Then without warning a call on the radio came right out of left field. Someone rudely broke into the conversation.

"Can I ask you, guys, is this something different? Is it a new type of catch and release?" Followed by complete silence.

Bryce, being a stickler for protocol on use of the VHF radio, immediately abused the rude interloper about it. Following this the unknown radio operator broke back in again.

"I may have interrupted you guys. But I can tell you one thing. It was the easiest and choicest bit of wild pork that we've ever had to eat! Over and out!"

We all cracked up at John's story telling, but by now time had rolled on and it was time for Jim and me to make tracks, so we headed for home. Besides, I was breaking my neck to have a closer look at Jim's new rifle, so we bade our farewells and departed homewards.

CHAPTER SIXTEEN

OF RODEO RIDERS AND ROMEOS

Over the next few days the weather was bloody horrible, only fit for ducks, and boy did it pour down! There were floods everywhere. Then it gradually lifted and all we had to do was wait for the bush to dry out a bit to give us the opportunity to try out Jim's new rifle; besides, we were just about suffering a dose of cabin fever!

Several days later, Jim and I were up before first light eager to get in amongst the deer. But this time without the dogs, and boy did they look brassed off!

Anyway, we'd been told just how good this particular area was for deer. So with fingers crossed that there'd be plenty of them around, we headed for the hills. With darkness all around we drove in as far as we could, leaving Jim's Rover at the end of a narrow twisting track. Then, with the light fingers of dawn in the east, we were gradually able to make out some deer tracks and there sure were plenty, both old and new. According to the locals, this area had last been milled in the late twenties, quite a few years back. Never having been here before, we were trying to piece together the instructions that had been given to us.

We were as careful as possible, trying to not create any noise and ensuring that the wind remained in our faces, stalking onwards until we found ourselves looking through a light screen of ponga fronds onto the side of a large slip. On the far side was just what we'd come for - deer, two hinds and a stag feeding. As Jim and I had arranged beforehand, he was going to christen his new rifle.

Slowly he eased a shell into the breech and, even though it was a barely audible click of the bolt slipping home, this alerted the deer and immediately their heads were up, their ears flicking, searching intently for the foreign sound. Jim lined the telescopic sight on the alerted stag. At that moment it decided to take off precisely as Jim squeezed the trigger. The stag stumbled to its knees and then in the flicker of an eye, staggered back to its legs, disappearing into the undergrowth. By now the hinds were long gone too.

A muttered curse came from Jim. "Bugger it, I think I've only managed to wound it! Let's hope that it doesn't get too far."

So I got my two pennies' worth in as well. "Fingers crossed, eh Jim, I've heard that they can go for bloody miles before they drop! Guess we'd better cross this slip and start searching for any sign."

On arriving at the approximate spot where the stag had stumbled we searched fruitlessly, but to no avail. Just a few small drops of blood but no sign of the stag.

"Nothing but thin air!" Jim moaned. "Guess we should've brought the dogs with us, at least they would've got on to the scent and would have found it by now."

Then, strangely enough, Jim began looking a lot further up the side of the slip and then turned to ask, "Rolly, do you think you'd be able to climb up that slip and out onto that small bluff? With a bit of luck you might be able to spot the stag while I try scouting a bit further around here."

I looked carefully up at the bluff above and wondered if he thought I was a bloody mountain goat.

"Yeah, I could give it a go Jim, but you just remember, my name's not Ed Hillary. I'll tell you what, how about you shout the first jugs of beer, then I'll have a shot at it, okay?"

Starting the first part of it was difficult enough, but clambering up and onto the small bluff was no joke. In fact, I reckon this bit of mountaineering was worth ten jugs at least. One would have to do a bit more negotiating when we arrived at the pub, it was damn near vertical. Then with a struggle I was over the lip and looking down on Jim searching the scrub below me. I couldn't see any sign of the deer at all, but then I heard him give a bit of a grumble, "Jeez the bush lawyer is as dense as hell in here!" Followed by, "I've spotted a few more drops of blood!" Then he let out a whoop of excitement. "Yahoo! I've found it. It's here, I've found it!"

I watched Jim as he propped his rifle against some scrubby native. Withdrawing his knife from the sheath, he straddled the deer, pulled back an antler, and was all set to cut its throat. But the stag had other ideas and quickly lurched to its feet. Jim gave a yelp of surprise, and dropping his knife, hung onto its antlers for all he was worth. I couldn't believe what I was seeing and although the deer attempted to get rid of its burden, Jim was holding on like grim death. No way was he going to let go! I thought that it looked really funny and couldn't resist laughing. "Come on, cowboy, ride it, ride it!" I yelled. "Don't let it throw ya!"

Luckily the stag must've been on its last legs; weakening fast, and with its final dying efforts, it stumbled forward to its knees. Jim lost his grip, sailing head first into this dense patch of bush lawyer! Boy did I crack up, talk about bloody humorous. Reckon it's about the closest I've come to wetting my pants since I'd been in nappies!

When finally Jim managed to extricate himself from the clutches of the bush lawyer, he turned, waving his fist. I was searching for a safe way down and it took me a fair old while. By the time I'd reached Jim he'd had enough time to cool off a bit.

"Hell's teeth, Rolly, I was shit scared! I didn't have a clue what the bloody animal was going to do next and those bloody antlers looked as sharp as hell. As for taking a dive into the lawyer head first, it sure isn't a joke, I can tell you. All these scratches are stinging like hell!"

He gingerly wiped his face with a shirtsleeve, certainly was no oil painting.

I couldn't keep a straight face, and responded by smirking. "No joke, you reckon? You should've been up there with me, I had a real bird's-eye view of your antics! Much better than being at the rodeo!"

Seeing a wild gleam appear in Jim's eyes, I quickly altered my line of attack. "Tell you what, your face is a bit of a mess all right, looks just like you've been pulled backwards through a barbed wire fence, you've got blood all over the place."

Jim grimaced a bit. "I hope it's not too bad, remember we're going over to the stock cars tonight, and it's my first date with Jenny too."

I just wasn't able to resist another dig. "Wouldn't grizzle too much if I was you mate. Just think of all the sympathy you'll be able to drum up!"

I could just about hear the wheels turning, then he was back to his usual happy self, and abruptly changed the subject.

"Well, there's one thing I certainly learnt today, and that's to treat every animal as if it's alive, and I'm never going to straddle one again, especially with sharp antlers! I guess I can count myself lucky to have only a scratched face!"

I looked at Jim and thought, 'Ah what the heck,' I had to get in one final dig.

"One thing you can bet on is that you hold the world record for stag riding, and probably the only record at that. Nobody in his right mind would go in for anything like that! Anyway, it's about time we got stuck in and dressed out this deer, and seeing you're the great white hunter, you can carry the head out to the Rover. I'll carry the rest out, okay?"

About an hour later we arrived back at the Rover and in the process worked up our usual thirst, but before we called into the pub, it was back home to hang the deer and feed the dogs.

Jim wasn't very taken with his reflection in the mirror and bemoaned his fate. "Bloody hell, what a mess. I look just like something the dogs have dragged in!"

I left him to wash off the blood and I must admit there was a slight improvement when he'd cleaned himself up a bit.

Then it was off to the old watering hole, that's what cowboys do isn't it? But one thing for sure, Jim was going to have to put up with a fair bit of leg pulling over the next week or so.

As per usual, the beer was as sweet and as cool as. In fact, it was extra more'ish after our exertions and the successful hunt. But, like I had hinted, Jim copped heaps of remarks about what was little more than a one-man deer-riding rodeo. And guess who had a great time just stirring the pot from time to time? But all in all, Jim stood up to the razzing pretty well.

I was all for staying at the pub and continuing the session and not bothering taking the girls to the stock cars, but Jim kept pointing to his watch, so after we'd had several more for the road, we pushed off home.

A quick shower each and we were into our glad rags and off to collect the girls. I did have to admit it, they both looked very attractive for their night out. Like I said before, after they'd got over the sight of Jim's face, there was heaps of sympathy and he certainly made the most of it! I reckoned he was a bloody crawler!

As for the night out, I enjoyed the tucker at the restaurant, the beers, and the stock cars. But as for the rest of it, meaning my half of the date, it was a bit of a dead loss, starting with the parking when we were getting ready to go into the gates. I was packing a few beers in the chilly bag and my half of the date let me know all about it!

"You're not taking beer into the stock cars are you? Don't you reckon you've had enough to drink already?"

Well, I've never been known for taking a backward step and I wasn't going to take one now! "My oath! You can bet your bottom dollar on that one!"

And so it went on, those little digs, they got under my skin a bit. The finale was when we'd parked out the front of Charlie's, and Jim, with his 'darling love of thee' Jenny, disappeared around the corner of the farmhouse. I placed my arm around Nancy, just to be friendly like, when out of the blue - pow! She belted me right in the kisser, and was out of the car, slamming the door so hard that it damn near flew off the hinges, then into the house without so much as a kiss my foot. So that was the end of that little episode, the only thing that I got out of the night was a bloody shiner. Curly was right about one thing, that Nancy could pack a punch all right!

But as for Jim and Jenny, they really enjoyed each other's company, scratched face or no scratched face. During the evening I could see all the signs of that little joker with wings and a beaming smile; he'd aimed his little bow and arrow right on target. They were both well and truly smitten with each other. It was the beginning of the end of the road for Jim, and I could see it would eventually create the downfall of another good keen man!

CHAPTER SEVENTEEN

A NEW HUNTING MATE

As the days and weeks rolled by, Jim's interest in hunting diminished somewhat and why shouldn't it, as he was spending more and more of his time with you know who – yes, Jenny! So in the end, I was doing most of my hunting with Curly, or with our next-door neighbour Danny. Boy, he was as keen as mustard!

Now, Danny hadn't any experience at hunting, but at least he was really enjoying it. One particular time out we were just coming to the crest of a pretty long steep slope. It had been a fair old climb up, with both of us blowing like a pair of old draught horses. Danny was carrying the rifle leading, with me just a step or so behind him, carrying a camera, in the hopes of getting a few good pictures of the dogs bailing or holding a pig. As the steeper ground gradually levelled off the bush thinned out, becoming a little more open, and on stepping out of the scrub into a sixty yard clearing, there, facing us, were four hinds. I stopped, waiting expectantly for Danny to raise the rifle and fire. But no, he just kept trudging forward, making no attempt to try for the deer. With a quick flick of their tails they all took off for cover and disappeared into the bush, so a nice feed of venison was missed! I lunged forward four steps to tap Danny on the shoulder and it was only when he turned to face me that I could see the reason why he hadn't seen the four deer. His glasses were so fogged up with sweat and heat from his body that he probably couldn't see more than half a yard ahead, let alone fifty. As he wiped his glasses clean,

I told him how the deer had taken off into the bush. Poor old Danny was disappointed as and quite put out at not having seen them, let alone not firing a shot at them. I felt a bit sorry for him, but them's the breaks at times, so I attempted to reassure him.

"Don't let it worry you, Dan, hopefully there'll be plenty more up ahead, so with any luck we'll drop onto a few more before the day's over. Anyway I betcha we won't be going home empty handed!"

He didn't know it but my fingers were crossed behind my back. After another hour or so we were perching on top of a steep old slip for a breather and a smoke, while keeping our ears pricked as we hadn't seen hide nor hair of the dogs for quite a while now. Just tossing about a bit of small talk.

Danny mentioned a time when he'd been running a small carrying business. One of the places that he'd been delivering to was an electrical-outfit-come-radio shop that also sold a small range of musical instruments - guitars, ukes and what have you along with the odd harmonica or two…

Well Rolly, it all came about one Friday night, when I'd dropped in to buy my Mum a couple of Scottish records, you know, those old forty-fives, and I walked into the place to the sound of music, with the owner tickling the ivories on the piano, his wife was on the violin and another woman playing a piano accordion; they sounded pretty good!

I listened, and when they'd finished playing a medley of tunes; for the life of me I can't remember what the tunes were-but they were popular hits of the day, the owner came across to see what I wanted.

"Good day Danny, now what can I do for you on this beaut evening?"

Just for an opening gambit I laughingly said, "Evening, now all you need is for someone who can play a set of bagpipes and you'll have a great group!" Then I asked him if I could see what Scottish records they had in stock. There were only about half a dozen Scottish records, so it didn't take long for me to pick out a couple for Mum and then I was on my way. On departing I thanked him and said my farewells to everyone, and I also remarked, just as a parting gesture, "Remember, all you need now is a set of pipes!"

About two weeks later, I received a message from the music shop owner saying that he wanted to see me and could I please call in when it was convenient.

'That'll be good,' I thought to myself. 'He'll be wanting me to deliver some more freight.' So early the next day I walked into the music shop, where the owner was beaming from ear to ear and pointed to a set of bagpipes sitting on the counter.

"Here's ya set of pipes, Danny, got them specially brought in, and had a bit of a job locating them! They're all the way from Dunedin! So now you'll be able to join us won't you?"

Bloody hell! Talk about being embarrassed! I didn't know which way to look, or what to say. Man, what a thing to happen! I'd only been making some small talk and joking around in the first place, and he'd taken me seriously! But the worst part of all was that I couldn't even play a tin whistle, let alone a set of bagpipes. Every time that I had to go in there, my eyes always went straight to the pipes under the glass counter, hell it was so totally embarrassing. One thing I can tell you now though, I'm bloody careful about whatever I say to

204

people! And to cap it off, it seemed like years and years before he managed to quit those bagpipes. Every time I had to go in there I just wished that the floor-boards would open up and let me disappear down the gap!"

We both grinned and it reminded me of one my most embarrassing moments in my younger days.

"Well, Danny you're not the only one who's had a damned embarrassing moment! In my mid to early teens I was always keen on the fairer sex and I liked being with them heaps. Anyway, I had arranged to meet a girl that I was pretty keen on at the local beach for a swim together. I was pretty fit in those days and ran everywhere; besides, it saved me heaps of money in bus fares. Well, I arrived at the beach and there were quite a number people there already, so I jogged along to where I spotted her and thought that I'd give her a surprise and sneak behind her. All that I wore in those days was shorts and I was as brown as and carrying just my towel. As I got close behind her, she stood up looking out at the sea and did she look alluring in her togs, so in a twinkling I thought 'Great, I'll just give her a quick flick near her beautiful bottom with my towel!' But just as I flicked the towel she took half a step back. The flick was probably one of the best I'd ever done, it must've really hurt!

She grabbed her bum and, screaming loudly, spun around facing me. The trouble was, it was the wrong girl, a complete stranger! Man, was I embarrassed, all I wanted then and there was for the sand on the beach to open up and bury me! I tried to apologise but all she did was to scream and cry, with all the people crowding around. Then two fairly big guys grabbed hold of me, and talk about things getting worse. I struggled with these guys trying to profess my mistake, and then I

205

recognised the local cop jogging towards us. A sergeant no less, and worse was to come. He made me get down onto my knees to apologise. I felt small enough to have hidden behind a grain of sand. Anyway there was even more to come my way, as in the crowd there was a reporter who snapped my picture! So then I ended up as front-page news with the disappointing result that none of the girls I knew would have anything to do with me and even today, when I return home to my old stamping ground, people still point the bone and boy do I wish that I hadn't been such a bloody idiot!"

Danny and I both chuckled at our inappropriate actions and embarrassments.

Then with there still being no sign of the dogs catching up with us, and given the pleasant scene of the stream meandering through the bush about fifty yards below us, it couldn't have been more satisfying spot to be at, so we settled in for another smoke.

No sooner had we started puffing away than Danny said quietly. "I know you reckon that I'm as blind as a bat, but what is that down there, near the bed of the steam?"

I looked to where he was pointing, but was unable to pick out anything. Just what was he talking about? "Danny, where exactly do you mean?"

Again he pointed the spot out. "Do you see that dead tree, just to the left of the tight bend in the stream?"

"Yep, now I do," and I began scanning the area carefully.

"Well, see that scrubby bit of bush in front and slightly to the right? Now watch, just where the stream disappears under it."

We both stared intently for several more minutes and I was beginning to have my doubts as to Danny's eyesight again, until I finally caught a movement and then a stag stepped out from under the bush, slowly making its way towards the stream. It was feeding from the bank. What a great picture it made, and I completely forgot all about the camera I was carrying!

Whispering quietly I said, "You're not as blind as you thought, Danny, it's a deer all right, a nice stag at that. Good on ya' and seeing as you spotted it, you can drop the bugger!"

With Danny sprawling full length on the ground, he eased the bolt forward, the shell was in the breech, he sighted and fired!

"Damit, I've missed it!" he muttered as he levered another shell into the breech.

I had seen where the bullet had kicked up a bit of dirt, slightly above and beyond the stag. "Danny, your shot was a bit high; remember, it's always the same when shooting downhill, aim slightly below where you want to hit."

The stag spun around trying to locate where we were. It didn't have a clue where the shot had come from and it took two more shots before Danny downed it. He was over the moon at finally having shot his first deer. His adrenalin was pumping, leaving him completely tongue-tied, and as I shook his hand, I could feel it shaking badly. I congratulated him.

"Great shooting Dan, and well done for seeing it in the first place! I reckon I'm the one who needs glasses, not you!"

We then had to clamber down the steep hillside, hanging onto whatever slowed our downward momentum through the bush, to drag the stag out of the stream. I looked at Danny. It was, as I'd said, his first ever deer; he was elated, but had tears in his eyes. I guess in some ways, he was sorry to have killed such a magnificent animal.

On carrying the deer out to the car we had stopped and were having a breather when Danny said, "You know something, Rolly? I enjoy the hunting, but when I saw the deer lying there in the stream, I thought about what a fine looking animal it was, and what a shame that I'd killed it. But - and a big but it is - no killing, no deer, no venison, and I sure do enjoy my venison!"

About half an hour after we arrived back at the car, Gray and Speck turned up with tongues just about dragging on the ground. Whatever they'd been chasing, it was still alive and running. Luckily I'd brought a flagon of water and they made short work of it. Then it was home for us via the pub for a couple of cold beers, where we bumped into a couple of other keen pig hunters so the few beers turned into quite a fair old session! Various topics of interest were shared across the table.

Well, one of these guys began telling us how he'd been doing a bit of maintenance work at the local RSA a few days previously on his own…

The phone rang and continued ringing for some length of time and in case it might be for myself I answered it. But when I said "RSA here!" a voice I thought I recognised asked, "to whom am I speaking please?" And then it hit me that the voice sounded like Terry's.

"Is that you Terry?" I asked.

There was complete silence for a moment and then the voice asked again. "To whom am I speaking please?"

Yes, I was pretty sure that it was Terry all right, and I didn't really like him at the best of times. So I was pretty quick off the mark and snapped "Listen if it's Terry, stop buggering me around would you?"

There was more silence and only some deep breathing. I said, "Right if you don't say what you're on about I'm going to hang up!" And I did.

Well anyway, immediately it started ringing again so I picked up the receiver again and the same voice was there. "Don't hang up please, it's Terrance Constance speaking and I just wanted to know who I was speaking to."

I was getting annoyed at being stuffed around by him, he'd been a long time member of the club but in all honesty he wasn't as popular as he thought, and a bit of a con man too. Always borrowing money and being chased up for what was owed.

"Listen Terry, I've just about had a gutsful! It's Ron here, what do you want, get to the point will ya?"

This time the reply was immediate. "Okay Ron, it's just that I don't want everybody at the RSA to believe what they will be reading in the paper, because it's not true. I am not dead! I'm alive and kicking; it's just that I need some way to get the creditors off my back. So I've put my own obituary notice in the paper to give me a bit of breathing space! I'd be most grateful if you'd pass the word around the club members that I am definitely not dead, but alive and kicking!"

It took me all my time to stop from bursting with mirth so I said, "Okay Terry, I'll get the secretary to put something on the notice board!"

A plaintive squawk from him broke in, interrupting me. "No, no, just word of mouth, I don't want all and sundry to learn, I could get sued and I couldn't afford that anyway!" Then there was complete silence and I thought that he'd hung up so I put the phone down, not giving it any more thought. Anyway when the president of the RSA arrived about an hour later I told him about Terry's request.

The president did his nana! "That bloody bludger, he's got a bloody cheek! And what's more he owes me ten quid as it is! Just wait until I get hold of him then he'll be needing a bloody obituary notice well and truly, I can tell you!"

Anyway I returned first thing next day to finish the job and noted that the flag was flying at half-mast. Being the first person there, I thought 'somebody's snuffed it' and I wondered who, but then immediately got stuck into finishing my job off.

Later on, when the secretary arrived and opened the front door, he spotted me working.

'Morning Ron," he said. "Did you notice that our flag is flying at half mast?"

"Yeah I did. Who was it, anyone I know?"

He pulled a sour face. "You wouldn't read about it, a real sponger he was, and in fact the bludger still owes me twenty quid, bugger it all. I know we shouldn't really speak ill of the dead but I reckon he deserved it anyway! He was that bloody freeloader, and of all things to have occurred, he was killed while using a pay-free phone box! I guess it was pretty ironic that he was flattened when a septic tank truck turning a corner rolled over onto it. It's a wonder you haven't guessed who I'm on about, Ron. That bloody Terry Constance, and you wouldn't read about it, even his membership wasn't up to date. So I reckon that it was appropriate that he was killed by a load of shit!"

We all looked at Ron, not too sure of how we should react. But then Ron started to chuckle. "And do

210

you know something else? That bastard still owes me ten bob too, so in some way I guess I got the last laugh. But it cost me ten bob to catch up! So it just goes to show that one shouldn't tempt the hand of fate just like he did. Fancy dying, being killed by a truck load of shit."

At that we all grinned and chuckled at the guy's demise.

Not too long after that Danny and I headed for home, as by then we'd taken aboard a fair old skin full, but we'd had a damned good day all round. And not only that, we had a peace offering, a nice chunk of venison to placate Dawn with. So you could say that all in all we'd come up trumps all round.

CHAPTER EIGHTEEN

THE GREAT WHITE HUNTERS

It was another Saturday night when Danny and I had been to the pub and downed a few too many beers.

Talk about being full of bull and false bravado, we decided to have a night's shooting for rabbits, nothing quite like a full pot of 'underground army' stew, we both reckoned.

When I called in next door for Danny, his wife Dawn was giving us a damned hard time, slinging off about us.

"The two great white hunters going off to shoot those poor hapless bunnies! Just remember, you've both got a skinful and in that state you'll be lucky to hit the side of a barn, let alone a little bitty rabbit. All I can say is that you're both nuts and I reckon there'll be nothing to show but empty hands when you get home!"

It's amazing how a few beers will make a man's tongue work overtime and Danny couldn't resist getting a last word in.

"Don't let it worry, my dearest, we're the two best shots this side of the Tarawera Ranges, aren't we Rolly? You wait and see, we'll be bringing home heaps of the buggers, so you just make sure you've got your pots ready!"

Then it was off out the door and some fifteen minutes or so we arrived at the area where we intended hunting. After we'd been on the go for about an hour, we'd gradually worked our way through the rough tracks in the scrub and hadn't seen a solitary rabbit. Perhaps

Dawn's prophetic words were going to come true, as normally there were heaps of rabbits popping up all over the place around here.

Then we spotted our first rabbit of the night, frozen in the headlight beam. I slapped on the anchors and Danny, who had been perched astride the mudguard, leapt off, raised the twenty-two, and let rip four shots in quick succession. Bang! Bang! Bang! Bang! And then much to my astonishment all that happened was that the rabbit started running flat out towards us, directly back into the beam of the headlights. Danny fired again, and still nothing happened, it kept on running unerringly straight towards the light. It wasn't slowing or hanging around for anyone or anything for that matter. Then finally, much to my amazement, Danny stepped forward and let fly with a big number twelve sized boot, and talk about connect! The rabbit sailed high up into the air, somersaulted a couple of times, and fell to the ground stone dead. Didn't even give so much as a twitch.

I couldn't resist letting out a hoot of laughter, yelling out the window, "You can't shoot for nuts, but you sure can kick the buggers to death! Reckon you might as well leave the rifle in the car and just boot 'em instead! Think of all the ammo it would save!"

With a big grin across his dummy Danny turned to me and gave the universal sign for 'that's two BBQs you owe me!' When we later checked the rabbit over we found that he'd hit it twice, so I guess two out of five isn't so bad after all. But of course, we mustn't forget Danny's right foot drop kick!

We continued driving around searching for more of those elusive cottontails for quite some while, but it was looking more and more hopeless. So much for all these heaps of rabbits we were going to take triumphantly home.

Eventually, on stopping for a smoke, we cracked the top off a couple of beers, giving us enough time to sort out where else we might possibly come across a few more of those elusive cottontails. One beer led to another, and after we'd happily knocked off a couple more tops it added to the effect of our feeling next to no pain and a couldn't give a damn attitude!

So once again we moved off, with Danny perched over the headlight on the mudguard and his feet on the bumper, continuing our search for the elusive quarry. "Look out you rabbits, here we come."

Around a few more bends we came across a possum, it was transfixed in the glare of the headlights right in the middle of the track. Bang, one shot only and on the move too, down it went in a heap. Old four-eyes Danny had dropped it dead in its tracks! I pulled to a stop most impressed with the shot, because of all the possums that I'd ever heard about being nailed, it had always taken more than a few rounds before they'd were stopped, as tough as old boots, the buggers! Then I watched in amazement when Danny leapt to the ground, walked forward, and picked the possum up by the tail.

I couldn't resist taunting him.

"What in the hell are you going to do with that, make yourself a fur hat, Daniel Boone?"

As he walked around to put it in the boot, he replied in all seriousness, "Nope!"

I was puzzled by what he was thinking of, so questioned him again. "Well, what's the use of keeping it then?"

He gave a short laugh. "Leave that to me, old son, it's gunna be rabbit stew! You wait and see!"

214

I couldn't believe my ears and disparagingly scoffed, "Rabbit stew, you must be off your rocker! Dawn will do her block if you try to get her to cook up a bloody possum and another thing, what in the hell will it taste like anyway? Is it any good? It might be absolutely bloody horrible eating!"

Danny's happy reply was full of optimism. "I can't see why it shouldn't be all right, it's as much a vegetarian as the old bunny and seeing as it spends lots of its time up in the trees, it would have less chance of picking up disease I reckon!"

All I could do was to shake my head in astonishment and I was already planning to make myself pretty scarce if Dawn seemed in the least bit suspicious about our so-called rabbit.

Not too long after this it began to drizzle, so we had to toss the hunting in and headed home with our bounty for the night.

On arriving back at Danny's, we went directly into his garage where it only took us about ten minutes to clean and skin the rabbit and its counterpart, the possum, Boy, what a job it was dressing it out and skinning it, but by the time we'd cut off the tail and removed the claws, it just looked like a real big rabbit.

My comments to Danny as I headed for home were, "It's on your head, Danny. If Dawn asks me what, when or how, I know nuffink. You hear? I know nuffink!"

With that I made tracks for home but did it take a hell of a lot of hand washing to get rid of that possum smell!

Fairly late the next day, I had just given the dogs a run and was putting my feet up when there was a knock on the back door; it was one of Danny's kids. He handed me a note, which read 'Rolly, mate, c'mon over for a quiet beer or two.' And never being one turn down a beer I thanked the youngster. "Say thanks to your Dad and I'll be there in two ticks!"

Clambering through the hole in the fence I parked myself down on the back steps next to Danny. He handed me a cold beer and after the usual pleasantries, I quietly asked, "How's things with Dawn? What did she have to say about the rabbits?" I emphasised rabbits!

Danny smiled happily. "No problems mate. But she gave me heaps about the fact that we'd only got two of the buggers and reckons that we were both absolutely chock full of hot air. But another thing she said was that even her Dad, who was a damned good rabbit hunter, had never shot one as big as that second one we'd bowled!"

I exclaimed in disbelief. "We! Listen you bugger don't try dragging me into this! You're a bloody rat bag, you bowled it and remember it was all your idea to get it cooked!"

At this point, Dawn must've somehow latched onto what we were yakking about and came out to the top of the steps.

"Hi, Rolly, that's the biggest rabbit I've ever seen, are you sure it's not a hare?"

There's no doubt she was a bit suspicious. 'Oh no,' I thought, 'was the proverbial going to hit the fan?' I mentally crossed my fingers.

"No worries, Dawn, one thing for sure is that it's definitely not a hare!" I bravely replied.

She returned to the kitchen.

I winked at Danny and called to Dawn. "You know something, your old man's a real deadeye dick as far as kicking them to death goes, you should've seen him last night. I reckon he should be in the next All Black trials as a fullback or first five! Talk about a drop kick!"

216

Her humorous laugh floated out from the kitchen, followed by, "He told me about that, but I'm glad that he's hung up his boots, as all he ever seemed to do on the field was to get into arguments and fights! Oh, and by the way, I saw Jim taking off with Jenny a while back so I've taken the liberty of setting an extra place at the table for your dinner and don't go making any excuses, it's no good eating by yourself, so dinner will be on the table in about twenty minutes, and that's final!"

I wanted to turn it down, but that was a bit like stepping into the lion's den and if I tried to back out now, it would probably upset the apple cart well and truly. I'd already prepared my meal, but I was now caught in a cleft stick. Looking at Danny I raised my eyebrows giving him the message about it as I resigned to my fate.

"Thanks Dawn, it'll be nice to have someone else prepare a meal for me."

Danny and I had just finished off our beers when his youngest came out. "Dad, Rolly, tea's on the table, and we're having casseroled rabbit." He looked quite excited at the prospect.

Danny and I looked at each other, uh oh, was the proverbial really going to hit the fan? Somewhat on the apprehensive side, I whispered to Danny, before we ventured into the house.

"I hope you and your bright idea hasn't put us in it up to our necks, you bugger! There's no doubt about it, our goose looks definitely cooked!"

On entering the dining room Danny smiled and said to Dawn, "Junior tells us you've cooked rabbit for dinner? Smells pretty good to me!"

"Yes, I've done one of the rabbits, it'll be a nice change from wild pork or venison. We used to have rabbit a couple of times a week at home when I was younger, so I'm looking forward to it again and I hope you two are feeling the same way as well."

"Sure am, dear!" What else could he say?

I didn't say anything, just decided to go with the flow, but must admit as I looked across at Danny, I wondered if we'd done the right thing. He just shrugged his shoulders slightly and looked back hopefully.

Then Danny's daughter said, "Mum, do you want me to say grace?"

Smiling happily Dawn replied, "Of course, dear, that's nice of you!"

While grace was being said, even I fervently hoped that everything would turn out all right. Then somewhat hesitantly, I speared a piece of rabbit meat with my fork and waited until Danny did the same.

Then the waiting was over as Dawn said, "Mm, this rabbit is nice, it's just like old times. We'll have to make it a regular meal, that is, if the two great white hunters are able to get any more of them."

With that I sampled a bit, and it certainly was nice, a big load off one's mind and thank goodness that Dawn had cooked the actual rabbit and not the possum. Danny and I looked at each other, big grins of relief showing on our faces, and then we both chuckled.

Dawn looked at both of us and frowned, "What's up with you two anyway? Had too much to drink again?"

"No, no!" smiled Danny disarmingly. "It's just a joke between me and Rolly! Boy this underground army mutton casserole is really beaut, isn't it Rolly?"

"Sure is, sure is!" I agreed, but I was very relieved just the same.

Then Dawn quickly got in. "In that case Rolly, seeing as you enjoyed it so much, you can join us for tea on Tuesday night when I cook the other one."

218

I was about to make excuses as to why I couldn't, but Dawn was two steps ahead of me.

"Now, Rolly, I expect you to be here on Tuesday. No excuses, and if you don't come, then you won't be invited over for a meal again. Do you understand?"

My fate was sealed, there was no way out of Tuesday dinner, not without letting the cat out of the bag and upsetting her.

"Okay, Dawn, I'll be here. Thanks very much!" I sure was on the hook all right.

The rest of the meal was very nice and uneventful, even ended up with us doing the dishes for Dawn. But each time we laughed and chuckled, Dawn glanced at the two of us. She even commented a couple of times about how we were acting like a pair of over-grown kids, and that we weren't setting a very good example to the children at all.

With the dishes done Danny and I went outside to where we had an enjoyable game of bat down with the kids. I then said my thanks for the meal but as I was about to climb through the fence on my way home Dawn called out again.

"Rolly, don't forget about dinner on Tuesday night!"

Did she really have to remind me? I called back, "Thanks Dawn!"

With the arrival of Tuesday night, I climbed through the fence with half a dozen under my arm and as there was a bit of misty rain we sat on the saw stools in the shed.

"We might just need this bit of Dutch courage," Danny said quietly as we downed the first beers.

Next thing there was a call from in the house.

"Dad, Rolly, dinner's ready!"

We filed in and sat at the table. Another lot of grace was said, with my mind on just one thought only, 'please God let it taste all right'.

With the first mouthful of the rabbit it was a relief, I could hardly taste the difference from the other night. I looked at Danny, and then we both grinned and laughed as our nerves happily settled down. Once again, Dawn got into our ears about the poor example we were setting for the kids. Afterwards Danny and I did the dishes again, but kept laughing about how we'd been worried about the possum and how it would taste. Well, eventually Dawn had had enough and got us bailed up in the kitchen, and there was no escape!

"All right, you two, what's the big joke? Why all the stupid laughter? And acting just like a couple of kids? I know something is going on, what is it? What's up?" She waited hands on her hips demanding an explanation. I could see that she was fair dinkum and no doubt about that.

Danny looked at her for a few seconds. He was thinking of how he could be diplomatic, before stepping into the lion's den, so to speak. Hesitatingly, he said, "You know the two rabbits we got?"

He waited for a few seconds. Dawn was still standing expectantly, hands on hips, looking pretty grim and she wasn't going to let things alone.

"The biggest rabbit, well, it wasn't a rabbit and we were desperate to come home with more than one and it looked like drizzle was going to set in. Anyway as we came around the corner it was transfixed in the beam of the headlights so I shot it!"

He hesitated, and Dawn didn't wait, she was in like a robber's dog!

"So you shot it? So what was it?" she demanded.

There was no chance of beating around the bush any longer.

"It was a possum." Fearing the worst, Danny then continued with as much bravado as possible, "Yes, it was a possum dear!"

"Possum? You're telling me it was a possum? A bloody possum! Are you two mad? I just knew you were up to something odd by the way you were both carrying on, and I thought it was too big to be a rabbit. You're just a pair of bloody rat bags!"

Then looking us both in the eyes she took a deep breath and stated; "One thing I'll tell you and that's for sure, if you ever bring another one home, don't you dare mention a word about possum, because if you do I'll tell you right now, I won't cook it, so now do you get the message?"

We both breathed a sign of relief. I was quite relieved, and amazed how Dawn didn't really even turn a hair.

Danny spoke up. "Thank goodness you're not upset my dearest. We were really worried!"

"Now listen you pair of buggers!" Dawn broke in. "Like I said, if you don't tell me what it is I'll cook it. Besides, I couldn't tell the difference between the two of them, apart from the size."

Very relieved at the final outcome, I decided that it was my turn to be counted so said, "Dawn, one thing I'm happy about is that when we ate the possum tonight it tasted pretty good to me."

Dawn grinned widely and then started laughing her head off. "Tonight? Tonight, you say? We ate the big one, the possum, on Sunday night!"

Once again Danny and I looked at each other and roared with laughter and Dawn joined in with us, so all our misgivings and worry had been for nothing. It just goes to show, there's nothing wrong with a feed of casseroled possum as long as you don't know what it is. It was surprisingly good tucker!

CHAPTER NINETEEN

GET A REAL JOB

As I'd said before, Jim and Jenny were spending more and more time together. All the signs were there, true love was alive and blooming. Anyway I'd only just stepped back in the door from giving the dogs a run before nightfall when in came Jim. Boy, was he happy, a smile beaming all over his face. I could see that he was on top of cloud nine, and talk about glowing!

"Rolly, old son, how'd you like to shake hands with and congratulate your old mate?" He pointed to himself.

I thought quickly, 'betcha he's popped the question to Jenny going by the look on his dial'. I decided just for the hell of it to pull his leg a bit, deciding to act all dumb.

"Congratulate you? What in the hell would I want to have congratulate a joker with an ugly mug like yours for? Have you won lotto or something?"

He was just too happy to take the bait and completely ignoring my jibe, threw his arms excitedly into the air. "Because Jenny and I are going to get married! It's wonderful isn't it?"

"You must be joking. Jenny's agreed to get hitched to a fella shaped like a Taranaki gate? Where's her taste?"

"Yep," he replied, his smile a mile wide with elation. "And her old man's all for it. Charlie has given us the go ahead, just a matter of setting the date and we'll be able to spend the rest of our lives together!"

I didn't have the heart to pull his leg any more. "In that case, James," I thrust out my hand, "my most sincere congratulations because if ever there were a couple made for each other, it's you two and I reckon this certainly calls for a little celebration. What do you reckon, do you think we'd better have a drink on it?"

I headed off to where I'd stashed a few beers for such a possible occasion. After we'd knocked some back, the conversation got around to the future, and about jobs that'd bring in a bit of dosh. And as Jim said, he needed one, because he only had enough cash to cover the costs of an engagement ring. I agreed with him that it was about time that we both got back into the work force, because even though we'd been able to sell a few pigs there was no real future in it. Besides, a man seemed to spend a bit too much time in the boozer on the end of a beer.

Soon Jim located a couple of back copies of the local rag. While there were several jobs advertised, one looked as though it'd suit me and all that I needed to do was go to the advertised address in the morning to see about it.

The other fitted Jim to a tee and as our phone hadn't been working very well for a while now, Jim headed down the road to the phone box to make a call. On arriving back, he looked like the cat that had been licking the cream. "Well, Rolly, it must be my lucky day all right. The joker I rang wanted a diesel mechanic, said he was desperate for a qualified tradesman. I gave him my life history and he told me the job was all mine, so all I have to do is turn up with my tools and trade certificate in the morning!"

I was overjoyed for him. "That's great news Jim! Isn't it fantastic when things start to fall into line?

Congratulations again, and here's another beer, but most of all, here's to it being as good a job as one could ever find. Cheers!"

It was up early the next morning for us both. Jim was heading off to his new employment and me to find out about mine. We both wished each other well and went in our pursuits.

I arrived at the depot that was advertising for a grader driver who had all the necessary licences. The reason I'd selected this as a possible job was that it had offered the highest hourly rate.

I drove into a big yard with odds and sods of earth machinery parked here and there. Right off I got the feeling that I'd be able to get on pretty well with the fella that owned the outfit. Walking into the office, I found a guy behind a desk that was covered with mechanical bits and piles of paper. A gruff voice enquired, "Just what in the hell do you want?"

When I told him that I'd come about the grader driving job, he perked up a quite bit and didn't mince his words. "What type of machines have you handled in the past?"

"Both, Cats and Inters. Tracked and on rubber."

"How many hours do you reckon you've knocked up and what sort of work have you done in them?" he asked pointedly, as he carefully watched and weighed up my reactions.

"As for hours I reckon, at a rough guess, about twenty five thousand with odd spells of breaking in land for farming and some general roading. Also a fair bit of time in constructing parts of the International Airport at Auckland."

He nodded. "Where's your driving licence?"

Reaching into my wallet I fished it out and passed it over. He scanned through it.

"You've had these for a fair while, all these classes of vehicles. So would you call yourself an experienced, competent operator?"

"Yep!" I replied.

He was pretty quick on his assessment.

"I see you've got no endorsements. Okay, I'll give you two week's trial. So next thing is, when can you start?" He certainly didn't believe in letting the grass grow under his feet.

"Tomorrow morning, if that suits you?" I replied.

He nodded happily. "That suits me right down to the ground. By the way, I'm Reg, what's your handle? What do your mates call you?" he said as he reached out and we shook hands on the deal.

"Just Rolly, nothing fancy," I replied.

"Well, Rolly, if you'd like to come out into the yard, I'll show you the machine you'll be using. We'll leave all the paperwork for now and fill it out tomorrow."

As we were walking across the yard, the phone back in the office began its strident ring and as he went back to answer it, he pointed to a corner of the yard. "There she is over there. I'll be back as soon as I've gotten rid of whoever is on the other end of the blower."

I strolled the rest of the way across to the grader he'd pointed out. Seeing it was nearly brand new, and one of the latest models at that, this would be a piece of cake to handle. I checked the hour clock, only seven hundred and eighty hours, great stuff, it's hardly even run in! My scrutiny was interrupted by Reg, as he returned chuckling and scratching his head whimsically.

"That joker on the phone was after the job that you've just got, but talk about being a real bright bastard!" He was chuckling away to himself. "As you know, the ad said, 'only experienced operators need apply'."

I nodded my head in agreement.

"I'm also on the lookout for another joker to operate that motor scraper over there in about three months, so I thought I'd chat him up a bit, asking him about what sort of machines he'd been driving. I don't know what sort of an idiot he took me for, but do you know what he said?" He was grinning widely at what had tickled him.

"Haven't a clue?" I matched his questioning grin.

"You just won't believe it!" Again he spluttered with laughter, but managed to get out, "Yellow ones! Bloody hell, would you believe it, bloody yellow ones! He must've thought that I'd come down in the last shower, cripes, just wait until the boys down the pub hear this one!"

Recovering from the joke about idiots and yellow ones, we started going over the machine, discussing all its attributes. Eventually, we rolled ourselves a smoke each and squatting back against one of the wheels, discussed earthmoving equipment in general.

Gradually the talk got around to personal experiences and Reg said, with a faraway look in his eye, "Ya know, Rolly, this story's going back a fair bit now, and not so long after I started driving, about thirty five years back…

Anyway it must've about six months or so after I'd started worked for this cocky. Boy, was he a real unusual bloke. I wouldn't say he was as nutty as a fruitcake, but he was pretty close to it. We were breaking in quite a few thousand acres of scrub into farmland. Well, when I wasn't crushing scrub with a roller, I was putting in tracks and roads, even built a dam or two. All the time I worked with him, this damned cocky was dead scared at the thought of fires, and always on my back about smoking and how it could lead to a fire. Talk about a cracked record, I was sick and tired of hearing about it all and I'd go as far as to say that he was paranoid about it. Anyway he made me tow this big clumsy water tank everywhere I went. Jeez, it was a bloody struggle at times, as awkward as all hell hitching up and unhitching it all the time. After about six months of this I was getting pretty hosed off, had an absolute gutsful! Then it dawned on me that it would be a lot simpler if I quietly cracked open the water valve a fraction so it would gradually all empty out. After that I was as happy as a sand boy, it was one hell of lot easier for me to handle. Every time the cocky was around, I kept on saying to myself, fooled you, got ya bluffed ya old bugger! Besides it had been raining off and on in the last month, so the chance of there being a fire was at the barest minimum anyway.

My plan was going real beaut until the old bugger happened to see me shifting the water tank and realised it was empty by the way it was leaping about all over the place. He waved me down, I stopped and you should've seen the way he was bouncing as he shot around to check the water level, and of course, I knew that it was as dry as a wooden god - not a drop in it! He came around the back of the tractor like a Bondi tram, and talk about move, his bald head gleaming in the late afternoon sun just like a warning beacon. He clambered up the tracks, I could see he was going to blow a fuse all right and he glowered at me yelling, "Why's the water tanker empty? You should always keep it full!"

I was pretty quick off the mark in those days myself, and besides I'd been thinking about tossing in his job for a while now; I'd already made a few enquiries around and new jobs weren't hard to come by, so I made my thoughts quite plain.

"It's empty because it's too damned difficult for me to hitch and unhitch, especially when I'm on my Pat Malone! Besides any fool can see it's been raining off and on for the last few weeks, everything is wet through anyway! Even the Devil would have a helluva job starting a fire using a flame-thrower around here!"

I was about to say a bit more, but he beat me to it. "That's not the point, there could be a fire and what steps would you intend taking then?" he demanded.

Well, I'd had more than enough of his paranoia about fires and the whole job in general. I yelled back at him, "What steps would I take? What do you think? Listen you, steps like I intend taking right now at this very moment. Big steps and bloody great long ones at that, just like I'm gunna do right now, as far away as it's possible from here! So now you can just take your bloody job and shove it where the sun don't shine!"

And I was on my way, only too happy to toss the whole kit and caboodle in, leaving the damned job and the old mudguard head well behind in my tracks.

Reg took a last drag on his smoke at the end of his yarn. I was curious about the term 'mudguard head' so I asked him about it.

"Reg, what's the story about calling someone old mudguard head?"

He chuckled to himself. "Haven't you heard it before? The cocky, he was as bald as a badger and shiny on the top and all shit underneath, just like the fender on that truck over there. Mudguard head."

I chortled to myself, "Very appropriate!"

Then the strident bell of the telephone rang out across the yard again. Reg again left me to answer it and when he returned said, "That was the county engineer and I've got to straighten out a couple of things with him. So I'll see you here at seven-thirty tomorrow morning okay? By the way, do you take any interest in rugby?"

"Yep, I try and get handy to a radio whenever there's a rep game on, that's if I can't go and watch it."

Reg's eyes gleamed happily. "So who are ya backing next Saturday? The Northland Taniwha, or the Bays Hori BOP?"

I grinned back at him. "Reg, I reckon the Taniwha will do the Hori BOP's like a dinner. The Bay hasn't got a dog's show, you wait and see!"

"If you're so sure, Rolly, will you have a jug on it?"

I smirked as I replied, "Like taking milk off a baby!"

Reg.was enjoying the banter between us. I thought to myself, 'let's hope that he's always in this frame of mind'.

He laughed at me. "That's what you think, Rolly, those jokers from up in the winterless North don't know what a game of rugby is about. Besides, their two dandelion to the acre country needs at least a tonne of super and a shower of rain every day, just to keep everything growin'! They might as well stay at home and give the game a miss, they haven't got a snowball's chance in hell!" Then as he walked through the door to his office, he called out, "See ya tomorrow."

As it happened, Reg was right about the rugby and I had to cough up for a jug of beer, but he insisted that I share it with him. He enjoyed a bet at any time and everything in life was a happy challenge to him. I found him to be a good and very fair-minded boss, and boy did he love his rugby and jugs of beer!

Also Reg enjoyed nothing more than relating stories and little anecdotes from the past and as it happened we'd had quite a spell of exceptionally wet weather. This meant that we were unable to do any of our normal contracting work, and having run out of any other maintenance and undercover work, it meant extended smoko breaks, and then Reg was in his element relating bits and pieces from his past. One that I recall is as follows…

Had a mate of mine who lived in Hawera. One of the best mates I ever had in all my life and even when very young, Don could turn his hand to just about anything. Repair motors, radios, clocks, you name it, he was able to turn his hand to any old thing and make a good fist of it. Even got a pilot licence to fly at the very young age of eighteen, so all in all, he was one helluva pal and we had some great times together, getting up to all sorts of adventures.

Don mentioned that on odd occasions he used to earn some extra money for flying lessons by helping out with loading the hopper of a converted tiger moth with superphosphate. Reckoned that it was bloody hard, sweaty, filthy work but at least he was able to do his greatest love, continue flying. When Don and the pilot were working on this particular day he said that the farm ran right to the high cliffs above the Tasman. Anyway this cocky was getting pretty pissed off with a Japanese trawler that was coming right into shore and catching fish well inside the international three-mile limit. Now this had been getting right up his nose, so Don had a bright idea and suggested to the cocky that they load up the hopper with as much yucky rubbish as they could and then the pilot could fly over and dive-bomb the Japs with the lot, giving the bastards the message about fishing well inside the three-mile limit! The cocky was over the moon at this idea and early the next morning they were going to let rip and cover the boat with all sorts of horrible stinking stuff.

When the hopper was loaded to the brim with the most horrible brew that it could carry, the next morning the pilot gave the cocky and Don ten minutes to drive to the cliff edge so that they could watch the Tiger Moth doing its thing. Luckily the cocky had thought to bring his binoculars so it was a very simple matter to take all the trawler's particulars and to see the crew's reactions under fire.

They must've thought because they were miles from the nearest port there was no one able to catch them out, but suddenly there was the sound of the Tiger Moth engine at about seventy knots heading directly out towards its target, the trawler. The crew of the trawler turned, looked at the rapidly approaching diving twin winged plane and all waved as though to say hi! But then the pilot jettisoned about half of his load. Don reckoned that the crew of the trawler were caught with their pants down well and truly with the stinking mess of disgusting rubbish that was spread from stem to stern! The crew frantically scrambled into the wheelhouse, and there was a belch of black smoke from the exhaust as the diesel engine started, followed by white foam from the prop as the trawler frantically turned seaward. The topdressing pilot then quickly zoomed up and around to again release some more of the vile yucky rubbish, and down it went adding even more mayhem to the trawler's decks, including one of the crew who'd been stupid enough to appear out of wheelhouse to wave his fist at the pilot. By this time the trawler had moved about four hundred further yards out towards the three-mile limit. The pilot dove down to just about sea level and gave the crew a disparaging signal, drawing some of the crew members out of the wheelhouse where they were gesturing with rage. Then, without giving any warning, the pilot pulled the nose up, flicked his plane across directly above the wheelhouse, and let go the last of his load, again showering even more onto the departing trawler. Then he shadowed it for another five minutes.

The pilot then returned shoreward and even executed a victory roll at about hundred feet or so above us, where we could easily see his elated actions, grinning and triumphantly waving his fist. Don and the cocky then quickly returned to the airstrip to join the exuberant pilot and in celebration they had a great feed of freshly baked scones and toasted a cuppa to the success of the sortie.

One other thing that Don mentioned was that if the trawler hadn't been poaching inside the three-mile limit, surely there would have been one helluva diplomatic international furore. So it just shows a good old bit of kiwi ingenious thinking could handle any situation!

As the day was nearing an end Reg glanced at his watch and declared, "Well, Rolly, the weather has really set in and I can't see us being able to do anything else today, so what's say we head off to the old rubbity dub and have the enjoyment of a few beers?"

Following the adjournment to the pub and several beers later Reg came out with another yarn about his great mate and their travels…

Don's suggestion was that we take our Christmas holiday in his soft-top Austin Seven tourer, even though it'd mean that we'd be doing it on a shoestring as neither of us had much money in those days. A round trip across to Rotorua, visit all the sights, geysers, mud pools etcetera and then continue on via Lake Waikaremoana to Wairoa, and then down to Napier and back home, stopping at Palmerston North, then Wanganui with just a final leg back to Hawera and home.

Don and I had a great time in the penny divers country, what with Rotorua's mud bores, geysers and hot pools. The only trouble was we didn't have a lot of money left in the kitty so had to try and keep as much as possible aside for petrol. Anyway, by the time we reached the Wairoa River, we were forced to sleep under a bridge to save money. We'd filled up the tank on the car and the spare jerry can with petrol, leaving us with enough money for a feed of fish and chips, boy, we were right on the bones of our backside and getting pretty hungry at that. So that night we went to sleep with food on our minds, and both woke pretty early. Being hungry does that to you! Anyway, we were loading all our bits and pieces into the car when Don excitedly exclaimed, "I know where there's some food!"

I stared at him in astonishment as he began tossing all the gear that we had packed in the back out of the car onto the grass. Then out came the back seat.

I was waiting expectantly as Don reached down into the recess and triumphantly pulled out a big cake tin. "This is the Christmas pudding that Mum made for us! It'll soon get rid of all our hunger pangs!"

In anticipation he wrenched the lid off. But what a sorry sight the pudding was, it had turned into a big hairy fungus, and being right over the hot exhaust pipe each day had caused it sweat, making it absolutely inedible. There was nothing for it so Don heaved the tin and the pudding in great disgust far out into the river.

"Let the bloody eels eat it!" he yelled out after it, his voice full of frustration and anger.

After we'd repacked everything back in we headed southward on our travels absolutely starving, but all that could be done about our hunger was to tighten our belts up a couple of notches. And I must admit we were both ravenous by the time we arrived some six hours later at Don's relatives' place in Napier where we were given a real decent meal and were also able to borrow some money from his uncle, more than enough to complete our journey homeward.

When we did arrive back at Don's house, his mum cooked us up a great feed, the best we'd had for most of the trip. Boy! Talk about good tucker. During the meal we were telling her about where we'd been and what we'd done during the trip.

She then asked us, "What was the Christmas pudding like? Did you enjoy it?"

Don despondently told her how it was ruined from the heat from the exhaust pipe, and it was only fit for the eels so he'd tossed the lot tin and all out into the river. His mother broke into gales of laughter and neither of us could make out just what was so humorous about it all. To us at the time it had been a catastrophe as we were as hungry as hell.

Don asked his mum imploringly, "What's so funny about throwing the Christmas pudding into the river Mum? We were just about dying from starvation at the time."

Still laughing and wiping the tears from her eyes she replied. "I thought when you guys were starting the trip that your finances were pretty thin on the ground, so I filled the Christmas pudding with money, it had about two pounds in small change, sixpences and shillings inside it, and you tossed the whole lot, money and all, into the river!"

It was only then that we caught onto the funny side of it all and even now when we get together we both laugh about this stroke of misfortune.

But, do you know something Rolly? In those days we could have lived like kings on that amount of money. Petrol was only a shilling a gallon, and it was more than enough money for us to easily get back home again. So I guess the moral of this story is, eat your Christmas pudding! You might just be lucky enough to find some gold or silver in it!

So, all in all Reg and I certainly had some very good times, but also I had to get stuck in to get through the workload that was expected of me. But we both knew when to call it a day and not to overdo it.

CHAPTER TWENTY

BRASS MONKEY WEATHER

About three months after I'd begun working for Reg, he sent me to do a job in the middle of the North Island, putting through a new road and widening an existing one that led onto it.

I was living at a single men's camp for five days a week, then back home for two nights which at least gave me the chance to enjoy a few beers with the boys and catch the odd pig or two with Gray.

Now, I've lived in some damned cold places, but when the southerly blew down from the mountains, boy was it bloody cold and I'm telling you, it could freeze the balls off a brass monkey before you knew it! But to add icing to the top of the cake, the local radio station had proudly announced that this particular morning was the coldest in history, for as long as records had been kept, maybe the last fifty years or so. Everything was frozen, even a bucket of water kept inside each of the huts for fire fighting was solid ice!

Anyway, on this particular morning there were about twenty of us waiting for the cookhouse door to open, to let us get out of the freezing cold. It was dark, 6.30am, and added to this was the southerly wind. We were all bundled up with heaps of extra jerseys, balaclavas and gloves - anything to keep out the cold! Must've looked like Michelin men, stamping our feet trying to keep the freezing cold at bay, impatiently waiting for the cooks to open up.

One big fat fella there, he was about six foot odd, and nearly as wide across as he was tall, I reckon that he would've weighed at the very least twenty-five stone. Boy, was he moaning to the group around him.

"Those bloody doors should be open by now, those bloody cooks, they must've slept in or something. I only hope to God they hurry up and shake a leg, 'cos I'm bloody well nearly freezing to death out here! Just look at how heavy the frost is everywhere, and as for this wind, it isn't helping one little bit!"

At this point he was interrupted as a pair of headlights appeared from out of the darkness followed by the roar of a motor. It was an articulated truck and trailer unit loaded with a stack of steel beams. It rolled to a stop just in front of us, and the next thing this little driver leapt down from the cab. Well, he was a real short-arse, all of five foot nothing. Just how he was able to see over the steering wheel, let alone reach the pedals and drive at the same time, was anyone's guess! When he leapt down from the cab onto the frozen ground, we saw much to our astonishment, all this little guy had on was steel-capped leather boots, black socks and a real tight fitting pair of thin black rugby shorts topped off with a skimpy black sleeveless singlet. But most astonishing to us, his bare legs, arms, neck and head were wide open to the bitter freezing cold! Just looking at him was more than enough to make a man begin to shiver. He then nonchalantly leant back against the tray of the truck and began rolling himself a smoke. After looking us all over for a while he spoke in the direction of the big fat guy.

"Ehoa, when's breakfast due round here?"

The big guy looked down unhappily at him and muttered a muffled reply. "These bloody doors are supposed to be open by now, the sooner the better too! Any longer and I'll be bloody frozen stiff!"

The driver nodded. "Thanks Ehoa, I guess I'll just have to be patient and wait a bit."

He put a match to his smoke and for about five minutes he happily puffed away, showing not a concern in the world about the freezing situation around him. Not a single goose pimple on the bare areas of his skin. All the time, we were staring at him in amazement. Then this big guy in our group just couldn't take it any more, he shuffled forward and looking down on the diminutive truck driver, said in disbelief, "Hey man, aren't you cold? Surely you must be freezing to death dressed like that?"

The little driver nonchalantly looked back up and down the big guy, took another drag on his smoke and as he breathed out, bent down, and taking hold of the top of a sock in his fingers replied quietly,

"Cold, you reckon?" He paused for a second or two and with a real straight face, replied to the big fat guy, "What do you think I'm wearing these bloody socks for?"

At that we all pissed ourselves laughing. I've seen some hard rugged little fellas in my time, but there's no doubt that he was the toughest little rooster I'd ever bumped into. Not only that, he had a damned good sense of humour to go with it!

CHAPTER TWENTY ONE

NOT AN EMPTY TANK AGAIN!

It was great when that job down country had been completed and I was back home again every night. No longer having to put up with the freezing frosts and cold winds and really enjoying being able to go down to the pub and enjoying a few beers with the boys after work was just great in every way.

On one occasion I was offered a proposition from a guy who wanted to buy Gray. He'd heard how good a pig dog he was, and it took a fair while before this guy finally got the message.

"Look mate, Gray's definitely not for sale so why don't you go back to your beer and leave me to enjoy mine in peace?"

But this also brought back to mind that Gray was not only a good pig dog, he was very loyal and a great mate at that. Recently, on a couple of odd occasions I'd had the misfortune to run out of fuel in my old bomb. You see the petrol gauge hadn't been working so well, and the only way to find out just how much petrol was left in the tank was by using a wooden dipstick, a piece of dowel to check what the level was.

Not out of bloody gas again, surely not? The car had spluttered to a stop again! Then it came to me that I'd only just filled the tank the day before, so some bugger must be flogging my petrol by using a siphon hose, and probably in the dead of the night at that. So from then on, I tied Gray up to a post on the front terrace with a piece of twine, knowing that he could easily break free if necessary. The petrol thief was going to be in for a bit of a shock!

My old bomb only had a rubber cap to keep out the rain and also I had never bothered locking the car at night, in fact no one living around here seemed to worry about locking their cars and none of them seemed to get pinched. Anyway, nothing seemed to happen and all was quiet for a week or so, until in the early hours of the morning there was a hell of a ruckus outside! Gray was out the front of the house on the road and boy was he going to town! Leaping out of bed, I grabbed the torch and threw open the front door to where the twine had snapped. Gray was running around the car growling and snarling and in the light from the torch I saw a couple of jerry cans on the ground and a length of hose half in and half out of the filler for the petrol tank. The owner of these articles was nowhere to be seen. I shone the torch up and down the road into the shadows, but there was no one around. Long gone, I thought, but at least he'd be thinking twice before trying to flog petrol from my car again. As I walked back to the car I whistled to Gray to give him a pat, and tell him what a great dog he was, but for once he wasn't interested, he was still going to town round and round the car, then he got up onto his hind legs growling even more menacingly as he looked in the window of the back door. Then the penny dropped, the only place the thief could've gotten away from Gray so quickly was to open the door and take refuge inside the car. I shone the torch in, and there on the floor crouched down by the back seat was a cringing form with a very white scared looking face and a pair of terror-stricken eyes staring back up at me. Aha, got you, you bastard! So taking hold of Gray's collar, I held him very firmly and slowly opened the door, then with a helluva lot of venom in my voice, I growled out, "Listen you! Whatever you do, move very, very, slowly, or I won't be responsible for what could happen to you! This dog thinks he owns this car and right now, he wants to kill you! So get out, and remember do it very slowly. Any fast moves and I won't be able to hold him back!" I really wanted to put the shits up him.

As the petrol thief began to get out, I gave Gray's collar a slight tug and this was enough to have him lunging forward, snarling something horrible, so it was just as well I had a good grip! The thief just about went through the hood lining of the car and going by the damp patch on the front of his trousers, he'd pissed himself. I asked him his name and address, and could see he was far too scared not to tell me anything but the truth and all the time Gray continued his vicious snarling. One thing for sure this joker was going to need more than a change of underwear. My final words were full of threat and venom, and I really laid it on.

"Now! You, listen to me very carefully! If I ever hear so much as a whisper about any more petrol being stolen from vehicles anywhere around here again, I will have the greatest of pleasure in contacting the police and passing along all of your details! Now, I'm going to give you a ten second start before I let the dog go, and there's nothing more that he would like than to take great chunks out of your arse!"

I paused, letting it all sink in, and to have an even more desired effect roared, "So get the bloody hell out of here now!"

With that he was on his way, boy did he go for it! Absolutely flying. At the same time I shook Gray's collar, and did he let rip again and even I would've had wings on my feet if Gray hadn't been my own dog. He certainly sounded bloody ferocious with his growling and snarling and needless to say, never again did I have any more petrol troubles. No doubt about Gray's abilities, what a kuri. What a mate!

TWENTY TWO

STICKS AND STONES

Most days when I returned from doing my stretch at the coal-face, I would give Gray his freedom for an hour or so. He had his favourite spots he checked out and one of these was always Danny's place next door, when he usually managed to come home with a bone. Dawn reckoned she had seen him lie down with her kids and he was just so contented lying there, lapping up all the fuss. The kids would climb all over him, pulling his ears and tail, and all he'd do was wag his tail for more and wait until Dawn gave him the bone, after which he'd head for home. Whenever he came past me, his tail would go nineteen to the dozen. He seemed to be smiling and saying 'just look at what I've got'. Then he'd proceed to chew away with great enjoyment.

On one occasion when he'd finished his bone he disappeared for a while, and on his return I noticed that he had a pronounced limp. On checking him out I found that somehow he'd damaged his left foreleg and he wasn't too happy about my touching it. So it was off to the vet, who on checking the leg over said there seemed to be a small broken bone. He thought that Gray had probably been hit with a stick or a stone.

I then had to wait for Gray to heal naturally, so it was no hunting or running about for a few weeks for either of us. Well, with Gray it was easier said than done!

After the enforced rest, the leg was well on the mend, he wasn't limping, and there were no signs of

244

tenderness when I checked it out. So it was back to our every day routine.

Arriving home from work one day I'd just let Gray out and he'd headed off towards the front of the house. The next thing I heard was the sound of a bike crashing and a scared voice yelling frantically, "Let go, you brute! Let go!"

I sprinted round to the front of the house and out onto the road where I took everything in pretty quickly. There was this joker on the ground all tangled up with his bike, and Gray worrying hell out of his trouser leg. I called Gray off, very puzzled because he'd never done anything like this before. It just wasn't like him at all.

"What've you done to him? He's never had a go at anyone before!"

Untangling himself from the bike the joker replied, "Oh, hasn't he just!" He snarled as he looked down at his badly torn trousers. "One thing for sure, he's not going to get another chance because I'm going straight down to the Police Station to lay a complaint and get him put down!"

With that he got astride his bike and wobbled off down the road.

I was a bit concerned about what had occurred, but hoped that he was all just full of hot air and that nothing further would come of it.

About an hour later there was a knock on the door. When I opened it my heart dropped deep into my boots. There stood a cop; one that Curly had introduced me to. Also there was this joker; the one that Gray had had a go at.

"Good evening Rolly. This chap said that Gray knocked him off his bike and had a go at chewing his leg off. Is this right?"

Much to my dismay, I had to tell him what I'd seen. But I also wasn't going to let it be all so one sided. I stuck up for Gray as best I could and when I'd had my say the cop had his. "I have to warn you that if ever your dog takes another go at anyone, even if he's the best pig dog around, we will have to take action and you know what that means? Another thing is that you'll have to pay for a new pair of strides!"

I nodded and said, "I'll be very careful officer."

This joker was really disgruntled at not having something more positive done about Gray. He threatened, "If ever I get the chance, I'll fix him for good, you wait and see!"

With that they both left and I was told later on that I'd have to pay for the torn trousers when this joker showed a receipt to the cops. I was to drop the money off at the Police Station. I was still puzzled about Gray's attitude. It just wasn't like him at all but after that I never let Gray have a run without me being very close to hand. Over the next couple of months it was only on a few occasions that Gray was away for any length of time, and all it took was a whistle and he was back like a rocket.

One night, I'd just finished feeding Gray and giving him fresh water, when down the drive came the sound of footsteps. I turned, seeing the cop there, and with disgust and heaps of apprehension, there was the same joker who had laid the complaint about Gray in the first place. My heart dropped. 'God I thought, whats going on now?'

On the back foot I blurted out, "What the hell?"

It was the same cop who had warned me about Gray's behaviour. He could see the alarm on my face and held up his hand so I could see he didn't want any trouble. I didn't know what to do or how to react.

"It's all right Rolly, sorry to bother you but this joker here owes you an apology!"

I was reassured by his words but baffled, wondering why in the hell would this joker be apologising to me, and what for? I gritted my teeth, as all he meant to me was trouble!

Then this bugger began explaining, "I've only just bought a car and when I turned into your road, I thought to myself that if I got the chance I'd bowl the dog over. Taking things into my own hands, I was about thirty-five yards down the road when I spotted him so I put my foot hard on the throttle. Soon I was only about twenty yards from him and thought, 'that's funny, that dog's got six legs.' Then it dawned on me. I braked rapidly and came to a stop. That dog of yours was leaning against a kiddie, just a toddler, pushing him towards the open gate next door, then through it. I was badly shaken. If I'd continued on I would've hit the kiddie as well!"

At his words I was starting to seethe. I wanted to clobber this bugger!

He then continued. "Anyway, about my complaint, what really happened originally was that I was riding past when the dog came running out and I've always been scared of big dogs, so I used to carry a stick when I rode my bike. On that night when he got near me I lashed out and hit him on the leg. I'm sorry about that, and the rest you know. So really, when he knocked me down, your dog was only getting his own back! I shouldn't have reported it to the police. I apologise."

I was fuming! The cop must've seen the look in my eyes and stepped in between us.

"So, you're the bloody idiot," I said. "I ought to take a lump of wood to you, just to see how you'd like it!"

The cop managed to calm me down by saying, "One good thing has come out of this Rolly; Gray has got a completely clean sheet as far as we're concerned."

Then, glaring at the joker beside him said, "As for you mate if I was you, I'd bugger off smartly while the going's good. Also you'd better watch your step in future. We know where you live and we know your car, so make sure you keep your nose very clean from now on!"

He left in a hurry looking very crestfallen and I was very happy to see the last of him. All I could think was good riddance to bad rubbish. I hoped that I'd never see him again. My rage was murderous and I knew that I wouldn't be holding back!

For a while the cop and I talked about the whole event, then he took his leave, shaking my hand as he went. "And by the way Rolly, let's have a chat over a beer sometime and I'll shout the first round," he offered as he departed.

So that was another saga in Gray's life that will remain with me forever. Fancy that, Gray guiding Danny's toddler off the road and pushing him in through the gate to safety. I was both thankful and elated to think that Gray had the ability to have protected Dawn and Danny's toddler.

Some day when the time's right, I'll relate the story to Danny and Dawn. Maybe. Perhaps over an enjoyable dinner of casseroled possum!

CHAPTER TWENTY THREE

WHAT, NO RABBITS?

One Friday night Danny and I got up to our usual tricks; had a few beers then decided to head out after some rabbits, and with a fair skinful at that. The rabbits had proved to be very few and far between on this night, none to be seen anywhere, and we were on our way home empty handed. It looked like the great white hunters were about to miss out again with not even any possums.

As we passed a bit of a rundown farm Danny said, "Hold it Rolly, slow down and put the anchors on quietly. I've just spotted something that'll more than take the place of rabbits. There's a load of turkeys roosting on the top of the fence battens over there, so if we're quiet enough we just might be able to nab one!"

When we'd coasted quietly to a stop he told me what to do. "Switch off the lights. Now, where's that old bayonet that you were going to cut down to a hunting knife? And remember now, whatever you do don't make even the slightest noise or else they'll be well gone!"

I carefully dragged the bayonet out of its scabbard from under the car seat and passed it to Danny with a whispered warning,

"Be careful! It's bloody sharp!"

Before we left the car Danny explained in a whisper. "When we get up close, I want you to slam your hand down on the top wire of the fence, and then when the turkey pokes its head up to see what the noise is about, it'll be all over. As good as in the pot, eh boy!"

We moved as quietly as possible, sneaking back on the grass verge up the road and across to the fence where the turkeys were roosting with their heads tucked under their wings. Danny got himself all set and I slammed my hand down hard onto the top wire. It twanged, and immediately the turkeys' heads lifted in alarm. And with one quick movement, the bayonet removed the nearest one's head. Danny also grabbed a wing as it was flapping and carrying on, with a fair bit of blood squirting all over the place. He was copping a lot of it, mostly on his clothes. By now all the other turkeys had taken wing and were long gone, but their rapid departure had caused some dogs about a hundred yards away to kick up bobsy die! This in turn aroused someone in the house to get up and switch on an outside light.

"C'mon Danny, let's make tracks before whoever owns this farm lumbers us!" We high tailed out of there.

The following day, Dawn stuffed and cooked the turkey, and it was certainly nice eating, but she only had one comment about us getting the turkey, next time Danny could wash his own damned blood-covered clothes because she wouldn't be!

One thing I know for sure, we'd never have had the cheek to knock the turkey off if we'd been sober. Another thing that I learnt in a hurry was it doesn't pay to whack your hand down onto a barbed wire fence, especially in the dark. It puts bloody big holes in the palm of your hand, it's bloody painful as, and bleeds like hell!

Saturday was a day of overtime that seemed to be dragging. Especially as throughout this particular day a strong gusty westerly blew, lifting the light sand and pumice dust high into the air, half blinding and choking me in the process. By mid afternoon I'd had a real gutsful, so I called it a day and being as dry as a wooden god I took big steps to remedy it. As Reg would say, 'bloody great long ones at that, in the direction of the boozer!'

Walking into the bar I spotted Jim and Curly, so I collected a couple of jugs on my way over to join them. This was going to help put an end to my raging thirst. Arriving with the jugs at the corner table where they were parked, I was greeted by Curly who was bubbling with glee.

"Did you happen to know that your mate here is a champion square dancer?"

I motioned for him to hang on for a minute and downed a couple of beers in quick succession and they didn't even touch the sides! They were just what the doc ordered, washing some of the dust and grime from the back of my throat.

I then queried, "Now what's all this about Jim goin' square dancing?"

With gleam in his eye and grinning widely, Curl' resumed his story. "We took Gray and Speck out to the back of Charlie's place to have a go at another pig he'd seen hanging around.

When we arrived at the back paddock we'd only just let the dogs out, and they went straight through the fence, latching onto a boar. A good sized one at that too! I was still lacing up my boots at the time, but Jim went over the fence like a champion hurdler. I heard the boar give a bit of a grunt and begin kicking up a fair old racket, squealing like hell! Then old Fred Astaire here…" Curly was grinning from ear to ear as he pointed at Jim, "starts yelling, 'Curly, Curly, hurry up. Giv'us a hand, quick!' I wondered what in the hell was up. The boar was still kicking up bobsy-die, and I could also hear the dogs holding another pig a bit further off, so they were doing their thing, certainly getting stuck in. I scrambled over the fence and through the scrub to where Jim was and found him hanging onto the pig, struggling to keep its back legs up in the air. He was dancing the pig around in circles and it was kicking like hell but he couldn't get it off balance and onto its back, it was just too damned strong for him and he couldn't let go. He was dead scared it'd turn on him, so he was into a real no win situation, but it certainly looked bloody humorous and no doubt about it!"

Jim butted in, "Look Rolly what really happened was, as I grabbed one back leg I slipped on a rock and only just managed to grab the other leg to regain my balance. Then the dogs thought I had everything in hand so they took off and latched onto another pig! When this bloody great ape arrived on the scene he thought it was just one big joke! He started singing out and clapping his hands 'Swing your partner round and round, even if it's a pig!'. The only way I could get him to give me a hand was to threaten the bugger that I'd let the boar go when it was pointing in his direction. Boy! Talk about a quick reaction, it soon made him jump in and give me the hand that I needed. Well, that was the end of the square dancing debut. Meanwhile the dogs were still latched onto the other pig, so we took off after them and in next to no time had that one in the bag as well. All in all we had a good morning's hunt but I'm not a damned square dancer!"

Needless to say I had a good laugh at Jim's expense!

Shortly after Jim's tale had been related we were joined by a couple of hard case guys we'd met up with occasionally and had enjoyed a few beers with in the past. Curly was not one to let things lie and remarked, "I'd like you two fellas to meet the greatest square dancer of all time. 'He pointed to Jim, relating the tale again, much to everyone's amusement. But I must admit, Jim took it well.

After a few more beers all round Curly said, "Hey Tom, I hear on the grapevine that you've been visiting your old hometown. Anything worthwhile happen while you were back in the old stamping ground?"

Tom thought for a few seconds and gave a bit of a chuckle.

"Well, yeah, I guess there was something that could be what you might call of interest to you fellas…

Ya see there's this old coot, he's been living in the town for as long as I can remember, one of the real old identities, just about a legend! Always going to the pub on most Saturday nights for years, as regular as clockwork, and he liked his drink or two. Wilson is his name, first name too. Anyway, as per usual, he'd gotten a real skinful on board, maybe even a bit more than usual evidently. Anyway as he was staggering his way home from the old rubbedy dub, he was having a fair bit of trouble navigating so decided to take a bit of a short cut home through the old cemetery. But halfway across somehow he got a bit bamboozled and crash, he fell into a freshly dug grave, knocking all the wind out of him. Reckoned that it took a fair old while to work out what exactly had happened and where he was. So at first he tried jumping to get out, but that was of no use because only his legs were bending at the knees, just a waste of time. With the sides at six feet he had to give it up as a bad job. So being in no fit state for any sort of athletics he started yelling, hoping that someone would come to his aid, but soon gave that up as a bad job too because who in the hell would be hanging around in a graveyard in the middle of the night anyway. Besides, his drunken yells would be more likely to scare someone away than bring anyone to give him a helping hand. In the end Wilson decided that there was no way he was going to be able to get out without assistance, and since it was a nice warm balmy night, decided he might as well stay put and not worry about getting out until it was daylight. So he curled up and nodded off in the corner.

Sometime later Wilson was aroused by a thump as something or someone landed at the other end of the open grave and a drunken voice began muttering, "Bloody hell, in one of these things before my number's up!" Followed by the scrambling sounds of feet as whoever it was tried getting out. Then there was a short silence and some more scrambling of feet when this joker then actually trod on Wilson's foot.

Wilson was still curled up in the corner hearing all this, and realising that this guy was in no fit state to get out either, decided a bit of free advice wouldn't go amiss, so out of the depths so he spoke up. "Look mate, you might as well give up. You're stuck in here for good!"

Initially there was no reply, just a very sharp intake of breath, followed by an agonised scream, "Hell no!" Then there was only the pounding sound of rapidly departing feet as this fella took to his scrapers!

Wilson reckoned this bloke, who ever he was, didn't even touch the sides on his way out!

Man, did we laugh, and poor old Curly just about choked on his beer. He had tears in his eyes!

As the beer flowed the conversation moved onto fishing and Tom's offsider, Eric, started telling us about his first job on arriving in the district. He was labouring on a hydro-dam that was being constructed…

After a few weeks he got to know the ropes and quite a few of the fellas who worked there. One guy in particular he reckoned really took the cake - a very shrewd Maori chap who was having a great time leading the local fish and game ranger on a real dinkum song and dance but always managing to stay at least two steps ahead. The one big problem for the ranger was that he was unable to legally go onto or to cross over the Ministry of Works site, and no way could he get permission, no matter what he did or who he spoke to, he was stymied. So there was only one way to get onto the opposite side of the river to nab the poacher and it meant he had to drive a fair way downstream from the dam site, hide his ute and cross over a narrow foot bridge. After that began a difficult scramble back through the dense scrub, toitoi and what have you that lined the bank. Even for a guy who was as fit as the ranger, and as determined to get his man, it was a struggle. All in all it was damned hard work, and no mean feat. So to put in a nutshell, his job of trying to catch the poacher was just about impossible. The poacher had everything going for him! Poaching the trout in the first place, and getting up to all sorts of tricks; no license, often using a hand line baited with huhu bugs, all completely illegal of course.

Each morning before starting work, or at smoko, this Maori fella would drop an illegally baited line in the river, leaving it there until he felt like pulling it in at lunchtime, or after he'd knocked off work at the end of the day. So it was not unusual for the poacher to end up with a nice sized trout at the final whistle!

Being very shrewd, he would purposely let the ranger catch a glimpse of him throwing the line into the water, but most of the time this was just a decoy and while the ranger remained hidden in the scrub handy to the line, the poacher was at another spot, somewhere else either up or down the river, pulling up his illicit catch!

This had been going on for some time, with the ranger getting more and more annoyed, making him all the more determined to catch the poacher. Then, during one of his many searches, he stumbled across a well-hidden line. Immediately he knew it was a fair dinkum line because when he pulled it up a bit he felt the weight and could see the gleam of the trout deep in the water. So, the ranger carefully lowered the line back to its original position and, making sure that he erased any marks he'd made in the soft damp soil, he carefully moved back into the scrub, crouching down completely hidden from sight.

No doubt about it, his thoughts were full of revenge!

"At last I've got you, you won't be able to make a fool out of me this time!" He squatted there, showing great perseverance and patience, hardly moving a muscle, even though the sand-flies were biting hell out of his bare arms and legs. There was no way he was going to give the show away by moving.

Much later that afternoon, he heard a slight movement just up river from where he was concealed. Still he remained motionless. Then at last he saw the poacher making his way towards the line. It'd been an uncomfortably long wait but it was going to be so worthwhile. He'd stay well hidden until the poacher began to haul the line up and then all his patience would be rewarded! A feeling of great elation flooded through him.

After taking a very careful look around, the poacher steadily began hauling in the hand line. This was the ranger's moment of glory and wonderful revenge and he leapt out of the scrub crowing, "Well, well, I've got you redhanded at last! I've been waiting months for this moment!"

The poacher spun round in agitation, "So it's you! The least you could've done was give me a bit of warning, you just about scared the living daylights out of me!"

The ranger snapped, "I don't give a damn if you'd jumped out of your skin and landed in the river, it's been worth every minute needed to catch you poaching and now I've collared you right in the act! The judge will really throw the book at you over this, when he reads my report!"

The poacher remained quiet for a few seconds before stating, "What do you mean, caught me in the act? My ancestors gave me the rights to catch as many fish as I like, whenever!"

The ranger gave a derisive laugh. "You know as well as I do, that's only legal with a license, a rod, and not a bloody hand line. So don't try giving me any bull about your ancestral rights!"

At that the poacher shrugged his shoulders and dropped the fishing line he'd been pulling up back into the river and derisively said, "Oh well, if that's the case, Mister Ranger, you can just pull up the evidence you want yourself!" then stepped back away from the riverbank.

The ranger certainly wasn't going to miss out on the evidence on the end of the line, and growled at the poacher, "This'll go against you in the court, you know."

"So what?" was the gruff reply.

The further the ranger pulled the trout up, the more he thought about the upcoming court case. He growled back at the poacher, "Ya know something, this trout feels like a big one, just like your fine will be, and I'm going to enjoy the judge's final sentence when he prosecutes you! It's going to cost you heaps!"

"Hmmmph," was all he got in reply as he continued pulling the line. He could see the fish gleaming as he pulled it in the last few feet and then yanked it out of the water and onto the riverbank. But he couldn't believe his eyes. He turned around, his mouth wide open, unable to utter a word for a moment. Finally he managed to blurt out, "A snapper, in fresh water?"

Of the poacher there was no sign, only mocking laughter and a voice drifting down eerily out of the scrub.

"Pai Kori, pakeha, you the greatest fisherman ever! Not even Te Maori can catch an eight pound snapper in the mighty Waikato!"

And then there were only the sounds of the rippling river left to mock the ranger as he stared down at the snapper in horror and disbelief.

His mind was slowly coming to the realisation of it all. He whispered to himself then moaned in unbelievable astonishment, "A snapper! A bloody snapper! No it can't be, surely not a bloody snapper?"

CHAPTER TWENTY FOUR

TALK ABOUT RAIN!

Time sure runs away when you're having fun. It was only two more weeks until Jim was getting hitched to Jenny, so it was decided that we'd better have a stag weekend away for the boys. Curly, who was going to become Jim's brother-in-law, knew of a great spot with plenty of deer and even a decent trout stream that was always good for a nice fat trout or two. Best of all was its isolation, as very few hunters could be bothered with the long walk in and it was bordering the forbidden military land. We were all looking forward to some good stalking but the only one thing we hadn't counted on was the weather turning sour.

We had just entered the outskirts of a small township on our stag weekend for Jim when old Hughie decided to really let rip. He threw a real wobbly and boy did it begin to pour, talk about raining cats and dogs. It was so torrential that the windscreen wipers didn't have a hope of keeping up with it. Deciding it was just too risky to continue driving, we stopped for a while to see what the weather had in mind. As we were sitting awaiting the outcome, it just so happened that the pub across the road opened its doors.

Now anybody would think that we'd stopped there on purpose but on this occasion it was just the luck of the draw. It didn't take too long and it was a unanimous decision to head across the road to partake in the local beverage. It looked like the rough weather had set in for the duration, and not being the types to look a gift horse in the mouth or twiddle our thumbs, we dashed through the downpour towards the pub. We were the pub's first customers of the day and we decided that the beer was sweet as. The radio report on the weather stated that it was only going to get much worse, so as the day progressed we settled in, enjoying a game or two of pool and the inevitable darts. The only trouble being that Curly was just too good at both, leaving Jim and me in his dust. We both reckoned that the only reason Curl was so good at playing pool and darts was because of his misspent youth!

Roughly about an hour or more on, a couple of fellows looking half drowned came in and we invited them to join us. During the games that followed, a few beers were consumed, with all sorts of topics being discussed, and these two guys who'd joined us began telling us how they'd just spent a fair bit of time recently in and around the National Park, trapping brumbies...

At first they'd bumped into an old codger, who'd told them how they could make a pile of gold in no time at all by catchin' the wild horses and knocking them off at the district livestock sales. As easy as falling off a log, nothing to it, he reckoned.

It didn't take long for the old codger to paint a pretty picture and he even took them out and showed them the grazing areas, water hole and seeps, and they took notice that there were quite a few head still on the loose so decided to give it a go too. However by the next sale they'd managed to catch sweet bugger all. It was a real kick in the pants when after a month or so of hard yakka they had nothing to show!

Anyway the old boy told them how it was that he'd been lucky enough to have latched onto a good sized mob. Most of the horses he had were in pretty good nick, and they fetched reasonable prices. So they asked him how come he'd got so many, what was the score? He reckoned that it was just the way the dice had fallen, and they'd probably reverse that and turn the tables on him in the coming weeks in time for the next sale. The main thing was that they just had to keep on trying, they couldn't expect to come out on top from the word go. 'These things take time y' know!'

Well, after they'd sweated out their guts for the next few weeks, they'd luckily enough managed to get a few head, but it was real tough going and once again the old boy was streets ahead with another nice sized mob. And all on his Jack Malone at that!

Again, they asked him how come he'd managed to do so well.

"It's like this, boys," and he looked around as though he was going to relate a big secret and beckoned for them to follow saying quietly, "c'mon over to that mare of mine that's tied up to the rails there an' I'll show you!"

Using a length of rope he tied it between two gateposts, a foot or so off the ground, and then leading the mare by the reins, he walked it forward until it had both front legs over the rope. Then he said, "C'mon now young fellas, just walk up to the horse's head and see what happens."

Now the old mare was a bit on the shy side and backed up smartly, but when it tried to lift its hooves the fetlocks came up automatically and caught under the stretched rope!

"See, she's trapped and is getting into a real tizzy, can't get away for love nor money, so now do ya see what I mean?" queried the old boy as he sucked away on his smelly old pipe. "So all you've gotta do is put wire around the water holes and soaks and you'll be in the pound seats!"

They were as happy as sand boys. At last they had the dinkum oil on how to get hold of plenty of these nags. So, obtaining a couple of coils of number eight wire, they got stuck into the job of setting it out, all in all taking about five days to do it. It was around a week before they realised that the old boy had them up the garden path well and truly. Sure, the rope or wire would work beauty on a horse that'd been broken in; it'd just back up; and stand there 'til it was led away or the wire was pushed down. But a wild horse wouldn't stand there or back up; he'd turn around and be on his way. And even if he got a fetlock caught he'd panic and prance around until he was free, then he'd be out o' there fast and be long gone in no time at all!

They were as wild as hell to have been made such mugs of, and as they were running out of tucker they took a trip into town for stores, and while in town they bumped into the stock and station agent. On mentioning how they'd had one put over them by the old boy, the agent kind of hinted to them that he was a sly old dog, and if they weren't too careful they would probably end up catching his nags for him.

On the way back to camp they got to thinking about the agent's remarks and decided to do a bit of snooping around. It was then that they found the first of his well-hidden traps! All the time they'd been chasing brumbies all over the show, they'd been filling his traps for him, just as he'd meant them to do. No wonder he was catching plenty when it was them who'd been chasing them into his hands! The only thing he had to do was to collect them up.

After they'd cooled down a bit, they started using his traps to their own advantage by chasin' them in pretty late in the day and collecting any brumbies caught in the trap, getting them out of there quickly.

They'd been doing this for a week or so when the old boy came over to see how they were making out and by then they had gathered up quite a few head for themselves, so he was a bit mystified. Keeping straight faces, they repeated his own words, 'just the luck of the game', and said that no doubt his luck would improve during the next few weeks. Anyway, he went off scratching his head. As sale day got nearer the brumbies were becoming very wary and much harder to catch and those they hadn't caught were making tracks for new and distant pastures. The area was pretty well skinned out and come sale day they had a reasonable number up for grabs. However when they came up for auction, the old boy spoke up and accused them in front of the bidders of rustling nags out of his traps. They were stumped for a reply, until my mate came up with just the right answer.

"Listen here, you old coot, you were the one who showed us how to go about catching them with a wire and backing them up into it, and that's how we did it, okay?"

Then the auctioneer came into the conversation and backed them up. "That's right, I saw you showing them in the yards with your old mare and a rope. Besides, none has got a brand on them anyhow! Looks like you've met your match eh!"

Boy, did the old coot look daggers at them, but the crowd told him to not be such an old moaner, giving a him a hard time. Evidently he'd taken just about everyone in the district for a sucker at one time or another, but nobody'd ever had enough proof to do anything about it. So perhaps the old bugger had met his match at last.

At this point these two ex-brumby cowboys reckoned that it was about time they made tracks. "Be seeing you, guys," they said, and were on their way out into the torrential rain.

With the bad weather not easing up one little bit we did what any group of guys enjoy. For the next couple of days we made sure that Jim's final days as a free man were just what he needed. We were as wet inside as the rain outside, but we also met up with quite a few other types who had a deep interest in pig hunting and deer stalking.

It so happened that a couple of guys that we'd been chatting to had been doing a fair bit of meat hunting and were reminiscing about some of the more unusual things that had occurred...

At times they'd sneaked in to poach deer in the forbidden no-go military zone. After hiding and carefully camouflaging their vehicle they headed into a spot where they'd often managed to bag some nice sized beasts; even though it meant a long carry back out to where they'd hidden their vehicle. So they had the long cold tramp in darkness, with the frosty ground crunching beneath their boots. And for once they were both very happy wearing gloves and balaclavas. The southerly breeze was a really lazy one; it didn't go around you, just straight through! It was as bitter as, to say the least. They walked the road in for the better part of two hours until fingers of light penetrated the darkness and it looked likely to be a fine but cold day ahead of them. Then as they rounded a bend in the road, there directly in front of them was a sight to

264

shock and dismay. They stopped and stared at a row of four army-style bell tents. There was no way that any hunting here was even remotely possible!

After a whispered conference in which they expressed their frustration, it was decided that as both were pretty fit they'd vent their disappointment by playing a trick on the army for mucking up their hunting plans. As there was no sign of a sentry the guy with the sharpest knife unsheathed it and crept silently towards the furthermost tent and then sprinted flat out around them slashing as many tight wet guy ropes as possible, and when the final tent was collapsing in on top of the rudely awakened members of the army, his mate rapidly fired a volley into the safety of a clay pumice bank and then they took to their scrapers leaving behind screams and yells of shock and frustration as the sleepers tried to fight their way free from collapsing tents!

They both reckoned that this run of theirs back out to their vehicle would have beaten any Olympian, by a hell of a distance! One thing for sure, they had no intention of falling into the military's hands, as their life wouldn't have been worth living!

Although we all cracked up with their tale, I for one wouldn't have liked to be in their shoes if they'd been caught!

The barman who was quite a character had been listening to some of the tales and joined in with a bit of yarn too, relating how years ago he'd been at a mate's send off and stag night in Auckland...

A group of the groom's mates had been downing a fair few drinks at the Railways Hotel in Auckland and the groom-to-be was getting well and truly pissed; he was out for the duration! So for a bit of fun, we decided that we would give him a really good send off to remember. Together we'd gathered up enough cash to purchase a ticket for the overnight express to Wellington, and in an inside buttoned pocket of his shorts we pinned more than enough dough to enable him to catch a plane back to Auckland. So all of us carried him to across the road to the train and placed him, still absolutely out for the count, in the carriage onto the gentle mercies of a hard slatted wooden seat. We watched as the express train's red guard lights disappeared out of the station. Next stop was Wellington, the capital, so there was no doubt that we'd given him a send off that he'd remember for the rest of his life!

This mate of ours later related what had happened during the night. The first thing he became aware of was just how cold it felt, and for ages he wondered what was the relentless aching and continuous thumping in his head? What in the hell had he been drinking? Clickety, clack all the time; would it never stop? It seemed never ending, just going on and on!

When eventually he was aroused by the ticket collector shaking his shoulder, he was unable to believe what he heard. It finally dawned on him; he was somehow in Taumaranui and outside there was a freezing eight-degree frost. And as per normal he was still only in working gear, lightly clad in shorts and a thinnish shirt, nearly suffering from hypothermia!

Fortunately the ticket collector took pity on him arranged to loan him a couple of blankets, and for sixpence he was able to rent a pillow. Then luckily he located the money we'd tucked into his pocket. So with a raging hangover he managed to get a bit warmer and slept off and on for the rest of the trip. In the morning he was suffering badly with the dry horrors and when I met him later on his arrival at the airport he looked much the worse for wear and didn't even manage to abuse me!

Nowadays, whenever we get together we have a damned good laugh but he reckons he never again wants to hear the clickety clack of the train wheels across the joins in the tracks! By the way I was the good mate and the Best Man who got it all organised for him. Even now Angela, his wife of some twenty years, has never forgiven me. And I can tell you, I know now right up to this very day I've got to keep my wits about me or he'll have his revenge!

Luckily for Jim he never got that pissed and besides it was fifty odd miles from the nearest railway station at least, so he had no worries about that possibility!

Jim's stag weekend wound to an end with three very knackered and rather fuzzy-headed mates returning home empty handed with no pigs or deer, but full of memories of how we'd certainly given Jim a fine send off into the bonds of matrimony!

One thing for sure, it took another few days back at work before any of us were feeling like another beer or two! You know sometimes you can have too much of a good thing.

CHAPTER TWENTY FIVE

JUST ANOTHER DAY AT THE OFFICE

Funny how things come about when they are least expected. Six days ago, Jim and Jenny had tied the knot and you could say it was the end of a good keen man. But that I guess is a bit of a bachelor's point of view.

Anyway, this was another day somewhat similar to the one when Jim and I had first met. Reg had me operating the motorised scraper, doing a job where I had to widen the narrow single lane road making it capable of carrying two lanes of traffic. This was to be my final job for him before moving onto greener pastures. Wanderlust had grabbed me and it was relentless. Reg was emphatic about me staying and continuing to drive for him, saying that there would always be a job waiting for me anytime I wanted it.

I had a couple of reasons to be moving on, one being that I was always wondering about what was over the next hill. In other words, I had itchy feet. Also with the two lovebirds being due back any day now, I was sure that they wouldn't want a hanger-on around the house to spoil their fun, now would they? Not to mention that I'd heard about a couple of good pig-hunting spots that needed to be given the once over. What greater incentive did a man need to pick up stakes and hit the road?

To widen the road it was a matter of cutting down two high banks, scraping load after load off parallel to the road, and following the verge for about a hundred yards or so. Then I'd take a right turn across the road and drop my load in a bit of a gully. It was sure filling up fast! Once again it was back across the road to pick up another load, and so on it went. In crossing the road, I always had to take the utmost care, making sure that there were no vehicles approaching. Believe me, at all times I really had to keep my eyes peeled, and some in the back of my head as well, because there were sure some pretty stupid drivers around, not to mention the impatient ones, especially on this particular section of the road. One driver in particular was up and down the road quite a few times every day ensconced behind the wheel of a big Yank tank, his head in the air acting as though he didn't have to wait for any man or machine. He always seemed to be roaring past in a hurry - no brains it seemed! It was just as though me and my machine didn't even exist. Then to cap it off he always seemed to arrive just as I was about to cross the road. At one time, I came pretty close to flattening him and his bloody great flash Yank tank. It was only by sheer luck that each time I had slowed down more than normal, or come to a stop as I began turning across. Even so, it still scared the living daylights out of me when he appeared out of the blue on the blind side of the machine. I'd waved my fist angrily, but he didn't see a thing, or even notice my annoyance, probably because of the pumice dust billowing out behind him. 'Bloody hell man,' I thought, 'what you need is for someone to give you a damned good fright! Maybe that'd wake your bloody ideas up and slow you down a bit!'

One good thing for sure, was that the indicators on the scraper were working well, big and very bright, so no one could miss them, and the signs at each end of the works were enormous and well placed, very easily seen, stating that all vehicles must give way to and beware of heavy earth-moving machines crossing the road. He must have been shortsighted, because even a half blind man could see the indicators flashing for miles. It just makes a man wonder about the saying, 'It's better to get there alive, than to arrive there dead in a hearse'!

Well for some drivers, and the small minority at that, it didn't make an ounce of difference to them. They just barrelled along the road at high speed, and if looks and gestures could kill I'd've been dead long ago, all because I wasted a few seconds of their precious time!

Gettin' on to mid-morning on this day, I decided to make this load my last before I stopped for smoko. Time to have a hot drink and feed the hungry worms. Ready to turn and cross the road, I switched on the indicators, looked behind, checked and saw no sign of anyone coming, so started to turn, making sure to take one more look each way to ensure the road was clear. Yes, it's all clear, good - so it's hard right and across the road she goes. About halfway across the road, the front of my machine jumped up a bit, began to climb rapidly, and there was a faint sound of a car horn above the roar of my machine's engine. I didn't have time to think. Automatically I slammed on the brakes and dropped the scoop which stopped the machine dead. Standing up, I could see the off-side wheel which had climbed up over the cab of a car, mangling it right in line with the front seat! Thoughts of horror flashed through my mind, my heart was in my mouth! My God, I've killed the driver! Nobody could survive that impact! Leaping down from the scraper I rushed around to the other side. Bloody hell, the wheel was at least three quarters across the front of the car's cab!

I reached the driver's door and there, hunched over the steering wheel, was the driver, as white as a sheet! At least he wasn't dead and that was a big relief! Amazingly, the wheel hadn't gone right across the car. I wrenched at the door but it was jammed solid. The weight of the scraper had twisted everything but luckily the glass window had popped out leaving a biggish gap. I frantically tried to help him out.

"C'mon, mate, do you think you can squeeze out of the window?"

Luckily no parts of his body were caught or crushed by the flattened cab of the car, but it was still awkward for him to get through the twisted window frame. When he was out at last I breathed a huge sigh of relief and watched as some of the colour slowly returned to his face. I then ran round to the driver's side of the scraper and turned the engine off.

In the time I was making my way back round to the car I thought of how, only a couple of hours ago, I would've loved to have given this guy, the driver of the Yank tank, a really good fright to teach him a lesson. Now I had bloody near killed him, as well as making scrap metal out of his car! I must admit it had all shaken me up a fair bit too, no bloody joke this!

Then abruptly my thoughts were interrupted as the Yank tank driver began to abuse me, up hill and down dale. He had his finger right in my face and I had to take a step back to avoid it.

"You bloody great idiot, you could've killed me! Look at my car, it's nearly brand new and now it's a bloody write off. I'll have the police on to you! You must be drunk, blind or something, or both. I'll have your license and every penny you've got to your name for this. Why didn't you look before you started turning? You would've seen me."

By then I'd almost gotten over the shock of the accident and these threats made me bloody furious! Who in the hell did he think he was, another bloody Rob Muldoon?

"You can talk! Look, mate, you ought to be bloody thankful that you're still in the land of the living and not injured! I did look and if it wasn't for my quick reactions, you'd be waiting here for a hearse or an ambulance. And another thing, there's nothing wrong with my eyesight. Ya see those things?" I pointed to the indicators that were still flashing away, "they're on because I was turning right and they're still flashing. Another thing, I've lost count of the times that I've had to take avoiding action when you've been coming down this section of the road. Always goin' like a bat out of hell and showing no consideration for anyone!"

"Rubbish!" he screamed. "Those indicators weren't on when I started to come on through, and if you'd had the good sense to look around, you'd have seen me coming. One thing's for sure, you're for the high jump and I'll make you bloody sorry for the accident that you've caused!"

It's amazing just how soon people gather after there's been an accident. They seem to appear out of nowhere, right out of the blue.

One little old guy stepped out of the crowd and said in a quiet manner, while looking up at the car owner who towered over him, "Aren't you making a lot of noise and accusations for a person who was completely in the wrong?"

"Me in the wrong?" the driver ranted. "Just because this bloody idiot driving this big machine that can't be damaged chooses to disregard the road rules and doesn't give a damn about other people's safety on the road!

272

Look as far as I'm concerned, you're just as big an idiot as he is! What would you know about the rules of the road anyway?"

The little old guy's head went back. "I beg your pardon? If I were you, I'd be very careful about what you've got to say. Surely you must realise that there are such things as libel and slander, and while I'm about it, let's get another thing straight right here and now! There are large signs at each end of these road works stating the speed limit and you were at least four times above that limit. Most of all, it says to give way to earth moving machinery crossing the road! Do I make myself clear?"

This really got the Yank tank driver going, making him more abusive than ever. "How in the hell do you know I was in the wrong? You look as though you couldn't even drive a kiddie's pedal car, let alone say how fast my speed was!"

I could see the little old guy wasn't going to be intimidated in any way, shape or form. He thrust his jaw out determinedly. "I'm sorry, sir, but you will be disappointed to hear that I do have a current driver's license, and I do drive a motor vehicle. At the risk of repeating myself about this incident, I saw the whole accident from that hillock over there. You were well above the restricted area speed limit, even above the current legal speed when this road is open to normal traffic regulations! As well as that, you began overtaking the scraper long after the indicators were flashing to indicate that it was turning right!"

The car driver, who was much taller and bigger than the little old guy, began to let rip again. "Who in the hell do you think you are? Throwing your weight around and trying to tell me that I'm in the wrong."

By now, I'd taken a real dislike to the driver. He was acting like a bully and was only being told the truth in the first place. Stepping a pace forward, I'd had more than enough of his stand-over attitude.

"Listen to me fella, it's about time you shut your trap because if you don't you're going to get my fist right in the middle of your kisser!"

The old boy interrupted me by stepping between myself and the driver saying, "It's all right son, don't let him upset you, I deal with his type quite often."

Then, reaching into his pocket, he drew out his wallet, opened it and as he showed his credentials, said, "Sir, I would like you to look at these and in doing so, just think before you say anything more."

The bumptious rooster looked at the old boy's credentials and boy did his face change. His jaw dropped and his eyes stuck out like organ stops. For a while he was like a stranded fish, his mouth opening and shutting with no sound coming out. When he did manage to speak it was little more than a whisper. "You're a senior magistrate?"

He then repeated it in amazement, and what little colour he'd had was fast leaving his cheeks again. "You're a senior magistrate? How was I to know, Your Honour?"

Even I was stuck for words!

Once again the old guy spoke quietly but in a very authoritative manner. "As it happens, I'm on holiday here and in no mood to have it ruined by you or anyone else, otherwise…"

And he paused for a second, looking down the road to where the sound of a siren wailed towards us. "Ah, here comes a traffic officer, I'm sure he'll take care of everything." Then turning to me, the magistrate passed me a business card. "If you require a witness, I'll be only too happy to be of assistance."

He walked across towards the police car and when it pulled up had a quiet chat to the officer. And wouldn't you know it, it was one of Curly's mates. So that was that, I wasn't in the wrong! This time I didn't get fired. How could I with a senior magistrate and the police on my side?

Once again, I'd managed to make front-page news and give all the locals something to talk about. And to think that something like this could have happened twice in a lifetime. Makes a man think he ought to head for home. Or grab the dogs and just go bush!

CHAPTER TWENTY SIX

TIME TO MOVE ON

It just happened that I'd already arranged with Reg to finish up at the end of the week which was only a couple of days away, so with all the loose ends tidied up and my reputation not in tatters this time round, I was moving on - to where, I wasn't quite sure. The newlyweds were due back and I'd already wished the happy couple all the best for the future, having said my goodbyes previously. It was with some regrets but with a feeling of anticipation that I tossed my gear into the old bomb along with Gray.

I'd already asked Danny to keep an eye on Speckle until the honeymoon couple turned up. Speckle and Gray had gotten together and she was due to drop her litter any day. I would've liked a pup from the litter for myself, but one thing for sure it just wasn't to be, not at this time. And if the pups are anything like their parents, there will be some damned good pig dogs in this area over the next few years.

On my way out of town I dropped into the pub for one last beer with Curly. Once again did he give me hell about the accident! So after more than just one beer, I left somewhat reluctantly, but knew if I had stayed there any longer I would definitely be in no fit state to drive.

So it was back on the road again. Which way? The signpost said Taranaki, so never having been in that direction before, that's where I headed, eastwards. With Gray sitting in the back like a king on all my gear we were on our way.

An hour or so later on the road we came across this little one-eyed place. All it had was a gas station, a motel, a pub, a home bakery and three small shops. I eased to a stop outside the pub and I wandered down the road a bit to where I could also see there was a small sawmill in action. Then at the bakery I bought a couple of pies. Gray was a real lover of them and he thought all his Christmases had come at once. But he only got the one. Then after he'd had a run around and done all the doggie things he wanted to do, he leapt into the back of the car, making himself comfortable. I myself headed to the pub - it looked pretty inviting so being me, I couldn't resist the temptation!

Lo and behold, when I stepped into the bar I bumped into a joker whom I hadn't seen for donkey's ages. He was havin' a beer with a couple of his cronies and they had been perusing the front page of the newspaper featuring the mishap, with graphic pictures and a detailed description of all that had occurred.

I was greeted with these words, "Talk about the bloody Devil himself, and then in he walks! What a bloody coincidence! How are you Rolly? Hey did you do this? What's the story? Is it true? What's the guts on this?"

The trio standing around the paper looked at me and waited expectantly.

I replied slowly, "Yeah, it's true. But, well it's just another story, so if you pour us out a beer, I'll tell you all about it! And by the way another thing, what's the pig hunting like around here? Is it any good?"

The End

GLOSSARY OF WORDS AND SAYINGS
According to the author's handle on things.

As ripe as	smelly
Aussie	Australian
Aussie salute	waving the flies away
One hundred yards	ninety odd metres
Baccy	tobacco
Battle-axe	domineering woman
Bays Hori Bop	Bay of Plenty rugby mascot
Bark a shin	scrape a shinbone
Barred	prohibited
BBQ	barbeque
Beak	judge
Beeline	direct line
Big noise	renowned in the area
Binder	meal
Blew his top	became irate
Blowed	expression of puzzlement
Blower	telephone
Bluey	traffic ticket
Bobsy die	a fuss
Bobby dazzler	the best
Boer war	War in South Africa 1899-1902.
Bomb	old car
Boneshaker	old car
Bonza	real good
Bottle store	liquor outlet
Broom	small exotic bush
Brumby	wild horse
Bullie	bulldozer
Bum up head down	working hard
Burl	try

Calling for Herb	throwing up
Cats and inters	earth moving machinery
Chain	22 metres (66 feet)
Chew the fat	discuss
Chinwag	to talk to
Chocka block	full of
Cleft stick	caught, unable to avoid
Codger	sly older person
Clobber	clothes, or to hit
C O	commanding officer
Cocky	farmer
Crusher dust	reject gravel from quarry

Day's grind	job of work
D C M	medal of honour
Dial	face
D I C	drunk in charge
Dosh, dough	slang for money
Dressed to the nines	well dressed
Dummy	face
Dummies, wooden	statues
Dutch courage	alcohol

Ehoa	mate (Maori)

Fair dinkum	the real thing
Fairy footed	clumsy
Finder holders	pig dogs
Five bob	pre decimal, fifty cents
Flog a few	ask for, borrow a few
Four by two	a timber size in inches

Four ten	small bore firearm
Fork out	pay for
Full as bulls	drunk

Galloot	idiot
Gander	to look at
Gasper	cigarette
Gawked at	stared at
Gimbals	hooks to hang animals
Grog	beer, alcohol
Gun shy	frightened of gunshots
Gut buster	real hard work
Guts full	more than enough
Gyp	pain

Hair of the dog	hangover remedy
Half a yard	just under half a metre
Half gallon	two and a bit litres
Half mile	just over 800 metres
Handle	name
Hangi	cooking food underground
Hard yakka	hard work
Harrowed	dug up bare ground
Hauraki	wind from the north
Hollywood	a big act
Hook grass	native grass with hook-like seeds
Hori	outdated term for Maori
Hot potato	too hot to handle
Humdinger	real good
Humping	carrying

Jeepers!	expression of surprise
Joker	a man

Kanuka	native tree
Kea gun	four ten small bore shotgun
Kehua	spirit (Maori)
Kick the bucket	to die
Kingpin	car steering part
Kit and caboodle	everything
Kuri	dog (Maori)

Land slippage	landslide
Laughing jackass	hyena
Leaner	a stand for beer drinking
Leg pull	to have on, tease
Line of bull	lies
Local rag	newspaper
Long drop	outside toilet
Lugging	dragging or humping

Mag	rifle magazine
Malone (Pat)	by oneself
Manuka	native tree
Master pin	steering linkage part
Mob	a herd of stock
Mocka	clothes
Monty	for sure
Moosh	mouth
Morepork	NZ native owl
Muffler	vehicle exhaust silencer
Mufti	plain clothes

Muldoon	former PM of NZ (very cynical)
Mutt	dog

Neck of the woods	in that area
Nectar of the gods	tasted good (ambrosia)
Knew his onions	knowledgeable
Nosey parker	inquisitive
Number eight-wire	galvanised wire size
Nut cases	idiots
Nutted out	thought out

Pai kori	very good (Maori)
Pakeha	white man (Maori)
Pat Malone	alone
Pig fern	dense bracken
Pint sized	of small stature
Pipiwharauroa	NZ shining cuckoo
Pissed	drunk
Piss and wind	full of wasted words
Pokey	jail
Pommy	immigrant from England
Possie	position
Pothole	deep hole in the road
Prowl car	police car
Puckarued	broken

Racket	noise
Ratbags	lowlife
Razzing	teasing
Really blue	swearing
Rolls	smokes

R S A	Returned Services Association
Rubbity dub	hotel (pub)

Scrapers	feet
Scratcher	bed
Secondary growth	old grown-over cut bush
She's jake	it's good
Shenanigans	mischief or nonsense
Shilling	pre decimal - ten cents
Shindig	a party
Shiner	a black eye
Shining cuckoo	native bird
Short arsed bloke	small person
Shot through	departed the scene
Shufti	a look
Slate wiped clean	forgiven
Slammed on anchors	braked hard
Smoko break	tea break
Snapper	NZ fish (sea)
Sparrow fart	at first light
Spigot	keg beer valve
Spitting tacks	wild, fuming
Square head	Dutchman
Steep pinch	hard climb up
Super	superphosphate fertilizer

TAB	totalisator betting agency
Taniwha	mythical monster (Maori)
Taranaki	Western area of North Is.
Taranaki gate	flexible wire-batten gate
Ten bob	ten shillings = one dollar
Ten quid	ten pounds = 20 dollars

Tomo	deep hole, cave
Three inches	pre decimal - 7.6 cm
Three-mile limit	legal fishing limit off the coast
Twelve-gauge	shotgun bore size
Two hundred yards	pre decimal-180 metres

Vet	short for veterinarian

WAAF	women's auxiliary air force
Waikato	type of beer (region)
Wash out	water eroded hole
WOF	warrant of fitness for car
Woolworths	cheap buying
Worry sheep	attack sheep

Yahoo!	exclamation of enjoyment
Yakka	real hard work
Yakked	talked
Yank tank	large American car

Graeme is currently working on the sequel to Deer, Pigs and a Little Bit of Bull, which will cover the next stage of Rolly's life as a good keen man.